Microsoft Dynamics 365 Project Operations

Deliver profitable projects with effective project planning and productive operational workflows

Robert Houdeshell

BIRMINGHAM—MUMBAI

Microsoft Dynamics 365 Project Operations

Copyright © 2021 Packt Publishing

Group Product Manager: Aaron Lazar
Publishing Product Manager: Alok Dhuri
Senior Editor: Ruvika Rao
Content Development Editor: Nithya Sadanandan
Technical Editor: Gaurav Gala
Copy Editor: Safis Editing
Project Coordinator: Francy Puthiry
Proofreader: Safis Editing
Indexer: Tejal Daruwale Soni
Production Designer: Jyoti Chauhan

First published: April 2021

Production reference: 1160421

Published by Packt Publishing Ltd.
Livery Place
35 Livery Street
Birmingham
B3 2PB, UK.

978-1-80107-207-6

www.packt.com

This book is a milestone of the big project that is my life! The largest milestone was when my wife, Barbara, agreed to join me on this journey of life, and she has since been an incredible force for good! She has always expected the best from me, our life together, and our business pursuits.

I gratefully acknowledge the impact of many people in the Microsoft Corporation and partner firms. Without Microsoft's continued innovation and product development, we would still be drawing Gantt charts on paper! I also acknowledge the partner firms who have put so much into my career. These firms continue to innovate and meet the needs of their clients, thus building a better business world.

I also acknowledge my clients, past and present, who have collaborated with me over the years to build incredible solutions and bring great business, processes, and technology together.

I especially thank the following people at Packt Publishing: Alok Dhuri, whose vision for this book lit the spark that will become a flame! Ruvika Rao, I thank you for working with me through the early chapters and bringing out the best in me! Nithya Sadanandan, you picked up in the middle of the book and really brought this book together. Prajakta Naik, thank you for keeping our project on track for success!

To Friyank Parikh, my technical reviewer, thank you for leveling up the content of this book and bringing together the best read for our readers!

This book and the Packt Publishing team have been a real joy to work with – I look forward to many successes with this book and others!

Contributors

About the author

Robert Houdeshell has over 24 years of project operations experience, with deep knowledge of the end-to-end processes that professional services firms utilize to deliver their projects.

Since 2004, Robert has worked with Microsoft Project Server and online versions that were integrating projects and ERP systems before there was a CRM-based PSA solution. In 2013, Robert's years of CRM, project, and ERP/accounting experience came together in the first end-to-end professional services automation solution of its kind. Built upon the Microsoft Dynamics technologies, this cloud solution was deployed in enterprise and mid-market companies. Therefore, when Project Services was released by Microsoft in 2016, he quickly saw the value of the solution we now call Project Operations.

Robert has worked with the Microsoft Project Operations solution since its beginning and has deployed the solution across multiple enterprise organizations, including a large multi-national Silicon Valley firm and a large Microsoft cloud solution partner. Robert has practical experience in enterprise and mid-size firms, helping them benefit from solution modernization. Excited about Project Operations, Robert passionately writes about his practical experience, offering solution observations and guidance for his readers to enjoy and benefit from.

About the reviewer

Friyank Parikh is an IT graduate from Mumbai University and has over 7 years of experience in Microsoft Dynamics. He is a certified Dynamics 365 Power Platform, Sales, Azure Data, and Azure Administrator Consultant. He is currently working as a senior consultant at Ernst and Young LLP. He is a technical expert with functional and business knowledge of multiple products of Dynamics 365.

He has vast experience with Microsoft technologies such as C#, .NET, MVC, and PowerShell. He has product expertise in technologies such as Dynamics 365 Sales, Customer Service, Field Service, and Project Operations. He has Azure expertise, including expertise in Azure Functions, Azure Logic Apps, Azure Data Lake, Azure Service Bus, and Azure Storage. He also actively participates in pre-sales and learning, and the development team at Ernst and Young LLP.

He has been recognized with many enterprise awards, such as the *I am Exceptional* award for the Digital Transformation category.

Table of Contents

3

The How-Tos of Setting Up Project Operations

Section 2:
Project Sales through Delivery

4
The Account Manager – Project Selling

5
Project Contracts and Pricing

6
Practice Manager Functions – We Won the Contract! What Now?

7
Resource Manager – Staffing for Success!

Section 3:
Project Delivery through Operations

8
Managing the Project to Success!

9
Team Member Activities

10
Approvals and Exceptions

11
Project Accounting and Operations

Assessments

Other Books You May Enjoy

Index

Preface

This one-of-a-kind book, *Microsoft Dynamics 365 Project Operations*, will help you deliver profitable projects with effective project planning and productive operational workflows. What makes it one of a kind is how we build a comprehensive story and working examples that the reader can follow along with and see the results of their efforts. It is designed to outline the foundations for project success while laying out recommendations that are the culmination of years of project operations experience.

Specifically, this book will cover project and sales methodologies, which combine to give the reader a clear picture of the life cycle, from the lead to project close. We will explain the implementation options, configuration, customization, and integration capabilities of the solution. Further, we will solidly present the sales processes from bid to win and the project processes from kickoff to revenue recognition.

By the end of the book, the reader will have a solid understanding of project processes, sales processes, and how they integrate to create an integrated solution for the project operations team. We will also explain the project accounting and operations processes with Microsoft Dynamics 365 Finance & Operations.

Who this book is for

This book is for project managers, project leads, business consultants and leaders who want to have a deep understanding of Project Operations and how it can benefit their business.

This book provides the reader with a solid understanding of how Project Operations builds upon the Microsoft 365 framework, leverages the Dynamics 365 platform, and brings the project manager into a modern Project for the Web environment.

What this book covers

Chapter 1, Introducing Project Operations, begins with the end in mind by understanding the key principles of project operations and how Dynamics 365 Project Operations meets the needs of a modern project business.

Chapter 2, Using the Microsoft Dynamics 365 Framework for Success, provides a foundational understanding of Microsoft 365, Dynamics 365, and all the components of Project Operations.

Chapter 3, The How-Tos of Setting Up Project Operations, dives deep into the heart of project operations setup and configuration. This step-by-step chapter is indispensable to the project implementation process.

Chapter 4, The Account Manager – Project Selling, explores the vital part of any professional services firm: selling. Sometimes called business development, account management, or other terms – the results are the winning of new business for the firm.

Chapter 5, Project Contracts and Pricing, provides you with the knowledge to structure multi-dimensional pricing and sophisticated contracts for your clients.

Chapter 6, Practice Manager Functions – We Won the Contract! What Now?, outlines decisions, the practice manager's concerns and duties, and how they will drive the firm's profitability.

Chapter 7, Resource Manager – Staffing for Success, focuses on centralized staffing. Centralized staffing is common among many professional services firms and project businesses. This chapter provides details on how best to accomplish these tasks.

Chapter 8, Managing the Project to Success, focuses on the execution phase, showing how managing the project timeline, budget, costs, and resources is imperative for the success of the firm.

Chapter 9, Team Member Activities, focuses on entering time and expenses, while effectively using Microsoft Teams and Outlook as a single entrypoint will also be outlined and leveraged in this chapter.

Chapter 10, Approvals and Exceptions, outlines project exceptions and how Project Operations handles them through many mechanisms that the project biller, administrator, and other authorized users can leverage.

Chapter 11, Project Accounting and Operations, outlines how billing and accounting for all the good work done through the Project Operations system is critical to accurately capture revenue and provide overall project net profit calculations. This chapter outlines the Project Operations billing integrations and revenue recognition considerations.

To get the most out of this book

To get the most out of this book the reader should have a desire to improve their project management and operations. Anyone concerned with being able to effectively set up, staff, bill, and recognize revenue will be interested in this book. The reader should have an average level of understanding of Microsoft technology, Microsoft 365 (Office 365), and Microsoft Dynamics. The following are some basic skills that you will need:

- Microsoft 365 framework administrator knowledge

- Microsoft Dynamics 365 CE administrator knowledge

- Microsoft Dynamics 365 CE customizer knowledge

- Microsoft Project knowledge

Code in Action

Code in Action videos for this book can be viewed at (`https://bit.ly/3abRHw7`).

Download the color images

We also provide a PDF file that has color images of the screenshots/diagrams used in this book. You can download it from `https://static.packt-cdn.com/downloads/9781801072076_ColorImages.pdf`.

Conventions used

There are a number of text conventions used throughout this book.

Bold: Indicates a new term, an important word, or words that you see onscreen. For example, words in menus or dialog boxes appear in the text like this. Here is an example: "Click on the **Close as Won** button."

`Code in text`: Indicates code words in text, database table names, folder names, filenames, file extensions, pathnames, dummy URLs, user input, and Twitter handles. Here is an example: "Required if you want to create a custom URL, such as `ProjectOperations.crm.dynamics.com`."

> **Tips or Important Notes:**
> Appear like this.

Get in touch

Feedback from our readers is always welcome.

General feedback: If you have questions about any aspect of this book, mention the book title in the subject of your message and email us at customercare@packtpub.com.

Errata: Although we have taken every care to ensure the accuracy of our content, mistakes do happen. If you have found a mistake in this book, we would be grateful if you would report this to us. Please visit www.packtpub.com/support/errata, selecting your book, clicking on the Errata Submission Form link, and entering the details.

Piracy: If you come across any illegal copies of our works in any form on the Internet, we would be grateful if you would provide us with the location address or website name. Please contact us at copyright@packt.com with a link to the material.

If you are interested in becoming an author: If there is a topic that you have expertise in and you are interested in either writing or contributing to a book, please visit authors.packtpub.com.

Reviews

Please leave a review. Once you have read and used this book, why not leave a review on the site that you purchased it from? Potential readers can then see and use your unbiased opinion to make purchase decisions, we at Packt can understand what you think about our products, and our authors can see your feedback on their book. Thank you!

For more information about Packt, please visit packt.com.

Section 1:
Foundation and
Framework of
Project Operations

Dynamics 365 Project Operations is a game-changer for a project-driven business. Combining the Power Platform and Dynamics 365 Project Operations unifies and optimizes the ability to deliver successful and profitable projects. Keeping large and small teams productive and collaborative means delivering promises that was made to your clients.

In this section, you will learn about the key principles of the Project Operations solution and how it works. You will start by exploring the key principles of Project Operations and understanding how it improves project planning and execution. You'll then learn how to successfully deploy Project Operations along with different integration strategies, and get to grips with the best approach for sales through project opportunities, project contracts, and pricing workflow implementation.

This section includes the following chapters:

- *Chapter 1, Introducing Project Operations*
- *Chapter 2, Using the Microsoft Dynamics 365 Framework for Success*
- *Chapter 3, The How-Tos of Setting Up Project Operations*

1
Introducing Project Operations

Microsoft Project Operations begins a new generation of project management capabilities combined with the power of the Microsoft 365 platform! Many years ago, Microsoft entered the *office solution category* and now Microsoft 365 dominates all other solutions. Project Operations is designed to provide you with the tools to expand your customer base by providing a connected environment from sales through delivery through planning to financial reporting and profitability.

Project Operations optimizes an already-proficient organization by providing optimized resource utilization and project economics. It allows you to amplify communication across project teams, collaborate externally and internally, and act upon up-to-date insights in a project. Furthermore, Project Operations simplifies time tracking and expense management while at the same time evolving with a modern and adaptable platform.

In this chapter, you will understand the key principles of the Project Operations solution and how it works. This chapter will help you to understand the key principles and concepts of the project business industry. People with the titles of project manager, practice manager or portfolio managers and consultants alike will understand the value of the solution and how it will improve project planning, execution, and accounting. Understanding where we intend to be is the first key to success. This chapter will define the success criteria of the Project Operations solution.

In this chapter, you will learn about the following concepts:

- Key principles and concepts for project managers, project leaders, or business consultants so that you know how you, personally, fit into the solution for your clients

- Project businesses at a glance to get to know how your company fits into similar industries

- The value of the Microsoft Project Operations solution so you can determine how this solution benefits your company, you (personally), and your industry peers

- Key performance results of implementing a Project Operations solution benefitting the firm by knowing your key performance statistics

- The overall solution value of a connected organization so you can connect internally and externally

- How to achieve more profitable projects in Project Operations so your firm benefits from the hard work performed

- Better decision making through better tools so you can spend the most time on the most beneficial activities

- Better customer/client relationships through communication, collaboration, and information so that you can enjoy the journey with your clients

Key principles and concepts for project managers

Congratulations! Imagine you have just become the project manager of that great new project your firm has won! You have worked hard to get this project and you want nothing but the best delivery of your solution for the client. You may be the program or practice manager who worked with the project manager to win the business and this is one of your many customers or clients (depending on your terminology). The chief operations officer may be looking at your portfolio as a part of a larger segment of business and thus looking at this new project as a part of a firm's overall services portfolio.

Project Operations pulls together the sales and delivery teams to provide a solution in which both sales and delivery can work. From the selling cycle, project contracts are created, which tie directly to the milestones that will be billed. Further along in the process, invoices are created, which drives revenue recognition in the accounting system.

Now, how do you deliver effectively for the clients that you have worked so hard to bring on board and keep happy? Now the project must be fulfilled to meet the expectations of the client. A hundred thoughts go through your mind. How do I turn an estimating worksheet into a project plan? How do I get the right people with the right skills on my project? What other projects am I competing with internally for the right talent? How can I manage all these moving parts?

Many project managers and others have lost many hours of sleep pondering these questions and trying to figure out how to deliver on the success promised to their client. Our goal with this book is to introduce you to a solution called **Microsoft Dynamics 365 Project Operations** that will be the tool you can use to relieve your mind and get more rest! The goal of this book is to identify the key principles and concepts for you as a program or project manager or business executive in charge of the **profit and loss** (**P&L**) of an entire firm.

Project businesses at a glance

First off, what does a project business do for their clients? Well, that answer is wide and varied. In fact, using the **Standard Industrial Classification** (**SIC**) codes, if you searched on project business categories, you will find a significant variation of business types within almost the same classification. One of my favorite examples from history has been how some firms classify **AEC** as **Architects, Engineers, and Construction**. Although classified together, architects, engineers, and construction firms have about as much in common as bakers, butchers, and farmers. They have some things in common but not common business processes. Thus, for the purpose of this book, let's identify the common thread within a project business. Project businesses deliver skilled and certified services by people to achieve a project's purpose.

The following is a representation of the common business sectors or industries included in the project business sector:

Figure 1.1 – The Project Business sector

Within the Microsoft world, we have consultants who are skilled (read experienced) and certified (having achieved Microsoft certification) on services (implementation and training) to set up and implement software for their clients.

Other examples are management consultants who provide business strategy and tactics to grow and build the performance of businesses as a result of a merger or acquisition or simply to grow the business. **Information technology** (**IT**) implementation firms may specialize in setting up cloud computing solutions for their clients. Furthermore, some **Point of Sale** (**POS**) or security solution companies may have massive hardware configurations they prepare for their clients to be deployed at a retail establishment that requires purchasing inventory, combining it with project business and onsite deployment.

These are only a few examples of what project business is. Let's also determine what project business is not. Project business is not personal services, automotive services, health services, or private services. These do not fit into the category of project business primarily because they do not have the project orientation that requires a level of management not readily available.

Some outliers that fit into the overall services category but may or may not fit into this category of project business include legal services, educational services, and membership organizations. If these businesses need to manage projects along with costing or pricing information they could benefit from Project Operations.

So, what is this *Project Orientation* that is so important to identify whether an industry is a project business or not? Well, it begins with the basics of a project itself. From the earliest moment of human history, we have been working on projects. From the Pyramids to the Great Temple to the Great Wall, projects have been the backbone of great achievements! I sometimes have mused about the project plan for the Great Pyramid… how many laborers of stonecutters would I need to cut a certain amount of stones to achieve the result of not just an architectural monolith but also an engineering achievement!? Oh, and to add pressure, it has to be done with relatively simple tools and within the lifetime of the Pharaoh! Now, talk about some pressure!

The Egyptians were some of the earliest recorded project managers and with the results of their projects, I would say they have achieved a lot, to their credit. They would have had to be concerned with the overall project (a pyramid), the timeline to get the project done, the labor, and the organization thereof. The resulting pyramid project also had concerns over materials and environmental concerns, emphasizing their achievements. Their projects took on a life of their own, very much like our projects, and a ton of support systems to achieve their desired results. There were support workers building roads and equipment, baking bread, and generally supporting the direct labor to the pyramid.

This is like a commercial construction project as constructed today. Commercial construction projects have very much the same concerns of the timeline, labor, and materials. Let's see what a Gantt chart of a commercial construction project looks like:

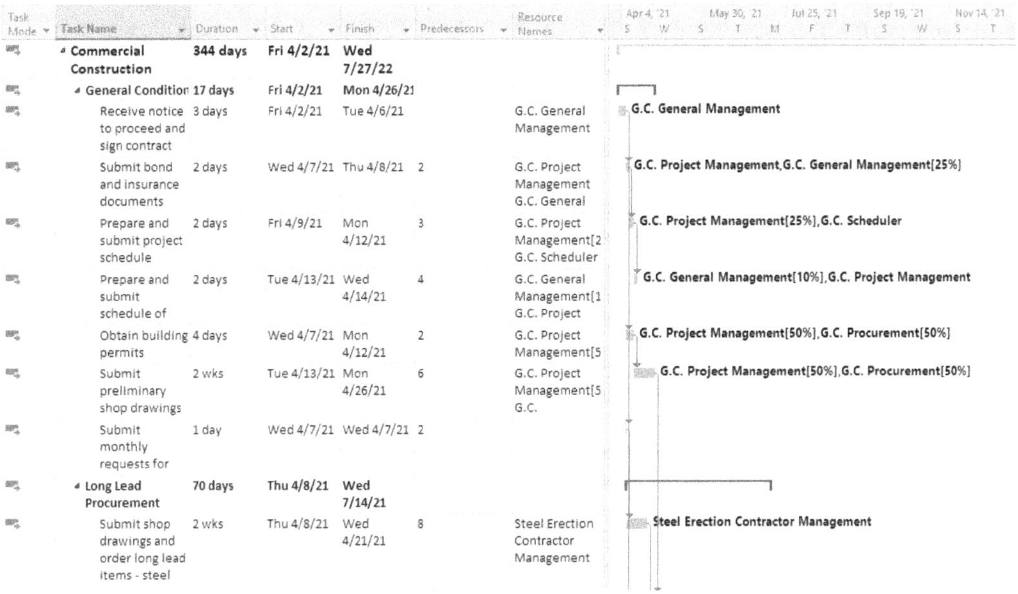

Task Mode	Task Name	Duration	Start	Finish	Predecessors	Resource Names	Gantt
	◢ Commercial Construction	344 days	Fri 4/2/21	Wed 7/27/22			
	◢ General Condition	17 days	Fri 4/2/21	Mon 4/26/21			
	Receive notice to proceed and sign contract	3 days	Fri 4/2/21	Tue 4/6/21		G.C. General Management	G.C. General Management
	Submit bond and insurance documents	2 days	Wed 4/7/21	Thu 4/8/21	2	G.C. Project Management G.C. General	G.C. Project Management,G.C. General Management[25%]
	Prepare and submit project schedule	2 days	Fri 4/9/21	Mon 4/12/21	3	G.C. Project Management[2 G.C. Scheduler	G.C. Project Management[25%],G.C. Scheduler
	Prepare and submit schedule of	2 days	Tue 4/13/21	Wed 4/14/21	4	G.C. General Management[1 G.C. Project	G.C. General Management[10%],G.C. Project Management
	Obtain building permits	4 days	Wed 4/7/21	Mon 4/12/21	2	G.C. Project Management[5	G.C. Project Management[50%],G.C. Procurement[50%]
	Submit preliminary shop drawings	2 wks	Tue 4/13/21	Mon 4/26/21	6	G.C. Project Management[5 G.C.	G.C. Project Management[50%],G.C. Procurement[50%]
	Submit monthly requests for	1 day	Wed 4/7/21	Wed 4/7/21	2		
	◢ Long Lead Procurement	70 days	Thu 4/8/21	Wed 7/14/21			
	Submit shop drawings and order long lead items - steel	2 wks	Thu 4/8/21	Wed 4/21/21	8	Steel Erection Contractor Management	Steel Erection Contractor Management

Figure 1.2 – A commercial construction Gantt chart example

Therefore, dear readers, this is a challenge for you as you have won this new project and built an additional business for your practice and your firm. I can imagine in that first project, someone was very passionate about their idea and project plan that they were selling to the client. This is not that different from you. You have a passion for what you are doing or you would not be successful and reading this book. Let's capture that passion and turn it into the burning heart that delivers upon your success.

If you are like most of the project management world, you are probably well immersed in the Microsoft world and use many of their products in your day-to-day life. One of the first applications you will interface with in your day is your calendar and your email. You will likely begin your morning (if you are honest with me) by looking at your smartphone and seeing what meetings you have on your calendar for the day or looking at emails that were delivered overnight. The infrastructure that supports this is what Microsoft calls its Microsoft 365 framework. We will go deeper in the next chapter into the overall infrastructure. However, just like you do not really think much of your electricity supplier when you turn on the lights, you really do not think much of Microsoft when you turn on your phone and see that someone put a 7:30 a.m. meeting on your calendar!

Once you have had a cup of coffee (or two), you will bravely fire up your laptop, surface, iPad, or Mac to begin the work of your day. You will likely open Microsoft Outlook for your email, calendar, contacts, and other functions. During the day, you will use many of the Microsoft Office 365 solutions, such as Microsoft Teams for meetings, files, collaboration, and messaging. Further, you might use Microsoft Word, Excel, PowerPoint, SharePoint, and maybe Microsoft Project to manage project plans.

> **Disclaimer:**
>
> There is no judgment in how you manage projects today. I just mentioned Microsoft Project and some of you may be playing in your mind the most erudite of thinking. Oh, yes, I *should* be using Microsoft Project but because of whatever limitations I cannot use Microsoft Project. Hey, there is no judgment here! I have managed many projects in Excel, Word, PowerPoint, and many other tools, so do not feel any need to level up to Microsoft Project before you read on! This is a safe place for all of us who are working hard!

Now that we have that out of the way, let's turn our attention to how we can grow through our project management capabilities. We know that we grow from level to level (or level up) throughout life. Where we are today is not where we will be tomorrow and we will grow from level to level as we progress in our careers. Thus, we should look at ways that we can grow quickly throughout the discipline of project management. We do know that to achieve more for our clients, we must focus on delivery processes and repeatability of success to continue to succeed from project to project. It is here that we do need to interject with some structure and tools to achieve the business objectives your firm has.

The value statement of Project Operations is to provide the overall framework together for you and your firm to connect your various systems and processes together to grow from one level of maturity to another. This is the value of Microsoft Project Operations.

The value of the Microsoft Project Operations solution

Looking at projects in a more modern way takes a modern solution approach. Furthermore, it requires collaboration, communication, and flexibility in the project delivery to be successful in tomorrow's world. In order to work best together, we need to have more modern tools and capabilities. This is the value of Project Operations.

The following screenshot shows what a project plan in Microsoft Project Operations looks like:

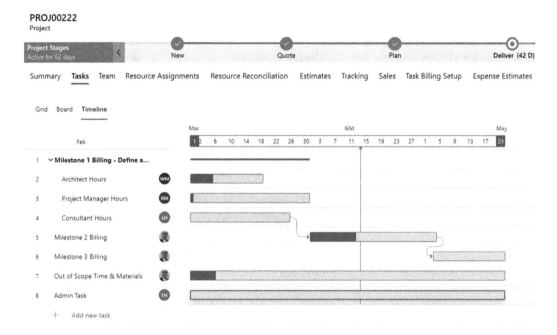

Figure 1.3 – Microsoft Dynamics 365 Project Operations

Like Neo in the movie *The Matrix* from 1999, you are about to swallow the red pill. The red pill represents an awakening that could be difficult and painful. Your world will be totally changed with the red pill and you will see the truth in the success you can have in your career with the right tools in place. You can take the blue pill if you want and go back to the cold comfort of believing that you have all your projects under control and you are delivering profitability to your firm. The choice is yours, Neo!

Welcome to the project awakening! Now that you are here, let's talk about some of the facts of the projects you have been managing. You have been doing a great job over the years and that is why you have been promoted so many times. However, the underlying understanding of your purpose is something that may be missing. Your purpose for the delivery of projects on time, on budget, and meeting your client's needs has been to meet and exceed the performance expectations of your firm.

With the tools you have used, you have achieved much success. However, you are now on the verge of realizing your full potential by connecting with your firm's purpose. Let's get that out of the way first. In a most capitalistic circumstance, your firm may be engaged to make a profit from every project, every time to a profit margin that is prescribed by the firm. In other firms, the purpose may be to provide the highest quality services and solutions to the clients within a given industry or solution segment. In other firms, you may be directly connected to the welfare of your customers and your ability to deliver will directly impact the success of real people and their lives and livelihoods.

Let's now connect this with the tools we use to gain more success and align more tightly with the end-to-end processes in your firm. Microsoft Project Operations is an end-to-end solution built upon the Microsoft Dataverse utilizing Dynamics 365 **Customer Engagement** (**CE**) for project sales, resource management, planning, scheduling, time and expense entry, billing, and project accounting functionality in one solution. The end-to-end integrated environment combines the power and functionality of the CE Project Operations solution with the accounting power of Dynamics 365 for Finance and Operations.

Embedded into the Microsoft 365 framework, Project Operations provides an all-encompassing solution to the project professional's daily life! The reason this is important is that when a solution is designed to work together in your daily life and support the end-to-end processes of a project, it provides the infrastructure needed to succeed.

Imagine, if you will, your home. Would you tolerate different settings on your faucets in different rooms? Hot on the right, cold on the left in one room while the opposite is true in another? How about your light switches? What if, randomly, they were different in different rooms? More so, what if your kitchen was wired for 230 volts while the rest of the home was 110/120 volts and had different plug configurations? Sounds like a mess, does it not?

Technologically, this is what businesses tolerate every day when they use one solution for the sales team, one for project task management, one for billing, and yet another for accounting. Yes, you can produce a *best of breed integrated environment* but the results are highly dependent upon the technical skills to pull this solution together. Furthermore, the solution is only as good as its weakest link and will break (not *may* break, *will* break) at the most inopportune time! These solutions proliferate through businesses today. Small armies of technologists support these solutions to keep them running and even at the best of their performance, they simply ensure an end-to-end transaction works through the system without error.

Building the right solution for tomorrow's project manager requires decades of innovation combined with the latest technological foundation. The entire solution must work seamlessly together while continuing to improve as workforces change, technology improves, and technical capabilities increase at exponential rates. Let's check how an end-to-end solution with Microsoft 365 works.

Understanding an end-to-end solution with Microsoft Dynamics 365

In a connected world, the project selling begins in a connected solution with the rest of the ecosystem. The people selling projects are typically business development managers seeking to sell new projects to new clients. These can also be partner-level players in a firm who are both landing or winning new accounts for the firm and/or keeping existing accounts active and happy with the firm's results.

In the following sections, we will be reviewing the components of Project Operations and how they apply to the different functions within a project business.

Customer relationship management (CRM)

The project seller works to bring business into the firm and works in the overall Project Operations solution, which includes account management, contact management, and entering and processing opportunities and quotes, which become the projects that you deliver against. The project seller is concerned with receiving leads in the system from the marketing team and qualifying them against the firm's known *sales methodology*. The sales methodology will determine how to qualify or make sure that the lead is worth the time to pursue business with. This will involve having contacts with the lead's main contact person or potentially a team of people who are asking you to pursue business with them. The kind of information shared at this beginning step in the process is critical to have throughout the entirety of the project delivery. Expectations set at the beginning of the sales cycle will be the same or more than what you are expected to deliver in the project delivery cycle.

The project business development life cycle includes the following:

1. Business strategy planning to create a sales methodology
2. Leads, which are the first marketing engagement with a prospective client
3. Opportunity, which is the first, fully qualified sales entity
4. A quote, which represents a proposal to a prospective client

5. A contract or project contract, which is a client's *order* to confirm the project contract terms

6. A transaction, which is the actual transactions produced through the project life cycle

7. An invoice, which is the billing produced as a result of our work

8. Profit and loss reporting, showing our firm's profitability

The expectations grow as the sale progresses through the lead qualification process and the potential sale is collaborated on with other team members. Once a project seller has qualified the lead, meaning that the lead truly intends to buy a service that your firm provides and has the budget, authority, and intention within a given timeframe to do so, it becomes an opportunity. Note that this qualification process may take days, weeks, or even months to process. Therefore, capturing all the information from the beginning is important as the project seller will be working on many leads and opportunities at one time. This will be critical to the success of the client relationship and communication that happens on an ongoing basis after this point.

When an opportunity is created, existing information persists and is visible from within the account, contact, and opportunity workplaces. The account is simply the business demographic and main information of the potential buyer. The contact or contacts related to the account are the people who you have been working with throughout the lead qualification process. In some scenarios, you may be working with one, a fully empowered buyer who has the ability to make decisions and see them through to completion. In other scenarios, you may be working with a committee of people who will make these decisions. Either way, being able to track their known preferences, buying habits, and other information will greatly increase your selling success.

The opportunity is where selling methodologies meet project methodologies. Selling a project is different from selling a product. A product has known specifications, quantities, and delivery methods. Project selling involves a team of people to be successful. The project seller will frequently pull in project estimators, delivery leaders, and others to build out a project plan that will be presented to the potential client. This involves a lot of different dynamics that combine to win business.

First and foremost is the currency of credibility. Every great project begins with building the credibility of the firm and its delivery teams. This begins with the firm's solid understanding of the project and being able to estimate the work that comes in at a budgetary number that the client has allocated funds. The better the estimation, the greater the credibility of the firm from the outset. Estimate too high and you lose credibility. Estimate too low and you lose your profit. This may seem counter-intuitive, but a potential client needs to know that you know their business, their project, and the complexity of the work involved.

This will directly impact and provide input for the quality of work delivered. The better we know the size, scope, requirements, and timeline of the project, the better we can schedule through the schedule board in Project Operations.

This is where Microsoft Project Operations comes in to solve this problem by providing all these frontend processes in a connected environment with the estimation of the project. Over the many years of a project firm's success, you will have learned what works for your clients and what does not work as well. Which kinds of projects like this have succeeded, and do they have templates that can be used and reused as a basis to begin? In Project Operations, we are continuing to build the data around the project being sold.

Work breakdown structure

In a project seller world, the estimates will be worked through many different versions before a draft version to move forward is agreed upon. At this point, the project estimates will become a draft **work breakdown structure** (**WBS**) that will be summarized and presented to the potential client. The level of detail presented and the level of detail tracked in the estimates are usually different. The client presentation is more a summary level and can easily be translated to hours, rates, and project pricing.

The following shows a traditional Gantt chart view of a project plan in Microsoft Project. Whether a Gantt chart, board view, or a timeline, the associated WBS (represented numerically with the hierarchy of relationship) is important for building out the necessary tasks and their relationships:

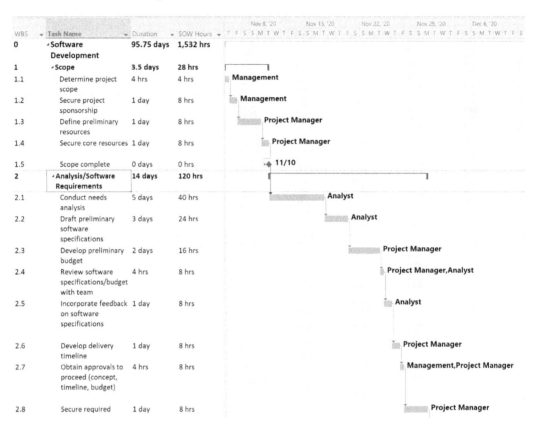

Figure 1.4 – A sample WBS

A solid WBS structure is a fundamental element of the project management methodology a firm chooses to use. Some firms choose to have very structured WBS numbering wherein a leading number of 1.x can mean an analysis phase, 2.x a design phase, and the numbering progresses from there.

Now that we have successfully sold the project and have a signed contract from the client, we need to onboard the project into the firm's delivery team. Let's check in the next section how to do this.

Statement of work

The **statement of work** (**SOW**) is the key document that we see across many project business firms. It guides and drives the work to be performed and outlines the remuneration expected from the client for this work. A SOW can be of different types: fixed fee, time and materials, milestone billing, retainers, and not-to-exceed contract types:

Statement of Work

Customer Name:	A Datum Corporation		
Project Name:	A Datum Project #1	Customer Requestor:	Bill Smith
		Practice Manager:	Joe Smith
Effective Date:	2/22/2021	CSM:	Mary McCoy

This Statement of Work dated 2/22/<u>2021</u> is entered into by and between Contoso Holdings, LLC ("Contoso") and A Datum Corporation ("Customer") and is hereby incorporated into the Master Services Agreement.

Scope of Services:

- Contoso shall assist Customer with the implementation of…
- The tasks included in this project are:

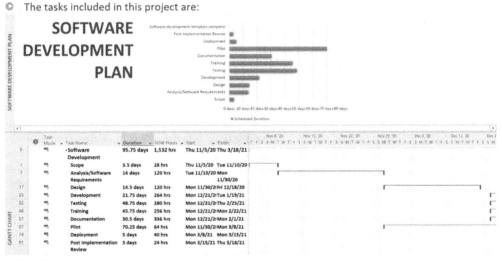

	Task Mode	Task Name	Duration	SOW Hours	Start	Finish
0		Software Development	95.75 days	1,532 hrs	Thu 11/5/20	Thu 3/18/21
1		Scope	3.5 days	28 hrs	Thu 11/5/20	Tue 11/10/20
7		Analysis/Software Requirements	14 days	120 hrs	Tue 11/10/20	Mon 11/30/20
17		Design	14.5 days	120 hrs	Mon 11/30/2	Fri 12/18/20
25		Development	21.75 days	264 hrs	Mon 12/21/2	Tue 1/19/21
32		Testing	48.75 days	280 hrs	Mon 12/21/2	Thu 2/25/21
48		Training	45.75 days	256 hrs	Mon 12/21/2	Mon 2/22/21
57		Documentation	30.5 days	336 hrs	Mon 12/21/2	Mon 2/1/21
67		Pilot	70.25 days	64 hrs	Mon 11/30/2	Mon 3/8/21
74		Deployment	5 days	40 hrs	Mon 3/8/21	Mon 3/15/21
81		Post Implementation Review	3 days	24 hrs	Mon 3/15/21	Thu 3/18/21

Deliverables:

Figure 1.5 – Sample SOW

Having the WBS properly structured is a key element of project success. It provides the project team with the ability to show summary level estimates that integrate into the SOW while simultaneously becoming a task-level plan that the team can succeed with.

The SOW budgets that are presented to the client are a factor in estimating a project's work effort or labor, the duration or time, the types of roles to be used, and the overall sequencing from one task to another. This may also include skillsets and desired resources. This is a common WBS that can perform all these requirements and more.

Project Operations' impact on profitability

In the Project Operations environment, the opportunity becomes a natural extension of the project selling. As we have been using Project Operations functionality all along, we have a consistent process flow from sales to project delivery, to planning to financial reporting and profitability.

Receiving this at project delivery means first off reviewing the WBS with the SOW and the project team roles outlined. Since we are using the Microsoft Dynamics 365 framework, integrated document management carries you right to the SOW. The SOW aligns with the summary of the WBS and you have a proposed team of people that may be explicitly stated by name or may be more implicitly stated by role or function. Either way, you have what you need to begin!

Now it is time to plan further and staff your project! Will the project kick off when it was projected? Are there any variations to the kick-off date that will adjust your project plan's start date or maybe the start date of the tasks? Because you have dependencies built into the tasks of the plan, no worries! All of your successive dates change and your plan is still intact. With the new dates, you have the roles of people that you know you need to work on the project. Their hours, duration, and plans are totally visible to you, which means that you are able to view a team member's availability through the schedule board in Project Operations as follows:

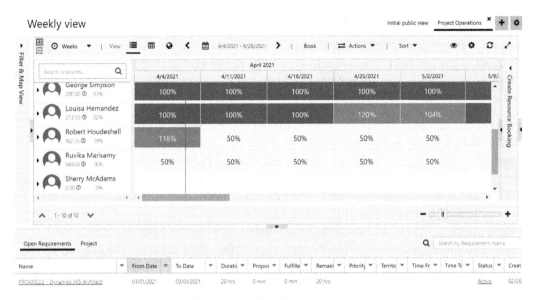

Figure 1.6 – The schedule board

The project may have begun with specific team members who were soft-booked onto the project to begin with. At this point, it is a good time to hard book them and commit their time to the project. This is a must to protect your project's resourcing so that others in the system will not be able to overbook your resources/team members.

While managing the WBS, you have the flexibility to manage the project in a traditional Gantt chart view while simultaneously viewing data as timeline and board views. This is important to be able to support today's agile project management. This is conducted through the embedded Microsoft Project for the Web functionality, which provides the most valuable functions of what many people have worked with previously, Microsoft Project. Integrated into the financial and project components of Project Operations, this solution pulls together and is the glue of the entire system.

Within the project management functionality, you will continue to collaborate with sales around any client expectations and this is all native to the Microsoft 365 framework. Your team can collaborate together with Microsoft Teams and OneDrive. As the project manager, you can see very clearly into the project schedule, potential overcommitments, and other schedule pitfalls.

You can also see the project's financial health of budget versus actual, project sales estimates, project labor cost estimates (with permission), and overall project status. Communicating the project delivery success is done natively through dashboards and views of data within Project Operations.

Team member time and expense entry

As a team member, I want to enter my timesheet and get on with my weekend! I want it to be quick, accurate, complete, and not rejected by the project manager. My managers do not want to remind me to enter my time and I do not need to spend weekend time on my timesheet.

For the project manager, saving time and improving accuracy are the most important factors to their success. The project needs to be managed and delivered accurately and that means being able to keep your fingers on the pulse of the project's success. Furthermore, keeping the project inputs (team members' time and expenses) accurate will improve the overall financial benefits of the project. In a time and materials contract, team members' time descriptions generally flow through to the project invoice. The project invoice is the most important client document to be generated on a regular basis. It needs to be accurate and timely generated. If inaccurate, you risk the client rejecting the invoice. If not timely, the firm's cash flow is reduced. Therefore, how you manage the billing interactions with the finance and accounting team will determine your project's financial health and performance.

For a project manager, approving, rejecting, and exception handling time entries and expenses is critical for the project's revenue. Not only will missed time cause missing revenue, but mishandled time will also cause further complications downstream in project accounting.

Your team members will log their time through the time and expense entry functionality. Time and expense entry is critical to billing and revenue recognition. Your team members can input a time entry through their Outlook calendar or through a simple-to-use weekly view of time in the Project Operations team member app. This makes their life simple as they can input time during the week and not bunch it all up at the end of the week. Across a team of 1,000 team members, if you save 15 minutes each and you bill out $200 per hour, the savings over a 52-week time frame is $2,600,000! This is baseline math as there are other productivities gained in time and expense entry beyond this example.

Project accounting and ERP functionality

With each project, there are a number of contract types that can be used to execute the project. This is where the project accounting and ERP functionality fit in. The project accounting and billing capabilities of Microsoft Project Operations supports the most common contract types in a project business. Contract types and are legally binding contractual obligations of performance and financial remuneration.

Project Operations billing modules tie all of your accurate work and timely approvals into project billings that are accurate and delivered electronically to your client's customers. On the finance and accounting side of the solution, the receivables management functionality allows a streamlined experience tailored to the project accountant's needs. Project profitability reporting gives the firm a project-by-project view of profitability rolling up into the practice and the firm's profitability.

A simple contract type can be a fixed fee contract where the firm charges a fixed amount of money to generally perform a fixed amount of work. Time and materials contracts are generally billed as hours performed against a contract/project. In a time and materials contract, for every hour worked, a rate is applied and those hours are billed. Time and materials may also include services, materials, or products bought to perform the work and typically direct expenses onto the project.

There are variations of each of these, including milestone billing, percent complete, time and materials to **work in progress** (**WIP**), and not to exceed types of variations. These are all really important to determine upfront as the contract type feeds directly into the Project Operations project billings functionality.

Furthermore, later in the project, changes invariably come into play, causing yet other accounting and project operational changes to apply to the projects.

All of these financial implications must be tracked in an accounting system according to **Generally Accepted Accounting Principles** (**GAAP**) and for some industries other requirements such as ASC606/IFRS15 revenue recognition requirements. Thus, having a combined, end-to-end solution, provides user-friendly frontend processes for sales and project operations while providing a robust, audit trail-enabled accounting and finance solution to support the project accounting needs.

Supporting the organization are the project financials and other financial reports that show project profitability, practice profitability, and overall firm financial health. These reports are critical to the success of the firm and their ability to react to market conditions.

Data analysis and presentation

There are several key performance results of implementing a Project Operations solution. Most notably, the firm will begin benefitting from the process, organization, and overall data generated from the Project Operations system, which will guide you through decisions based upon your key performance statistics.

The information processed through Project Operations is only as valuable as the ability to make sense of it later in the business. Therefore, encircling all this functionality are Customer Insights, dashboards, and Power BI capabilities to have visibility into customer satisfaction as well as overall practice and firm health:

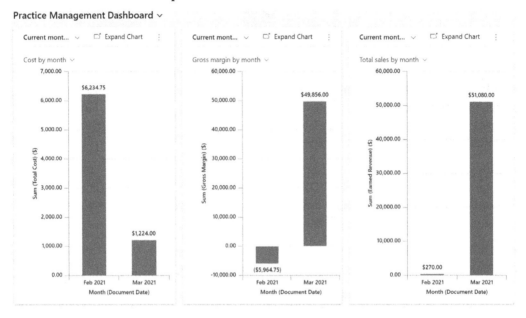

Figure 1.7 – Sample dashboard showing KPIs on a project

Power BI is part of the Microsoft Power Platform, which will provide you with the information you need to manage projects successfully. Having information is only one element, though. Acting upon it is another and that is where the power of the Microsoft Power Platform comes into play. Critical components of the Power Platform that play most well with the Project Operations system are Power Automate, Power BI, and Power Apps development.

Power Automate is used to perform a number of automation tasks revolving around the Project Operations solution. Power Automate has connectors and templates for a large number of Microsoft and non-Microsoft solutions. Power Automate can be used to perform workflow approvals, data integrations, automation of tasks, and much more.

Combined with Power Apps, you can have the power of decisions, approvals, and workflows in the palm of your hand. All power apps are built with a Unified Interface design, which works equally well on a laptop, tablet, or phone.

The Power BI platform allows you to take the information generated through the entire solution and puts it into the right data presentation form factor to give you the information you need to make better decisions.

Bottom-line benefits for the company

The overall solution value of a connected organization derived from Project Operations automates the mundane and accentuates the already great components of a robust project management solution. Gone are the days of reminding team members to input their time, manually generating invoices, or physically moving data from one system to another. Back to the house analogy, this is really the *smart home* version of project management and operations functionality.

As the chief operating officer, practice manager, firm partner, or other vested interest in the success of the firm after implementing Project Operations, you should expect a number of things to benefit the overall firm. First is that you should expect the firm to grow through this experience and be able to move up by one or two levels in your project management maturity. Typically, firms start off at level 1 by performing very entrepreneurially in their style and systems. This is how they succeed! As the firm grows, structure and policy replace ad hoc systems to bring the firm into some compliance. Growing from level 1 through to level 5, where you are able to not just collaborate but really benefit from collaborating across the firm brings value to every aspect of the business. With this, you win more business, more consistently and more profitably.

Gone are the days of having revenue leakage, missing targets, and deadlines, or having low-productivity solutions in place. Leadership, client relations, team members, delivery, and finance and operations are all aligned and working together toward the firm's goals. Furthermore, each of these areas is working together to drive the business strategically.

Bid-to-win ratios improve as core utilization rises and project profitability increases, which flow directly to the bottom-line **Earnings Before Interest, Taxes, Depreciation, and Amortization (EBITDA)**. The firm is able to deliver on projects with a level of optimization, which makes the firm an attractive place for the best talent, thus producing the further healthy growth of the firm. Utilizing the Project Operations system should provide the firm with bigger, predictably deliverable projects that add to the bottom line.

A solution such as Project Operations should bring value to the topline, operational, utilization, and bottom line with value concentrating in the areas most lacking today in your firm, meaning that if you are struggling today with winning new projects, focusing on the frontend, customer engagement processes will likely result in more business upfront that can be delivered through your delivery teams. Frequently, we see that the focus moves from one end of the project implementation process to another as we grow within the solution. Today, you are fixing sales. Tomorrow, operations... thus you can see the continuous growth opportunities this will uncover for the firm.

The remainder of this book is designed to lay out for you the plan to begin taking advantage of Project Operations in your firm or business. We are going to cover the Microsoft framework in the next chapter and then get into the setup and configuration of the system. This will not replace the technical expertise of certified individuals but will complement strong implementation methodologies in Microsoft Project Operations.

Summary

We have learned through this chapter that Project Operations is a solution built to make end-to-end processes for project managers a solution set, not just a toolset. The project business industry is built around delivering projects in a timely and cost-effective manner for their clients. The value of the Project Operations solution is that it is built upon the Microsoft Dynamics 365 framework, making the Project Operations solution an end-to-end, user-friendly system.

The functionality begins in the frontend with the CRM/sales functionality to support sales professionals who are building their project opportunities into SOWs. When provided to the delivery team, the SOW provides the contractual framework to engage in and work to completion of the project. While working on the project, team members can easily and effectively enter their time and expenses. Upon approval, this information integrates into the Finance and Operations project accounting functionality to perform billing, revenue recognition, and costing.

Underlying all this are the benefits to the firm, which are recognized through the financial improvements to the firm and visualized through the tools in Project Operations dashboards, Customer Insights, and Power BI.

As we proceed through the next chapter, we will dig deeper into the underlying technology that will be used to deploy Project Operations. This includes a deep dive into the Microsoft 365 framework, the Power Platform, and Dynamics 365 CE.

Questions

1. What separates a project business from other types of companies and organizations?

2. What does CRM stand for and how it is important to the project business?

3. What is a sales methodology?

4. What does WBS stand for and why it is important?

5. What is a statement of work and how is it used in a project business?

6. Bonus question: In the movie *The Matrix*, which pill (red or blue) does Neo take that opens his eyes to a whole new world of potential?

2
Using the Microsoft Dynamics 365 Framework for Success

Microsoft Project Operations is built upon an overall framework that Microsoft calls its Microsoft 365, Power Platform and Dynamics 365 frameworks. Formerly Microsoft Office 365, the Microsoft 365 framework enables the entire experience for users of Project Operations. This means that users sign in to their portal and upon authentication are presented with all the applications they are licensed to access. The Power Platform is the development platform which Dynamics 365 CE is built.

This chapter is designed to outline the interconnected environments of Microsoft 365, Dynamics 365, and the Finance and Operations solution. The result should be that as you begin deploying and utilizing Project Operations, you will be able to quickly license, set up, and configure the baseline configuration.

In this chapter, you will learn about the following concepts:

- The Microsoft 365 framework
- The Microsoft Power Platform framework
- Microsoft Dynamics 365 CE
- Microsoft Dynamics 365 for Finance and Operations
- The Unified environment

As a result of this chapter, you will learn the following concepts:

- Project Operations interconnectedness with Microsoft 365 and the Dynamics 365 platform
- How to leverage the Microsoft Power Platform framework
- How best to leverage the Dynamics CE/CRM framework
- How integration with Finance and Operations is performed
- The overall Microsoft Finance and Operations strategy

The Microsoft 365 framework

The Microsoft 365 framework is a fully encompassing solution that is available across Home, Business, Enterprise, and Education customer types. Microsoft 365 is, for many businesses today, an all-in-one solution that provides an underlying IT infrastructure that is highly secured with multi-factor authentication and defends against cyberthreats such as viruses, malware, phishing, ransomware, spam, and other threats. This means that as a business, you are able to leverage Microsoft technologies that protect your data, secure your devices, and manage your access.

Built on top of this are the applications that are available from Microsoft, such as Word, Excel, PowerPoint, Outlook, and many others; these are common to the daily tasks of users. Furthermore, Microsoft Teams collaboration provides the ability to easily chat, share files, add calls and meetings, and much more, to make team collaboration easy and effective.

The solution is delivered on a monthly (per-user, per-month) basis so the licensing is affordable for small businesses as well as large enterprises. The administrator of the environment can add users, remove users, add licensing as needed, and generally make all the adjustments needed to keep the environment secure. Users can access their favorite applications through a conventional desktop client, browser, or mobile/tablet device. All the data is securely stored in the Microsoft Azure cloud for safe-keeping.

There is a lot of technology that has come together quite recently that makes the Microsoft 365 and Power Platform so exciting.

Learning about the history of Microsoft 365

Let's rewind less than a decade and reflect on what the technology stack looked like then. Prior to 2012, most personal purchases and corporate licenses of Microsoft software were still based upon buying software on a CD-ROM and in some form or factor installing onto a PC (personal computer) or laptop. Once installed, you typically stayed on the same version of, say, Microsoft Word 2008 until corporately you were upgraded to Word 2010 or 2011. Between versions, everything was static. No changes, no improvements.

In 2012, Microsoft had less than a few years in the *online environment* with some offerings such as **Microsoft Business Productivity Office Suite Online** and **CRM Online**. The Cloud Rubicon had already been crossed into **Software as a Service (SaaS)** and was moving more to a subscription-based model in the Microsoft Azure cloud. Pulling this all together was the Microsoft Office 365 solution, which included online and client versions of the popular Office applications of Word, Excel, PowerPoint, and Outlook, as well as other applications such as Visio, Project, and others.

When Microsoft went all-in on the cloud, they changed some of the architectural framework underlying all of the Office applications to provide a more robust capability across the platform. What this meant for the users of Microsoft Office 365 was they could count on having an ever-current interoperable working environment with the rest of the organization.

With the addition of Microsoft OneDrive to the solution, when you save a file in the Microsoft 365 environment, you save it to a OneDrive cloud location that is allocated to your business user. This location will be a part of the corporate collection of documents that your firm will have control over from a security, compliance, and audit perspective. This does so much for the business user, such as version control, autosave, optimization, and security embedded in everything they do.

Microsoft leverages SharePoint document management as the underlying technology in OneDrive as well as the filesystem within Microsoft Teams. SharePoint itself is a frequently leveraged document management solution for many clients.

This makes the process of IT data and device management easy and simple and for the Project Operations user who utilizes so many applications across the organization, it means they can be assured that their data and everything meaningful to their day-to-day operations is readily available to them. Furthermore, Microsoft has produced mobile apps such as Outlook, Teams, and Dynamics 365 to further enhance the ease of access to business data regardless of location or device.

So far, we have learned how Microsoft 365 has evolved over the years. With the inclusion of applications, there have been changes in the licensing as well, which we will understand in the next section.

The licensing of Microsoft 365

Microsoft breaks out its Microsoft 365 solution to accommodate four major sectors of users:

- **Home**: Personal users of Microsoft 365
- **Business**: Small- to mid-sized business users
- **Enterprise**: Large corporate accounts
- **Education**: For educators, faculty, and staff

For the purposes of our book, we will primarily explore the Business and Enterprise editions as these are the common user base of the Project Operations solution. Home users would not typically use Project Operations, and Education is not a market for the solution.

Microsoft approaches Business and Enterprise differently. Business licensing is approached on more of a common, commercial type of transaction whereas Enterprise is typically worked through the Microsoft Enterprise sales team, meaning that the business is of such a size that Microsoft puts a different level of energy into managing.

Business editions of Microsoft 365 typically sell based on three major types:

- Microsoft 365 Business Basic
- Microsoft 365 Business Standard
- Microsoft 365 Business Premium

Enterprise editions of Microsoft 365 typically sell based on three major plan types:

- Microsoft 365 E3
- Microsoft 365 E5
- Microsoft 365 F3

In both scenarios, the solutions are sold and charged on a per-user/per-month basis. The difference is that the Business editions have no annual commitment levels whereas Enterprise editions have contractual obligations.

Within the Microsoft 365 framework, the apps (or applications) that are included are the same. The biggest difference is how they are deployed. For example, Microsoft 365 Business Basic gives you licensing for Microsoft Teams, Exchange, OneDrive, and SharePoint but they are all the cloud services-only versions – meaning web versions and not a desktop/client version. Standard and Business Premium give you access to more apps and the desktop/client versions of those apps. This means that you can use Microsoft Outlook as a client on your desktop/laptop, in a web browser, or on a mobile/tablet device with an app you download through the Apple App Store or Google Play Store (`https://www.microsoft.com/en-us/microsoft-365?rtc=1`).

The Microsoft Power Platform framework

Imagine being able to harness the potential of yourself, your team members, and others in the firm! Microsoft's Power Platform (`https://powerplatform.microsoft.com/en-us/`) does just this! The Microsoft Power Platform allows you to harness the skills and abilities of citizen developers and contributors within the firm, which can offer success to the team. This is accomplished by utilizing the low-code/no-code capabilities of the Power Platform.

The Microsoft Power Platform provides the ability to use Microsoft tools and technologies to perform the overall cohesiveness of the solution. With the Microsoft 365 environment, you have already authenticated with **Azure Active Directory** (**Azure AD**), which tells Microsoft what you are licensed for and which apps and data sources you have access to.

The Power Platform turns this into a cohesive solution by adding much-needed functions such as reporting and analytics (Power BI), development and mobile device solutions (PowerApps), integration and automation (Power Automate), power portals, as well as virtual assistants (Power Virtual Assistants).

Let's explore a few of the most integrated Power Platform applications and how they are used in Project Operations.

Power BI

Business intelligence (**BI**) applications have been around for a couple of decades. However, they historically have been very expensive and required specialized skills to build, maintain, and improve. Microsoft Power BI is the tool to create interactive dashboards and provide reporting, visualization, and performance indicators for a professional services firm. Power BI connects natively with and works through all the components of the Project Operations solution.

Furthermore, it is easy to engage with and begin using. Power BI is easy to pick up and build upon while simultaneously improving upon the visualization of reports and data. Many of the visualizations that are included in Power BI would typically cost many extra dollars but are part of the overall solution.

One of the complications of Power BI comes from its strength. Although it is a sophisticated tool, it takes a level of knowledge and vision to make meaningful informational presentations out of the firm's data. Power BI can present data from many data sources into one consolidated and unified environment.

There are other Power Platform apps that help you create new apps for your business. PowerApps is that tool within the Microsoft Power Platform.

PowerApps

Imagine if when you last said "Hey, it would work better like this," in a couple of hours you could have a working model of your vision! This is the promise behind the PowerApps part of the Power Platform. You can start building and launching apps using *templates* and *drag-and-drop simplicity*. You can deploy these apps quickly and couple them with Power BI and Power Automate to give the users of your information more promises without compromise. Furthermore, when you do need to move from citizen developers to professional developers, the professional developers can utilize app capabilities with Azure Functions and custom connectors to make a more robust experience.

Automating information is a powerful capability and to accomplish this, Microsoft created Power Automate.

Power Automate

As Microsoft has done so well, Power Automate brings sophisticated, usually expensive functionality to the typical business user. The result is that the Power Automate tool can be used to perform business workflow processing (approvals and workflow), as well as moving data from one point in the workflow to another.

Power Automate can integrate Microsoft Forms data from external users into Microsoft Dynamics **Customer Experience (CE)/Customer Relationship Management (CRM)**. Power Automate can take unstructured data and create structured data in your business systems. This makes the task of data integrity and quality easier to achieve as you have control from source to destination.

Extending automation, Microsoft has created Power Virtual Agents to automate actions within the platform.

Power Virtual Agents

"I am not a robot" does not apply here! With Power Virtual Agents, you can create a chatbot that makes sense for your business to integrate with the services and solutions you offer your clients. With handoffs to live agents and other **application programming interfaces (APIs)**, you can create a workflow that works for your clients in a Project Operations world.

The business applications Microsoft builds out for sales and marketing are all under the product name of Dynamics 365 CE, which is the CRM/CE application.

Microsoft Dynamics 365 CE

How do you build an app that needs to tie together the sales organization with the operational project planning and the accounting department? How do you build an application that needs the security of Microsoft Azure coupled with the framework of Microsoft 365? How do you extend that functionality across all devices and user types and through workflow and power applications?

The answer is Microsoft's development platform called **Dynamics 365 CE**, formerly called **Dynamics 365 Customer Relationship Management**. Upon its release, Microsoft's CRM platform was adopted by many people who chose to utilize it not only for CRM but also for additional functionality around the sales processes. Microsoft has previously called this the **eXtensible Relationship Management (xRM)** solution.

Today, the development environment that was Dynamics xRM is now a totally encompassing development framework that you can use to build a totally extended environment on top of Dynamics 365 CE. The Power Platform provides the tools of Power Automate, Dataverse, AI Builder, Power Virtual Agents, PowerApps, PowerApps portals, and Power BI in one complete development solution.

Let's rewind to 2003...

Microsoft introduced Dynamics CRM in 2003 as Microsoft Business Solutions Customer Relationship Management but was renamed Microsoft CRM 1.0 probably because customers could not say the original name without misplacing the words! The product was built to be extensible from its inception including even its most early adoption of **SQL Server Reporting Services** (**SSRS**). From versions 1.0 through CRM 2016 (released in November 2015), the Microsoft CRM solution was largely a server-based solution (on-premise software) with some online presence since 2008. Customers had to choose between a Workgroup, Professional, or Enterprise edition and perform complex installation and configuration.

It was in 2016 that we had solid idea of the direction of Microsoft's Dynamics 365 strategy. This included their direction in the professional services industry by releasing their **Project Service Automation** (**PSA**) solution on top of Microsoft Dynamics 365 CRM. Dynamics PSA, as we called it in the early days, was built very similar to how many successful apps were produced on top of CRM: as a **solution**. A solution in Microsoft CRM/xRM speak is a framework for packaging, installing, and updating software that is added into Microsoft's CRM solution. Ultimately, the ability to *solutionize* add-on apps became a large part of the Microsoft AppSource exchange.

Fast forward to today...

The app marketplace and approach have gained momentum over the years and Microsoft Dynamics 365 CE is now really a series of apps created on top of the Microsoft **Dataverse**. Dataverse is the database for the Power Platform formerly known as xRM. The Power Platform provides the entities, relationships, forms, fields, business processes, and much more that make up the universe of applications that are Dynamics 365 CE apps.

Think of it this way: when you license Dynamics 365 CE, you are licensing a foundation (Azure), a Dataverse database, and the apps you wish to deploy on top of these. So, for a regular sales team use of Dynamics 365 CE, you would likely license just the Sales app. Customer service would use the Customer Service app.

As shown in the following figure, for Project Operations, you use three different apps to provide the functionality to your users: **Project Operations**, **Project Operations Team Member**, and **Resource Scheduling**:

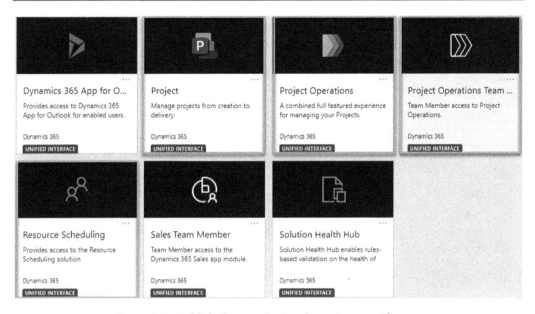

Figure 2.1 – Published apps – Project Operations specific apps

The **Project** app highlighted is a *project-only app* sitting on top of the Dataverse with three main areas of functionality enabled: **Projects**, **Settings**, and **Training**. For all intents and purposes, it really is just for the project's functionality on a day-to-day basis.

The Project Operations app is a full-featured app that most in a project operations role will know how to work with. The Project Operations app has the Projects area along with others, such as Sales, Resources, Settings, and Training. Project managers and related roles will typically work in the Projects area. However, they may go into the Resourcing Scheduling app to see schedules and book resources. A firm's practice management may utilize the Resourcing area to track utilization while the business development team and others may utilize the Sales area for opportunities, project contracts, and other related functions:

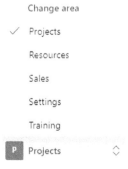

Figure 2.2 – Project Operations – full-featured areas available to the user

The Project Operations Team Member app is the most widely deployed app across the Project Operations population. The Team Member app primarily provides two functions, **Time Entries** and **Expenses**:

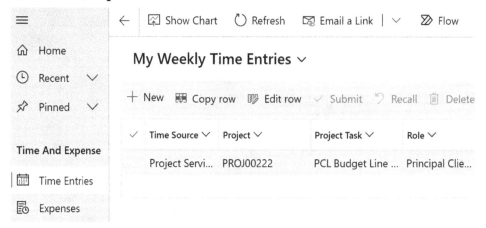

Figure 2.3 – Project Operations Team Member app

Finally, the Resource Scheduling app provides an app just for the Resource Management Office and other related functions. It primarily provides the resource requirements, bookings, resource (team member) lists, resource groups, and the schedule board:

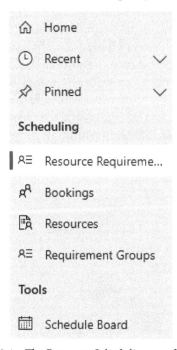

Figure 2.4 – The Resource Scheduling app functions

However, it does not have to stay this way! This is where you get to tailor the user experience according to the needs your users have. This is quite powerful as you can control access to apps, rearrange the layout of the user experience, and take away unnecessary apps.

With the Power Platform, you have control over the apps that are deployed. In order to do so, you can start in the **Advanced Settings | Settings | Apps** to launch the App Designer. You do need to have the System Customizer role to log in to this site. When you do, you will get a screen that looks something like this:

Figure 2.5 – Dynamics 365 CE App Designer

This is where you get to select what is included and excluded in your app! You take control and you get to define the amount of information shared in the app. For example, remember how the Project Operations Team Member app has both time and expense entry functionality to it? Well, what happens if you want to just have the user see time entries and not expense entries? You can remove it through App Designer portal. Since this is tied directly to your Dynamics 365 CE environment, your login and credentials will drive what you can and cannot do.

In this portal, you can modify the site map for the app as well. Remember how the first Project app I mentioned only had three areas: Projects, Settings, and Training? This is why, when you open the site map, it only includes these three areas and within the project and resources, you see the limited number of enabled screens:

Figure 2.6 – App Designer – Sitemap Designer for the main Project app

Furthermore, when you have data in your Project Operations environment, you may want to make your own PowerApps built off Dataverse and the data contained within. With PowerApps, it is easy to start from a Dataverse database and pull from your specific entities (database records) to create an app for the iPhone/Android or tablet world as seen here:

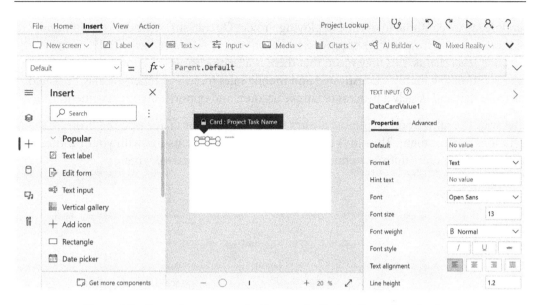

Figure 2.7 – Example canvas app built upon the Project Operations database

This app approach provides you with the power you need to pull information together for your users to augment the capabilities of the system. The difference between a Canvas App and a Model Driven app is this.

A canvas app can be built upon any database or data source. With canvas apps, you start with a somewhat blank slate. There is still a lot of programming functionality already built in but you are controlling the app programmatically. Model-driven apps are developed in Dataverse and can be integrated across systems. With a model-driven app you have more built in user interface as it adops the UI of the Dynamics 365 CE environment. Project Operations leverages model-driven apps, as we will see later as we modify some of them to suit our needs.

Microsoft Dynamics 365 CE – sales functionality

It is important to know that you are still working with a sales solution that in and of itself is a great enterprise solution. The Dynamics 365 CE sales functionality is built to provide a sophisticated level of opportunity management coupled with all other functions you would typically think of, including lead, account, contact, and activity management. However, coupling this with Microsoft Outlook (for email, calendars, and contacts), the user now has one solution that does it all for them.

Therefore, as we continue to outline deploying Project Operations, we must keep in mind that there is a sales frontend set of processes that should be addressed as well. For some enterprise-level clients, this may mean that there is a large, connected effort to fully deploy a sales solution to a highly sophisticated and mobile sales force. For others, it may be scaled back from that and largely a process of simple account and opportunity management.

Either way, the sales frontend almost always fits in one form or factor into the Project Operations environment. Thus, it is important to have this discussion with your business users and sales leaders upfront before getting too deep into the deployment:

Figure 2.8 – Project analysis built into Project Operations

Oh, and Project Operations also integrates well with competing CRM solutions such as Salesforce.com, SugarCRM, and others! This means that if your sales team is already deployed in a solution but you need the functionality of Project Operations, there is a solution!

To summarize, Microsoft Dynamics 365 CE integrates and seamlessly takes advantage of the Microsoft 365 environment. Having the Power Platform provides you with the ability to cohesively work across all data entry points, combining them for collaboration and teamwork and providing meaningful information through reporting and analytics.

Just as Microsoft has sales and marketing apps, they also have finance and operations apps that handle all of the accounting and finance work for a firm.

Microsoft Dynamics 365 for Finance and Operations

An exciting element of Project Operations is that it is an end-to-end solution from sales through delivery through accounting. This means that the solution must deliver upon the accounting requirements of a professional services firm! This is no small feat!

Historically, some professional services firms have implemented Finance and Operations to accomplish only part of what Project Operations does. This means that previously, customers have spent their efforts setting up a robust project accounting system to perform WBS and resource management, time and expense entry, billing and invoicing, and many other functions. The challenge they incurred was that this configuration was heavily accounting-oriented, which limited the scope of the number of users who could effectively contribute to the solution. This is why having purpose-built user experiences that match the need of the users working in the system is beneficial to a professional services firm.

The nature of project accounting coupled with **Generally Accepted Accounting Principles** (**GAAP**) requires many different ways of accounting for the project contracts that a firm delivers. For example, a simple fixed-price contract of $1,000,000 may be billed upfront and the money is collected upfront but the revenue recognized against that contract will be tracked over time, based upon a percent complete. *Why is this done this way?* The purpose is to match revenue with costs and represent the revenue across the accounting periods (months) based upon what has been earned through the percent complete. When the $1,000,000 is billed and paid, that revenue goes into a deferred revenue account and when the project is worked on, that account balance is reduced over time and revenue is earned (recognized).

That is for a fixed price. What about time and materials? Or time and materials with **work in progress** (**WIP**)? Or not to exceed? Or how about retainers? Each of these different contract types requires a different way of setting up the contract and contract lines, the billing methods, the revenue recognition, invoicing, and accounting for labor costs. All of this is with the goal of recognizing revenue according to GAAP. Furthermore, with SaaS and other monthly-based contracts, revenue now needs to adhere to ASC606/IFRS15 accounting.

Therefore, Microsoft has put a considerable amount of work into integrating into their **ERP** solution called **Microsoft Dynamics 365 for Finance and Operations**, sometimes called Finance and Supply Chain. This solution has the sophisticated project accounting capabilities needed to support a professional services firm and has had this functionality for many years. However, it is only recently that the project management and accounting functionality has been elegantly integrated into the professional services solution.

On the CE side of Project Operations, we have seen how sales connect with delivery. Now, delivery must connect with accounting through the time entries that are entered and approved, the expenses processed, and the resulting billing transactions with all of their nuances in billing and revenue recognition. This is accomplished through the dual-write integration technology and the integration journals that run between Project Operations delivery through to Project Operations accounting.

In the end, you want your invoicing to be accurate and timely so that you continue to maintain the best relations with your clients:

Project Service Invoices ∨

✔	Name ↑ ∨	Created On ∨	Status Reason ∨	Total Amount ∨	Customer ∨
	New Project Need	3/4/2021 7:37 PM	Billed	$50,000.00	123 Architects
	New Project Need	3/4/2021 8:01 PM	Billed	$2,500.00	123 Architects
	New Project Need	3/4/2021 8:07 PM	Billed	$1,350.00	123 Architects

Figure 2.9 – Project Service Invoices resulting from delivery and project management activities

More than just the billing, invoicing, and revenue recognition, the project accounting also needs to provide the right costing information so that the project's profitability is accurately measured and comparable to benchmarks. This is accomplished through roles, role prices, blended costs, and their application to projects based upon the work performed. As time is entered into the system and approved for a time and materials project, the result is generally a cost transaction for the team member or resource who did the work and a billing transaction based on the project contract. You can literally have a profit and loss statement for each hour. For example, we bill at $250 per hour, our cost is $110 per hour, our gross margin is $115 per hour.

Furthermore, project accounting has many other functions that a sophisticated firm will need to manage a project, such as dashboards and key performance indicators that identify trends in the projects and alert managers to problems ideally before they manifest.

The end-to-end capabilities of Project Operations are incredible; however, like the sales frontend, Project Operations too is capable of integrating with other project accounting solutions from competitors such as Sage Intacct and other project-oriented accounting systems.

The Finance and Operations functionality of Project Operations provides a purpose-built user experience that project accounting teams will naturally gravitate to. This app is made to integrate with the overall Project Operations solution, providing the sophisticated accounting controls a professional services firm requires.

Now, to bring all of this together is the Project Operations apps that Microsoft has published. These apps, combined with the integration framework, provide you with a unified solution to work in, across the firm.

The Unified environment – Project Operations apps

As we proceed into the next chapter, we will learn that there are three different deployment models of Project Operations to be chosen from. These deployment models will greatly influence how you use the solution going forward. Therefore, it is beneficial to dig a little deeper into the environment.

For the curious-minded, let's demystify this. When looking at the Unified environment, it is easy to forget all the capabilities across the Microsoft 365 framework that are working in your favor to give you a world-class project operations solution:

Microsoft/Office 365	Dynamics 365 CE Apps	Dynamics 365 F&O
Microsoft Office and Outlook apps	Sales app for business development experts	Project financial details for project analysis
Microsoft Project for the Web	Project Service Automation functionality	Invoicing and revenue recognition
OneDrive and SharePoint	Dataverse entities and PowerApps	Time and expense costing
Outlook integration throughout	Dual-write integration technology	Accounting integration for billing, costing, and revenue

Table 2.1 – The components of the Project Operations solution

All of these functionalities are available in a browser of your choice, through your phone, tablet, or any other device with modern browser interfaces. Let's understand the preceding table in detail:

- The first column represents the common Microsoft 365 apps that are in use as part of Project Operations. Of course, you have your Office apps and Outlook, and with Outlook, you have the integration to Dynamics 365 so you can work in Outlook and use Dynamics 365 CE functions. Furthermore, you have Project for the Web, which is the core planning functionality for Project Operations. OneDrive and SharePoint do your document management and Outlook is integrated throughout.

- In the second column are your Dynamics 365 CE apps, which include the baseline Sales app for client managers/sales professionals. Built upon Dataverse and integrated through dual-write integration technology is the Project Service Automation functionality, which controls the majority of the user experience in Project Operations.

- In the third column are the functions of the Finance and Operations accounting solution. These are specifically written for an accounting user to leverage and perform all the structured project accounting, revenue recognition, and costing functions needed for their compliance, audit, and reporting requirements.

With this, we will end this chapter and summarize our learnings.

Summary

Microsoft Project Operations was purpose-built for professional services firms' complex and sophisticated requirements. As an integrated end-to-end solution, Project Operations provides project, program, and practice managers with an overall integrated and easy-to-use solution for day-to-day operations. Project Operations solves the problem of disparate systems and disconnected work.

First, we learned that Project Operations is built into the Microsoft 365 framework so it leverages the sophisticated IT infrastructure that Microsoft provides. This controls your security, manages threats, and protects data.

The Microsoft 365 apps help with your daily workloads, including Outlook, Excel, and all other Microsoft Office apps. We learned that as part of the Microsoft 365 applications, we leverage Project for the Web as the task management core solution for planning resources and tasks.

We also identified how the Power Platform with its various components provides you with additional capabilities to report, integrate, and build applications with.

Knowing that Project Operations is built upon Microsoft Dynamics 365 CE, we learned that the solution is delivered through apps that work best for the user's experience. Integrated through Dynamics 365 for Finance and Operations, the best of project accounting is utilized to provide the GAAP accounting all businesses need.

As we proceed into the next chapter, we will determine our deployment model and identify the steps necessary for your deployment model to stand up a baseline Project Operations solution.

Questions

1. Which Microsoft app provides you with document management in the cloud?
2. Which structured document management solution in the cloud is used for more formalized contract and document retention?
3. Which app is used in Project Operations to track and manage tasks?
4. Which app is used in Project Operations to modify the site map of CE and is also capable of making your own applications?
5. Which Project Operations app gives you full functionality?
6. Which Project Operations app just has time and expense functionality?
7. True or false: Project Operations is only licensed on a 3-year contract.
8. True or false: Project Operations requires Dynamics 365 CE for Sales.
9. What is the accounting backend that is used in Project Operations?
10. What is the purpose of deferred revenue and revenue recognition?
11. What is project profitability?

Further reading

- Matthew Weston, *Learn Microsoft PowerApps*, Packt Publishing, 2019
  https://www.packtpub.com/product/learn-microsoft-powerapps/9781789805826

3
The How-Tos of Setting Up Project Operations

As we learned in the previous chapter, there is an overall, underlying framework to the Project Operations solution. In this chapter, we are going to review all the considerations necessary before going forward, one of which is deployment.

Deploying requires some pre-planning and decision making that will drive the deployment type your firm chooses. Decisions will depend upon corporate strategy, software solutions already deployed, types of users of the system, and many other factors.

This chapter will walk you through the decision points, provide you with guidance on the best paths forward depending upon your answers, provide real-life examples of deployments, and finally give a step-by-step approach for deployments.

In this chapter, you will learn about the following concepts:

- Understanding the deployment approach
- Non-dynamics integrated approach
- Upgrade path for existing customers

- Setting up Dynamics 365 CE – Sales
- Setting up Project Operations
- Dynamics 365 CE – Sales Customizations
- Data Import
- Integration strategies

By the end of this chapter, you will know how to deploy Project Operations for your firm's needs. Specifically, you will learn about the following:

- A functional, step-by-step guide to get started
- How to deploy Project Operations without Dynamics 365 CE customers
- How to deploy Project Operations without Dynamics Finance customers
- Integration strategies for moving data to and from Finance and Operations

Let's begin by discussing the deployment approach.

Technical requirements

To perform the tasks in this chapter, there are some technical requirements:

- An Office 365 account and an Azure **Active Directory** (**AD**) login
- A Microsoft Dynamics 365 Project Operations (CRM) license
- A Microsoft Project Plan license
- If integrating with Finance and Operations, a Dynamics 365 for Finance and Operations license
- Global admin rights in Office 365

Please visit the following link to check the CiA videos:

`https://bit.ly/3abRHw7`

Understanding the deployment approach

To begin your deployment of Project Operations, you should first work to gain understanding and agreement in your firm on some key decisions, as these will have (organizational, technical, financial, business, and political) implications that the firm will be required to live with for many years into the future.

In the following image you can see Project Operation's deployment journey:

Figure 3.1 – Project Operations deployment journey

To guide the decisions, let's ask a few questions and discuss the ramifications of the answers. Remember, we are attempting to outline, across three different areas of Microsoft technology, how to configure a solution.

To understand what is involved in Project Operations deployment, the previous chapter showed *Table 2.1 – The components of the Project Operations solution*, which outlined the pillars of the solution.

The table shows that there are some components that stand alone, such as the Microsoft 365 components. This deployment is valid and is actually in use in business today. The Dynamics 365 CE apps and Microsoft 365 components together create the lite deployment. Adding in the accounting software completes the integrated solution.

Therefore, there are some questions we should ask before deploying Microsoft 365 overall.

Microsoft 365 framework question

A very foundational question is this:

> *Are you currently using Microsoft 365/Office 365 for your IT infrastructure, Microsoft Office 365 apps, and related security, data protection, and compliance features?*

We have two answers, obviously:

- If the answer is *yes*, then your firm has already made a very foundational decision to move to the Microsoft 365 platform. If this sounds important, it is because it is. Microsoft Azure Active Directory and Authentication controls access to everything from your licensing to the documents you have access to and the systems you will use as part of your overall IT policy and infrastructure.

- If the answer is *no*, then you may be utilizing a competing platform such as Google Cloud Platform and the G-Suite of apps, or a best-of-breed environment of specific applications. Such examples are firms that adopted the G-Suite of applications to perform the same functions as Microsoft Office. Therefore, this environment is not a native Microsoft Azure Active Directory environment, and therefore the authentication model and all key components of the Microsoft 365 and Dynamics 365 environment are going to be a challenge to overcome.

There are a number of Dynamics-related questions that need to be resolved to move us forward.

Microsoft Dynamics questions

Dynamics 365 is a power set of apps that empower and engage the firm. Therefore, a few key questions should be asked, including this one:

Are you currently or do you desire to use the Microsoft Dynamics 365 CE Sales apps to perform selling in your firm?

Microsoft Dynamics 365 CE is a foundational sales application that many firms adopt to drive marketing, sales, and customer support efforts across the enterprise. Therefore, it is not uncommon for you to have already chosen this solution for your marketing, selling, and support functions. The solution may already be implemented or it may be a part of the implementation strategy of Project Operations. Either way, this foundational decision will benefit the organization with tight collaboration between marketing, sales, and Project Operations functions.

If, however, your firm is utilizing a different CRM system, such as Salesforce.com, Sugar CRM, or any other solution, this will not preclude you from utilizing Project Operations. It just means that the frontend sales functionality will be performed in an outside system and integrated into Project Operations using tools from the non-Dynamics CRM system.

Are you currently or do you desire to use the Microsoft Dynamics 365 for Finance and Operations/Project Accounting software to perform the finance and accounting functionality?

Microsoft Dynamics 365 finance and accounting functionality is an element of the Project Operations solution that can take on a life of its own. Furthermore, the use of Finance and Operations will largely be driven by the finance, accounting, and executive teams. Sometimes referred to as the ERP system, the decision to move from another system to Finance and Operations is one that would typically be made alongside a larger effort to determine a migration path forward.

However, if you are using an older ERP system, maybe something on-premises such as Microsoft Dynamics SL, Sage Intacct, or enterprise solutions from Oracle or SAP, integrating into these solutions is not uncommon. The line of delineation is the cut-off point of transactional information coming from Project Operations into the ERP system such as time entries, billing transactions, costing information, and other data.

Have you previously used Microsoft Dynamics Project Service Automation?

You may have already used Microsoft's Project Service Automation solution previously in the shape of its original release back in 2016, or in a subsequent version such as V3.0 prior to the release of the Project Operations solution. If so, you will be pleasantly surprised to find that the functionality of the solution is going to be familiar to you but with some added features. The highlights are that Project Operations added more contract type functionality for not-to-exceed and retainer billing, as well as changing out the planning function from the older model's *Gantt chart-only* style to a more modern project for the web functionality that includes task, board, and timeline views of the planning information.

If you have not been using Microsoft Project Service Automation, you may have been using a different solution with a similar structure. It has not been uncommon for some of the key concepts to roll forward from other solutions into the Project Operations solution with very similar types of functions. Other solutions have taken similar approaches to the needs of professional services firms.

This leads us to the organizational questions that will need to be asked.

Organizational questions

Organizationally, the move to Dynamics 365 Project Operations is a big endeavor! There will be a multitude of opportunities to work across the organization and collaborate with many of your peers and leaders who will contribute to the overall success of the solution. Furthermore, there will be opportunities to work with Microsoft partners who have been expertly trained and certified on the solution and will most assuredly bring a valued perspective to the deployment.

Are you currently working with or considering working with a Microsoft partner?

Implementing Project Operations is a strategic project that can benefit greatly from wise counsel, and there are many Microsoft partners who specialize in the Project Operations solution. Furthermore, if you're implementing the full solution from CE to Project Operations to the accounting components in Finance and Operations, there will be advanced topics to be covered above and beyond what is available on a self-service or research basis.

Do you have a team of cross-functional team members available to help with the implementation?

Undoubtedly, you will need more than a few team members, executive sponsors, and others across the organization to make the deployment of Project Operations a success. The best approach is to begin identifying upfront some of the key areas of operation that you or the firm intends to benefit from Project Operations. This will provide you with an overview of who from these areas will need to be involved. You will probably want to have managers, executives, and **subject matter experts** (**SMEs**) involved in the decisions leading up to and including your implementation strategy and execution.

Which deployment model will you choose to deploy Project Operations?

This leads us into the next few sections to evaluate each of the options for deployment and discuss their functions and the overall approach for each.

Lite deployment

The lite deployment option of Project Operations provides you with the functionality of Dynamics 365 CE plus the Project Operations apps that drive the project services capabilities. The solution provides a sales process (business process flow) for projects that extends Dynamics 365 CE Sales and provides your users with a guided selling experience.

The lite deployment is not actually "lite" on functionality. It is just a name that Microsoft has tagged it with. Within the lite deployment itself, there are a lot of decision points around functionality that will need to be made.

This deployment leverages Microsoft Project for the web to build a work breakdown structure and task management capabilities. The resource management functionality is built into the WBS to assign specific resources to a task, assign hours, and provide resource management through the use of the unified resource management schedule board.

When you deploy Dynamics 365 CE and utilize the sales management functionality in CE to provide opportunity management, quoting, and project contract management, you are able to create contracts easily and quickly. Contract management provides you with the basic functionality of contracts (time and materials and fixed-price contracts) plus advanced contract functionality, including not-to-exceed limits, retainer billing, and split billing. The combination of contract types will provide the project managers with the flexibility that will benefit the firm when billing out the project.

Advanced customer pricing supports multi-dimensional pricing models that allow for the creation and use of default selling rates, customer-specific rates, and project-specific rates built using chargeable and non-chargeable roles native to the Project Operations solution. Furthermore, roles are used to define not only the selling rates but also the costing rates that are applicable by role, so you can receive a project profitability view by project based upon the roles, hours, rates, and costs.

On the operational, day-to-day side of things, this deployment provides time tracking, approvals, and management. The team members have their own app that can be limited to show only the time entry functionality, should you wish for that. The time entry functionality provides the ability to enter time through the Project Operations interface in a browser or through the Outlook app for Dynamics 365. Time is entered weekly and submitted for approval with each line entry uniquely tied to a project, task, and hours worked basis.

Time can be imported automatically from resource assignments, resource bookings, and from a team member's Outlook calendar. With each of these options, the goal is to get a timecard entered quickly and efficiently. Furthermore, you can copy a week from a previous week and provide a baseline of entry from work performed previously.

Also, time entries for absence, vacation, overtime, and administrative or sales time can be tracked in Project Operations. The time entry capabilities are robust and sophisticated, providing for almost all time entry scenarios.

Approvals are sent to the project manager or other delegated approvers who can approve the time for the team member. Time can also be sent back to the team member for corrections with notifications and information on what needs to be corrected. Furthermore, time that has been approved can be recalled as well, providing the ability to have an overall time management continuum.

Basic expenses are a part of the solution as well. You can have chargeable and non-chargeable transactions and produce proper invoicing based upon the expense type. They are basic, meaning that you can categorize expenses with airfare, mileage, hotel, and so on, and you can enter expenses with attachments for receipts. However, missing from the solution is a sophisticated expense policy management infrastructure.

The options for that policy management and enforcement include using Microsoft Dynamics 365 for Finance and Operations (one of the other deployment options) to perform the policy and management. Alternatively, many organizations will use an SAP Concur type of solution and integrate the expenses into the project for costing purposes.

To perform billing and invoicing in this deployment, you will utilize what become actuals and journals from the Project Operations solution. These are produced through the act of approving time, expenses, invoices, and other billable transactions that become the actuals, thus generating an accounting transaction. Upon review and approval of the actuals, journals are created, and it is in this journaling that you can integrate into your third-party or other ERP system or accounting system. The integration approach you take will greatly depend upon the ERP system's capabilities. Some can leverage Microsoft technologies, others will require third-party integration tools.

Proforma and customer-facing invoicing can be generated out of Project Operations and rendered in a form that is customer-facing and accurate from a Project Operations perspective. However, missing from this will be a tax engine that will add taxes to the invoice and perform the sophisticated tax processing inherent in many ERP systems today.

This deployment model depends upon a number of key data setup tasks that will be discussed in future sections and chapters. Furthermore, we will discuss the impacts and options around the setup tasks.

An integrated Dynamics 365 CE to Finance and Operations deployment model may be right for some firms that are wanting to deploy all aspects of the solution in a unified environment.

Project Operations for resourcing

This deployment method builds upon the *lite deployment – deal to proforma invoicing deployment* method in a number of ways. In this deployment, you will receive and perform many of the same tasks that we have already discussed. You will still set up and implement the following areas:

- Sales process for projects that extend the Dynamics 365 Sales application
- Project planning using Microsoft Project for the web
- Multi-dimensional pricing
- Unified resource management
- Time tracking and management

However, you will have more sophisticated functionality around these specific areas:

- Full expense policy, entry, and management capabilities
- The ability to scan receipts with **Optical Character Recognition** (**OCR**)
- The ability to create proforma and customer-facing invoicing
- The ability to enact revenue recognition for projects

To enable this deployment, you will perform the same steps as in the lite deployment plus the configuration of Dynamics 365 for Finance and Operations. Performing this level of configuration will require a number of key IT decisions, purchases of subscriptions, and deployment of Finance and Operations. This is generally an accounting and finance task coupled with the IT team and the Microsoft partner.

At a baseline, setting up Finance and Operations requires four key components that all interact and work together to set up the accounting system:

1. The first area is the setup and configuration of the Microsoft Dataverse (previously Common Data Service) to enable the integration between Project Operations and the Finance and Operations accounting system.

2. Next, you will set up a project in Microsoft Lifecycle Services, also called **LCS**. The licensing for Finance and Operations will be provided by Microsoft and **your Cloud Solution Provider or CSP**. LCS is available at `https://lcs.dynamics.com/v2` and is the baseline to set up a new project in LCS to deploy Finance and Operations.

3. Setting up an Azure environment is a critical element of this deployment method. Azure is the Microsoft subscription and server configuration that will provide the underlying infrastructure for Finance and Operations. Deployed in the cloud, the end result of the Finance and Operations deployment will be an app that is accessible, being integrated into the same portal you use to access all the other project apps.

4. Setting up and configuring Microsoft's Dual Write functionality will enable an integrated environment that you will benefit from. The complete data model in Project Operations will integrate seamlessly into Finance and Operations.

The additional functionality will include the ability in the accounting system to set up expense policy and entry as well as approval and management capabilities. Adding to this is the ability to scan receipts with OCR to automate the entry of expense data from the expense receipt itself.

On the invoicing side of things, when creating invoices through the time and materials, fixed price, or other billing events, these invoices are transferred through the *integration journal into Finance and Operations*. This creates a proposed invoice resulting in a fully functional customer-facing invoicing system complete with sales tax information.

Furthermore, revenue recognition for projects is automated in the Finance and Accounting system to recognize revenue on a percentage basis and provide the ability to recognize revenue as needed for your project environment. *Chapter 11, Project Accounting and Operations* provides more detail on this process.

The high-level steps to accomplish the implementation of Finance and Accounting are as follows:

1. Set up LCS with a project to implement Finance and Accounting.

2. Set up Azure and configure with LCS.

3. Install Finance and Accounting.

4. Enable initial sync between systems.

5. Set up the dual-write integration.

6. Get started with configuration and personalization in Finance and Operations apps.

7. Configure your user interface in Finance and Operations apps.

8. Configure a chart of accounts in Dynamics 365 Finance.

9. Create fiscal calendars, years, and periods in Dynamics 365 Finance.

10. Configure currencies in Dynamics 365 Finance.

11. Configure ledgers and journals in Dynamics 365 Finance.

The end result of all this work will provide you with a unified environment that produces a solution looking something like this:

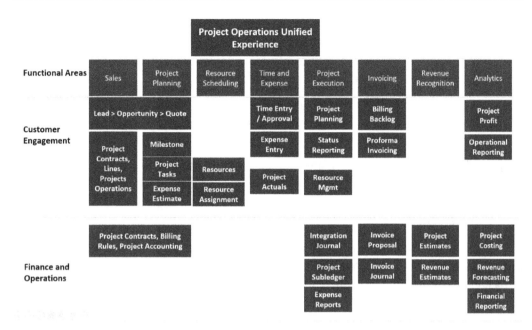

Figure 3.2 – Project Operations unified environment

Project Operations supports non-stocked/resource-based scenarios (discussed here) as well as stocked/production order scenarios in the same environment through legal entity-level configurations. As an example, a company (called Contoso in our demo database scenarios) can use the stocked/production order capabilities in their US manufacturing facility (legal entity = Contoso Manufacturing United States). Contoso can use the non-stocked/resource-based capabilities in their Contoso Robotics Arms servicing facility in the UK (legal entity = Contoso Robotics United Kingdom). So, let's now explore the stocked/production order scenario.

Project Operations for production orders

The Project Operations for stocked/production order scenarios is a deployment option available at the legal entity level within Project Operations. What this means is that you can have a mixed environment where, for example, you have a manufacturing or job shop configuration of Project Operations working in one legal entity while having a delivery or setup function in another legal entity. A real-world scenario that has commonly been encountered is companies that both manufacture and deliver their own products. The benefit of this deployment is that you can uniquely manage the needs of both legal entities and then combine them at a financial level to view the overall performance of the company.

With this deployment, you will use Project Operations (CE functionality) to perform project planning using Microsoft Project for the web, and you will use the work breakdown structures that we see used prevalently in Microsoft Project for the web.

However, in Project Operations (specifically, the Finance and Operations functionality), you will manage the project-based sales and marketing in Finance and Operations apps. Project pricing and costing will incorporate the cost rate and bill rate configurations in Finance and Operations.

Resource management, project progress, expense management with receipt capture using OCR, invoicing using sales tax and date-effective exchange rates, configurable project groups for **Work in Process (WIP)** accounting and accruals, and project revenue recognition are all performed in the Finance and Operations app functionality.

Procurement and consumption of stocked inventory to projects will be conducted utilizing a Finance and Operations app for Supply Chain Management. This means direct costing and consumption of inventory will be costed to a project (job) in Finance and Operations.

The results of this are that you will work in a project management system that manages inventoried items and job costing for internal and billable projects for schedules and financials.

The expense management system will provide you with a fully functional, policy-based expense entry and approval system to expense billable and non-billable expenses to projects.

Furthermore, you will be using a robust sales tax management solution that provides exchange rate engine processing to generate customer-facing invoices. Furthermore, invoicing can be conducted through intercompany invoicing, providing a robust invoicing method for the borrowing and lending legal entities. This is accomplished through intercompany timesheets, expenses, and vendor invoices. You can accrue the WIP revenue in the lending legal entity. This provides you with transfer rates for sales and costs so that project costing will be accurate across multiple legal entities. More advanced functionality such as pay-when-paid vendor invoicing and forecast models for project budgets are available.

Finally, at a financial level, you will be using an **International Financial Reporting Standards (IFRS)**-compliant project accounting and revenue recognition system. This means that, as a multinational corporation, you can utilize this deployment option to accurately report on all aspects of your project accounting.

There are some situations, though, where a firm may want to deploy only parts of the solution to begin with and then deploy more as the firm gets some wins.

Non-dynamics integrated approach

There are scenarios where the entire end-to-end Project Operations solution does not fully meet the requirements of the firm, resulting in a non-dynamics integration approach.

As much as there is a benefit to having an all-in-one integrated Project Operations environment, it is probably more common to take on portions of functionality that bring the most value most quickly when moving to a unified solution. However, as a case in point, some clients may start by implementing Dynamics 365 CE Sales and Marketing while also then implementing Project Operations. Let's look at both in the next subsections.

The CE Sales and Project Operations scenario

So, this type of client will typically deploy Dynamics 365 CE Sales first, or deploy along with Project Operations, and will perform the deployment method of lite deployment – deal to proforma invoicing. This then will necessitate integration into the ERP system that will manage the accounting activities related to the projects. The type of accounting software that can do these accounting activities ranges from entry-level solutions such as QuickBooks Enterprise with job/project costing to mid-size solutions such as Sage Intacct and high-end solutions such as SAP, Oracle, and Workday. The accounting software will be as varied as the integration technologies involved.

Some consistent factors exist, though. The first factor is that if the accounting system is to track the project costing, then there needs to be the feature of job or project costing inherent within the solution. This will allow more robust integration between systems with project costing information being stored in the accounting system at a project and task level. However, if that level of project accounting is not required, then some integrations simply take the project invoice data and compile it into a project invoice for the accounting system to consume. Upon consumption, it is stored as a standard invoice in the accounting system to be paid by the customer. Credits and rebills are integrated between the two systems to credit an invoice, back it out in Project Operations, and rebill in the Project Operations system to integrate again into the accounting system.

In this scenario, the accounting system is the system of record for all accounting and customer invoice information, whereas the Project Operations solution is the system of record for all project-related activity. Furthermore, some integration between the CE Sales customer records and the accounting system customer records will need to be in place.

The third-party CRM and Project Operations scenario

A recent enterprise-level implementation involved a high-tech client who re-platformed from Salesforce.com to Microsoft Dynamics for the high-volume side of their business but kept Salesforce.com for the enterprise side of their business. In this scenario, we deployed the Dynamics CE and Project Operations solution, but on the Salesforce side of things, we integrated project opportunities at a specific stage into Project Operations. This resulted in a completely uniform process for project initiation through closeout. The result of this is that salespeople do not need to do anything different in their business processes and the results are the same: a unified Project Operations platform to conduct project execution.

Upgrade path for existing customers

Project Service Automation (**PSA**) from Microsoft has been available commercially since 2016. Clients have worked on and implemented PSA since 2016 and have upgraded to PSA 3.0, which was commercially available until Project Operations in the fall of 2020. Upon the release of Project Operations, which supplants and deprecates PSA, the clients who are on PSA 3.0 will upgrade to Project Operations as a matter of the typical upgrade cycle in Dynamics 365.

In the Microsoft Dynamics Wave 1 release notes (`https://docs.microsoft.com/en-us/dynamics365-release-plan/2021wave1/finance-operations/dynamics365-project-operations/`), we see that the upgrade path for Dynamics 365 PSA clients is scheduled for September 2021.

On a related note, there are three other features that are listed as included in the spring release. The first is one that we will use in later chapters and this is the integrated task-based billing setup for projects. This is a significant improvement to address previous limitations and I have found it to be highly beneficial for a wide array of clients.

Another feature is an improved and seamless provisioning and **application lifecycle management** (**ALM**) experience. This is going to include better provisioning questionnaires coupled with automatic linking of environments and enablement of dual-write entity maps for new and existing environments. Furthermore, there is the new trials experience, which guides customers to the correct deployment approach based upon their scenario.

Tracking the pricing and use of non-stocked materials is a need for some Project Operations clients. These capabilities include estimating and pricing non-stocked materials during the sales cycle for a project as well as tracking the use of non-stocked materials during project delivery. It also includes integrating vendor costs from project-based vendor invoices for non-stocked items from Dynamics 365 for Finance and Operations. Also, there are feature accounts for project costs and revenue on projects.

With that in mind, let's explore the setup of Dynamics 365 CE sales functionality.

Setting up Dynamics 365 CE Sales

We are now going to utilize the information we have covered up to this point by taking all the information we have learned and putting it into practice:

> **Note**
>
> It is likely best to use Incognito/InPrivate browsing to perform the following steps. You may find it better to deploy using Google Chrome rather than Edge, but that is largely subjective and based upon the cache you have in your browser and the number of accounts you use.

1. Let's get started with the deployment of Project Operations by logging in to `http://portal.office365.com/` with your Azure AD account with administrator privileges. From here, choose the Admin/Settings icon, on the left navigation bar. From here, select **Users | Active** and locate your user who is logged in to the portal.

2. In the vertical ellipsis next to your username, select **Manage product licenses** and within the **Licenses and apps** pane on the right, you should have the following licenses enabled:

   Project Plan 3

   Dynamics 365 Project Operations

   Project for Project Operations

3. To perform this step, you must be a user in Azure AD, have a valid Dynamics CE license, and have global admin or equivalent access. Upon validation of licensing, navigate to `https://admin.powerplatform.microsoft.com/` to build a new Dynamics 365 CE environment. From the **Environments** menu on the left navigation bar, choose **New** at the top of the screen to create a new environment. Give the environment a name, choose **Sandbox** for now (you can promote it later), choose your region, and choose to create a database for this environment, as shown here:

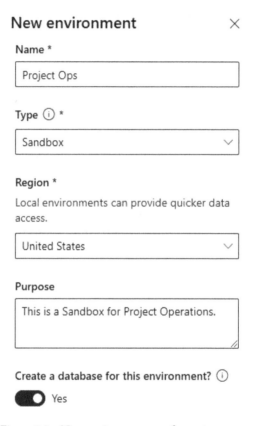

Figure 3.3 – New environment configuration screen

4. Click **Next** to proceed to the next screen. On the next screen, you will input the following option:

URL: Required if you want to create a custom URL, such as `ProjectOperations.crm.dynamics.com`. This must be unique for your organization:

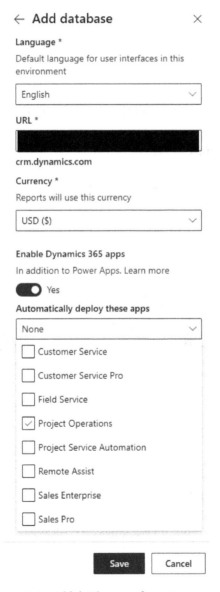

Figure 3.4 – Add database configuration screen

5.   From the **Environments** list screen, choose the horizontal ellipsis and choose **Open environment**:

Figure 3.5 – Environment list screen

Congratulations! You have just deployed Project Operations! When you open the environment, the following apps will appear:

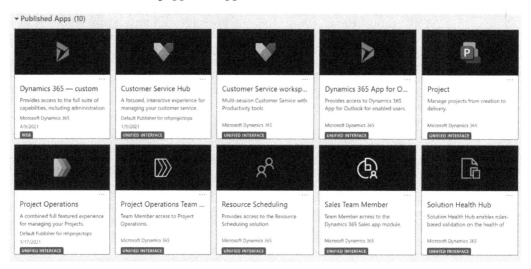

Figure 3.6 – Published Apps screen

From each of these apps, you can select their respective apps and pin them to the top of the portal for easy access. As an administrator, you can also open them in App Designer and manage roles for access control to each of the apps. Before we begin in Project Operations, let's first open the first app listed as **Dynamics 365 – custom** to begin some deployment discussions around Dynamics 365 Sales (as a foundation for Project Operations). Therefore, click on **Dynamics 365 – custom**.

In the settings area, select **Advanced Settings**, and let's review a few things that will drive the system functionality.

Advanced settings

The advanced settings area will drive a number of system-wide configuration choices that will impact all users in the system:

Figure 3.7 – Advanced settings

Although there are a number of screens in each of these subareas to review, some notable areas to be sure to validate and set up include the following:

- **Business Management**: You can set up everything from fiscal year settings to business closures, currencies, and connection roles.

- **Customization**: The customization area is where you have the ability to customize and/or configure the system with changes to existing entities (records), fields, forms, views, and relationships, as well as creating new ones. This greatly augments the system and allows it to be able to extend beyond the out-of-the-box functionality. Also, under **Publishers** in **Customizations**, you can set the prefixes for new entity names and other default behaviors.

- **Solutions**: These are packages of customizations to existing and new functionalities. Solutions allow you to group together all code to move easily and quickly from one system, such as a development environment, into test and then into production. You should use these solutions to group your customizations differently than the out-of-the-box grouping.

- **Microsoft AppSource**: This is the main marketplace to find **Independent Software Vendor** (**ISV**) solutions to add into Dynamics 365 CE.

- **Administration**: This will allow you to set your system-wide settings, autonumbering, and other administrative functions. In **Autonumbering**, you will likely want to set the prefixes and numbering schemes for contracts, quotes, orders, and invoices specifically for Project Operations. We will cover this topic in more detail in the next section.

- **Security**: This is where you will want to apply proper security roles to the users in the system. Note: best practice is to copy the security roles from the baseline system and modify them to be your roles to use as part of your deployment. The roles themselves define entity-level access across the full spectrum of the system, from the organization to the child business units, business units, and user level. Once defined, you will assign roles to the specific users to manage their access. Furthermore, note that if a user does not have access to an entity, they will not see or be able to access the data in that entity at the assigned levels.

- **Data Management**: This provides you with overall data management and controls such as duplicate detection settings, rules, and jobs. Data import is made easier by creating templates for data imports, setting up data maps, and managing the data imports through a wizard-driven interface. There is also the ability to import sample data, encrypt data, and set import field translations for localization.

- **System Jobs**: This gives you the ability to manage and control jobs that run in the Microsoft Dynamics CE environment.

- **Dynamics 365 App for Outlook**: This controls the deployment of Microsoft's integrated environment with your Outlook app on your desktop, laptop, or other device.

- **Processes**: The processes native to Dynamics 365 CE or custom processes, such as Business Process Flows, in Dynamics 365 CE.

- **Microsoft Flows**: These provide access to the workflow engine inside and outside of Microsoft Dynamics 365 CE and interact with the rest of the Microsoft 365 framework as well as many (hundreds of) external applications.

- **Apps**: This section provides you with control of and access to App Designer, providing the ability to change the layout of the sitemap as well as adding custom processes to the overall solution.

So, let's start with the setup.

System Settings

To manage the overall system capabilities, the **System Settings** function turns on functionality that is quite important to the system usage across the rest of the Microsoft ecosystem. Therefore, let's take a look at the **System Settings** screen for some more information:

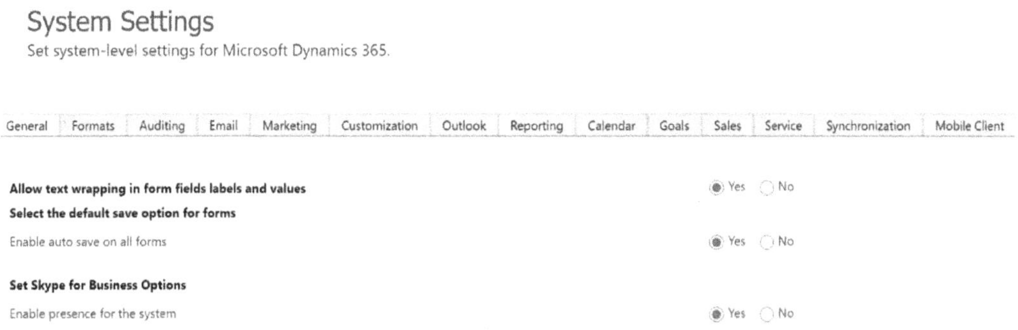

System Settings
Set system-level settings for Microsoft Dynamics 365.

General	Formats	Auditing	Email	Marketing	Customization	Outlook	Reporting	Calendar	Goals	Sales	Service	Synchronization	Mobile Client

Allow text wrapping in form fields labels and values   ◉ Yes   ○ No

Select the default save option for forms

Enable auto save on all forms   ◉ Yes   ○ No

Set Skype for Business Options

Enable presence for the system   ◉ Yes   ○ No

Figure 3.8 – System Settings screen

The **System Settings** area controls a significant number of system-wide capabilities. The list is quite exhaustive and as such we will briefly touch on a couple of areas and go deeper into two specific setup options.

Overall, Microsoft and the partner community can help you understand the overall implications of the **System Settings** screens. An important thing to focus on is to validate that your formats are correct for your firm. You will also want to focus on the **Email** and **Outlook** tabs and set them as per your firms needs.

However, in a project business, there are a couple of key considerations to focus on: **Bing Maps** and **Microsoft Teams**.

Setting up Bing Maps integration

Project businesses who arrive at their customer/client site rely on optimizing all time during the day. Wasted time in commuting is a wasted revenue opportunity with the client. Therefore, turning on Bing Maps is beneficial to integrate Bing Maps in the **Client (Account)** form natively. This is done by selecting **Enable Bing Maps** from the **General** tab as shown in the following figure:

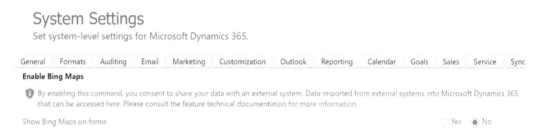

Figure 3.9 – Enabling Bing Maps integration

While working with your clients is the number one priority, most project businesses rely on collaboration across the firm to get results for the client. Therefore, Microsoft Teams is integrated with Dynamics 365 CE and the Project Operations solution.

Microsoft Teams integration and collaboration

Microsoft Teams is a highly collaborative and configurable environment to work together across the firm. I have worked with clients who use both Microsoft and non-Microsoft add-ins in Teams that provide a great deal of functionality, from wikis to lists, to embedded functionality such as Dynamics 365 CE.

To enable Teams integration, go to the **Advanced Settings** area, select **Administration**, and then **System Settings**. Within **System Settings**, you can select **Microsoft Teams Integration** to turn it on:

Figure 3.10 – Set Teams Collaboration

Once you complete the preceding steps, on an **entities** page, such as on **Projects**, you can click the **Collaborate** button in the ribbon bar and it will take you to the following screen:

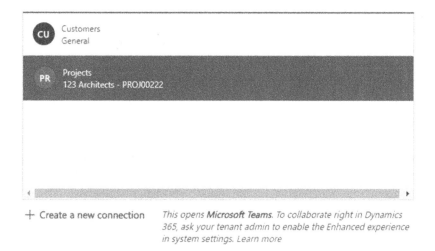

Figure 3.11 – Link Teams with Dynamics

Once linked, the project is embedded within Teams. You can now upload files and folders for document management shown here:

Figure 3.12 – Teams Collaboration around Projects

However, there are many more activities that you can do, such as having a wiki, creating new Teams channels, as well as clicking the **Meet** button to meet in the context of this project. As we have been building this, we need to understand that security is an overarching element that controls what we do and how we do it. So, lets take a look at this further.

Security setup

To accomplish this, in Dynamics 365 CE, navigate to the settings gear in the top right of the Dynamics 365 screen and select **Advanced Settings | Settings | Security and Users**. You can add users on the Dynamics 365 CE **Users** screen.

You can assign roles to each of the users by opening the user record and, at the top of the screen, choosing **Manage Roles**.

The following setup will represent some out-of-the-box security setups. However, if you want to customize the roles, first copy them and then rename them to `YOURORG.RoleName`, where you are making a custom role that will not be overwritten in future upgrades.

Account Manager

The Account Manager is the main project seller, business developer, or customer manager in your firm that will use CRM to develop sales activities. For out-of-the-box security setup related to the Account Manager type of user, you will need to assign them to the following roles:

- Sales Manager
- Project System
- Project User
- Potentially Project Manager (if the Account Manager will have any project management or creation functions)

Project Manager

The Project Manager will need to have access to all aspects of the project system in CRM to plan, deliver, and manage projects. For the Project Manager, you will need to set up the following roles:

- Project System
- Project User
- Project Manager
- Project Approver

Practice Manager

The Practice Manager, and sometimes a portfolio or program manager, will manage many projects or have oversight of them. For the Practice Manager, you will need to set up the following roles:

- Project System
- Project User
- Project Manager
- Project Approver
- Practice Manager
- Resource Manager – to view the **Schedule** board

Resource Manager

The Resource Manager, or resource management office, will provide resources (people or team members) to staff a project. For the Resource Manager, you will need to set up the following roles:

- Project System
- Project User
- Resource Manager – to view the **Schedule** board

Project Billing Manager

The Project Billing Manager will export out billable transactions to Dynamics 365 for Finance and Operations or another ERP/accounting system. For the Project Billing Manager, you will need to set up the following roles:

- Project System
- Project User
- Project Manager
- Project Approver – if they will need to perform ad hoc approvals
- Project Billing Administrator

Team Member

The team members are the resources (people) entering time cards and expenses against a project. For Team Member users entering times and expenses, you will need to set up the following roles:

- Project System
- Project User
- Project Resource

Each of these roles will have the proper rights set up for each of the roles. Some additional configuration may need to be conducted to get the right security for your organization.

As a new user of Dynamics 365 CE Sales, there are some key navigational techniques that are necessary to know in order to follow the directions in the rest of this chapter.

Navigation notes

Some general navigation notes in Dynamics 365 CE will be important to have going forward. The following is the main/home screen as you log in to the Dynamics 365 CE Sales app:

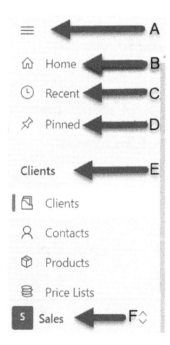

Figure 3.13 – Navigation tips

The following points correlate to each of the arrows in the preceding screenshot:

- **A**: The main Dynamics 365 menu bar navigation.
- **B**: The home screen will return you to your default home view/dashboard view.
- **C**: This will show you the screens and records you have recently accessed.
- **D**: This will show you the screens and records you have pinned to your environment.
- **E**: The menu grouping area, which shows you the menu items grouped together logically.
- **F**: The area menu will navigate you between the Sales, Service, and Training apps as they are published in the Published Apps section. Your Dynamics 365 CE instance can have multiple apps. Each app can have multiple areas, each area can have multiple groups, each group can have multiple subareas, and finally, each subgroup can hold a single entity, dashboard, or external URL.

While we have covered navigation at a high level, there are also personal settings that can be useful for your personal experience.

Personal settings

From the settings menu, select **Set Personal Options**; you will get the following screen:

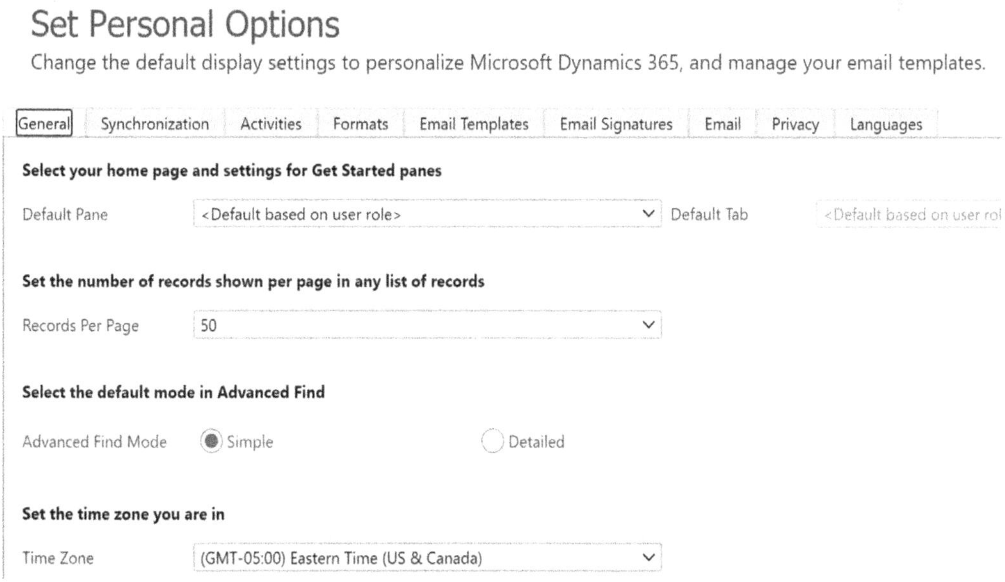

Figure 3.14 – Set Personal Options

Here, you can set your user-specific, personal options that are relevant to you only, things such as records per page. I personally prefer the highest setting of 250 so I can view a larger record set when I initiate views in the system.

Each user in the system will want to check out these settings to get the best user experience.

To further understand the Dynamics 365 CE system, let's review the sales entities that make up the system.

Sales entities

The following are some of the main areas you will need to know about relationships in Project Operations overall:

Figure 3.15 – Dynamics 365 CE – sales entities

We've covered each of the navigational elements, so now let's review what some of the main sales entities are. The navigation is generally broken down into subareas that group your work together. So, we will review these from the top down.

My Work

The **My Work** section covers the things most pertinent to you, the signed-in user. This includes the following:

- **Dashboards**: This area provides you with the system-provided, custom, and user-configured dashboards that you can use to manage and drive the business. Dashboards are built off of views in the system and therefore are totally configurable to you. You can choose different presentation elements and types of dashboards to view. Select the dropdown to choose from various dashboards. Once enabled, Power BI dashboards can be added to the list to enhance the user experience:

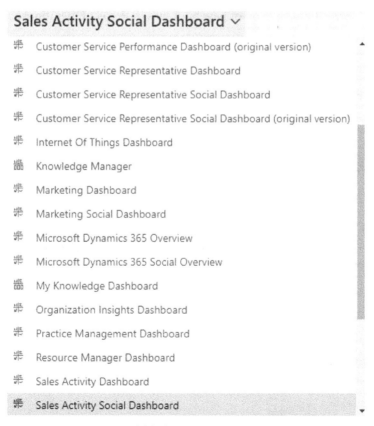

Figure 3.16 – Available dashboards in Project Operations

- **Activities**: These are your activities that are due or becoming due of all types. Activities can be broken down into the following:

Tasks – Things to do

Email – Messages to send

Appointment – Calendar events

Phone Call – Calls to make

Letter – Letters to write

Fax – If using faxes, faxes to send

Service Activity – If using Customer Services

Campaign Response – If using marketing – campaign responses to activities in **Marketing**

Booking Alert – To notify you of new bookings in Project Operations

Customers

These are your client records we use to track company/customer levels of information. There are two types of customers:

- **Accounts**: The *company*-level information for customers you work with
- **Contacts**: The *people*-level information linked to the account so that an account can have many contacts related to it

Sales

The **Sales** area is where an Account Manager will spend most of their time. The sales area is focused around primarily business development and selling so you have the following types of entities you work with:

- **Leads**: New interests from potential or existing customers to buy your services
- **Opportunities**: Qualified leads that represent the monetary potential of the business
- **Competitors**: If tracking, the competitors that may be going after the same business

Collateral

The **Collateral** area will represent a few different things in Project Operations, but we will talk about them here from a purely Sales perspective:

- **Quotes**: After qualifying a lead, typically the client will ask for a quote of services or products to consider doing business with you. Quotes become orders in the next step of the process.

- **Orders**: In the Project Operations world, these represent project contracts. However, in a pure-play Sales world, they potentially relate to a product or service not related to projects.

- **Invoices**: Orders become invoices when the client accepts the order and you are now invoicing them for the goods or service.

- **Products**: Specific products you are selling, tied to price lists.

As you can see, these areas are all related to the overall Dynamics 365 CE – Sales navigation and usage of the system. As an overview, this gets you started. There are more supporting entities in the backend that are not visible in the app but are used in processing and can be added to the app by customizing the sitemap in App Designer. Now, let's expand into Project Operations on the Dynamics 365 CE side of things and outline the key considerations around Project Operations.

Setting up Project Operations

Pressing the Dynamics home button will take you back to **Published Apps Menu**. However, if, for some reason, you are missing any published apps, click the **Sync** button in the top right. This should refresh your view with all your apps.

In Project Operations, the view will have changed significantly, as shown here:

Figure 3.17 – Dynamics Project Operations home screen

Notice that some things have remained the same and some have changed. The overall navigation remains, as do the **Home**, **Recent**, **Pinned**, and other dashboard areas. Other things have changed, though, including the Project Operations entities:

- **My Work**

  Time Entries – Timecard entry functionality for team members, Project Manager users, or anyone who needs to enter a timecard.

  Expenses – Expense entry functionality for team members, Project Manager users, sales managers, executives, or anyone who needs to enter expenses.

  Approvals – For time and expense, the approvals drive the behaviors behind each of the time and expense records. For example, some times or expenses may be approved and some rejected, based upon policy and criteria.

- **Projects**

  Projects – The main navigation page for viewing, entering, and managing the outstanding projects in your firm.

  Schedule Board – The main board, which will show you the schedule by team, skill, role type, or any number of setup criteria that your firm needs. It shows projected utilization and over-utilization so you can keep the team busy but not over the top.

  Resource Utilization – The main tracking mechanism to show historical utilization in the system. This shows historical actual work performed based upon time entries.

  Resources – These are the team members who make up your project team.

  Roles – These are the roles that define what kind of work a team member can do. Team members can have multiple roles and those roles can have different cost and selling prices by the organizational unit.

Now let's take a look into the Resource Manager view of Project Operations.

The Resource Manager view of Project Operations

To navigate to the **Resources** area, in the lower left of the menu screen, select **Resources**:

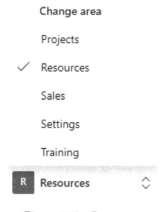

Figure 3.18 – Resources

We now see there are a number of additional entities that are visible. We've seen some of them before, since this is intended to be a person's main screen that they would log in to to do their work. So, as a Resource Manager user, these are some of the key areas I work in:

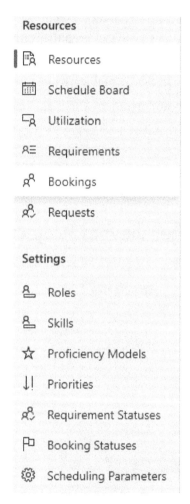

Figure 3.19 – Dynamics Project Operations Resource Manager menu

Some of the key elements of a Resource Manager user's view include these:

- **Resources**

  Requirements – Requirements are generated by the Project Manager user, who looks at a project and the generic requirements and generates project requirements that state the role type and the number of hours needed to fulfill a task for the project. These requirements then feed into the **Schedule** board for resource fulfillment.

  Requests – A step before requirements, generally a request is a submission to the Resource Manager user to fulfill what is to become a requirement.

  Bookings – Whether using hard, soft, proposed, or some other naming convention, a booking is a commitment of a specific resource (a team member) to a task.

- **Settings**

  Roles – Roles are entities that tie together pricing, team members (resources), skills, and others to work together in the Schedule Board and all throughout the system.

  Skills – What comes under this may be identified as skills, certifications, characteristics, or simply adapted to whatever naming convention your firm may have. Skills are user-configurable and have multiple levels of proficiency.

  Proficiency Models – Coupled with skills, proficiency models drive the level of skills attained by the resource.

  Priorities – The priority levels used throughout Project Operations are outlined here.

  Requirement Statuses – The statuses of requirements in Project Operations are outlined here.

  Booking Statuses – The statuses of the bookings in Project Operations are outlined here.

  Scheduling Parameters – The main settings screen for resource scheduling, including refresh intervals of the scheduling screen and other parameters.

The Resource Manager user's view will provide them with the most important screens for a resource manager or a resource management office. Remember, you can also add or remove screens to this view as well.

The Sales/Account Manager view of Project Operations

There is another area, Sales, specifically designed for the Sales/Account Manager user to work in. It contains all the relevant screens to drive the sales efforts of the firm. Some of them we have already reviewed, so let's look at the material relevant to Project Operations:

Figure 3.20 – Dynamics Project Operations Sales/Account Manager menu

Customers

Of significance to this section are the price lists, which drive the pricing that is specific to the firm (such as a rate card) and the pricing that is associated with a specific client or down to a specific project. This is called **multi-dimensional pricing**.

Alongside the price lists are the project contracts, and the associated lines and line items drive all the selling prices related to the project.

Transactions

In the **Transactions** section are a few areas of significance to discuss:

- **Approved Time** is a view into all approved time in Project Operations and has multiple views to see the information you need.

- **Approved Expenses** is a view into all approved expenses in Project Operations and it too has multiple views.

- **Journals** contains journals, which are used either as a correction from the approved actuals (time that was entered and approved) or other transactions; journals aggregate and post accounting system-level information.

- **Actuals** has information on the production of actuals resulting from approved time, expense, or other entries into the system; the actuals are part of the accounting system information.

Billing

The **Billing** section will generally be accessed by the project accounting team or others who work through the billing processes:

- **Retainers and Advances** is where to go to set up retainers or advances. It combines with **Available Retainers** and **Advances**, which is a view used to view the outstanding retainers and advances.

- **Fixed Price Milestones** is where to go to set up fixed price milestones in the system.

- **Product Billing Backlog** is used to view any not-to-exceed projects.

- **Time and Material Billing Backlog** is used to view any time and materials billings in the backlog.

- **Invoices** is where to go to view all invoices in the system.

Project Operations system settings

The Project Operations system has system-wide settings specific to Project Operations functionality:

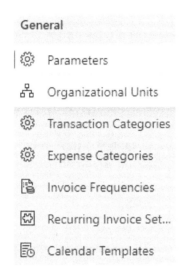

General

⚙ Parameters

🖧 Organizational Units

⚙ Transaction Categories

⚙ Expense Categories

🖺 Invoice Frequencies

🧩 Recurring Invoice Set...

🗓 Calendar Templates

Figure 3.21 – Dynamics Project Operations system settings menu

The following are the system-wide settings you will need to consider in Project Operations. This section sets up some of the system-wide functionality that will be used as part of the Project Operations system:

- **Parameters**: Allows you to enable multi-currency cost price lists, default organizational units, invoice frequency, default Project Manager and team member roles, and work hour templates and resource allocation modes.

- **Organizational Units**: This is where you set up each organizational unit, the unit's currency, and (a very important costing function) the cost price list for the roles that are related to this organizational unit – for example, different costs by country or region with different currencies.

- **Transaction Categories**: Here you set up unit groups and billing types, such as chargeable, non-chargeable, and complementary, to be used with pricing and billing customers.

- **Expense Categories**: Here you determine the various expense types that are then associated with expense reports.

- **Invoice Frequencies**: Here you determine the billing frequencies in the Project Operations system.

- **Recurring Invoice Setup**: Here you set up the batch jobs to perform recurring invoices.

- **Calendar Templates**: Here you define your default working times for a work template.

As you have seen, there are a number of areas that drive functionality within Project Operations. While that is great, there is also a need to make system-specific changes to support business needs. This is where customization comes into play.

Dynamics 365 CE – Sales customizations

We are going to begin with the baseline setup of Dynamics 365 CE – Sales. Note that without this information, you will not be able to work through the rest of the system. For example, to sell a contract, you need to have accounts (customers or clients) in the system. Let's begin with some baseline configuration changes, decisions that will help you go forward.

Customizations and configurations

There are a number of customizations and configuration changes that will help to make Project Operations a more friendly environment for your users. Microsoft has made Project Operations somewhat generic, counting on the partner community and the clients of Project Operations to further tailor it to their businesses.

Dynamics 365 Project Operations uses the process of *solutioning* each group of customizations as a way to perform customization in, for example, a development system, and then transfer into a test system for testing before a final transfer into production for production usage. This *solutioning* capability provides portability and future-proofing of the customizations that you create for your firm. This can be automated with an Azure DevOps *Continuous Integration/Continuous Deployment (CI/CD)* pipeline.

So, let's create a couple of example customizations to learn from that we can use throughout our solution.

Let's begin with a very practical application.

Changing Account to Client

One of the first things you will want to perform as the system customizer is to create a solution in CE to begin compiling your changes into. Use solutions to extend the capability of Dynamics 365 and group together your customizations so that you can build them in a development environment (sandbox) and test them in a test environment (sandbox) before applying them to a production environment. This will greatly benefit the overall development strategy and will help you move customizations around:

1. To begin, navigate to **Advanced Settings | Settings | Customizations | Publishers** to create a new publisher for your customizations.

2. Next, navigate to **Advanced Settings | Settings | Solutions** as shown here:

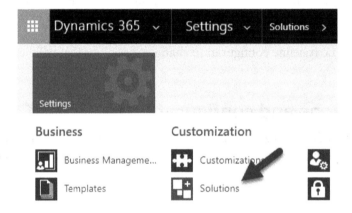

Figure 3.22 – Solutions

3. From this area, select **New** and fill out the fields as follows:

Figure 3.23 – New solution creation

4.   From within this new solution, select **Add Existing** and then choose **Entity**. Choose the **Account** entity and select **OK**. Next, click (in the upper right of the screen) **Add All Assets**. Click **Finish**. Then, if you see a **Missing Required Components** box, choose **Yes, include required components.** and click **OK**.

5.   Now, open the **Account** entity and change the display name to **Client** and the plural name to **Clients**. Next, select the **Fields** icon under **Accounts** and rename **Display Name** for **Account** to **Client**.

6.   Let's now change the form data. Click on **Forms** and choose the **Account** form. Change **Account Name** to **Client Name** as shown here. Also, while you are here, change the **Section** name from ACCOUNT INFORMATION to CLIENT INFORMATION:

Figure 3.24 – Changing Account to Client

7. Alternatively, you can change the field name in App Designer as shown here:

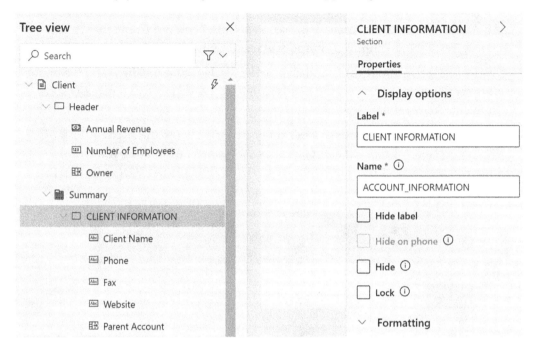

Figure 3.25 – Changing Account to Client in App Designer

8. Next, click the **Save** icon and then the **Publish** icon.

Next, navigate to `admin.powerplatform.microsoft.com` and log in. Note that you may want to use Chrome/Incognito mode for this. Find and select the horizontal ellipsis to choose **OPEN IN APP DESIGNER**:

Figure 3.26 – App Designer mode

9. Once in App Designer, choose to edit **Sitemap**. Change the **Customers** section to **Clients** and change **Customers** to **Clients**. Click **Save** and **Publish**:

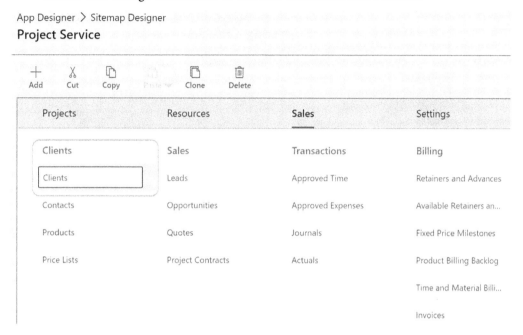

Figure 3.27 – Sitemap changes

10. This should now have renamed your menu section to **Clients in Project Operations – Sales** and your form should be all cleaned up to represent the **Client** nomenclature versus **Account**:

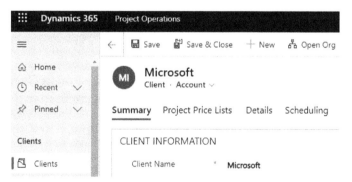

Figure 3.28 – Resulting change from Account to Client

Although to some, this seems like a small change, the implications for user adoption of the system are tremendous. Similar terminology changes will provide great communication across the teams using the same words.

Opportunity customizations

Using the same solution as you used for the prior customization, we will add the Opportunity entity to the solution so that we can add some specific customizations that will be used in the Lead to Opportunity business process flow.

Following the same steps as before, add the following fields to the **Opportunity** entity:

Name	Schema N...	Display Name	Type	Field Type
new_architectassistancerequi...	new_Archit...	Architect Assistance Required	Two Options	Simple
new_linktosow	new_Linkto...	Link to SOW	Single Line of...	Simple
new_linktostatementofwork	new_Linkto...	Link to Statement of Work	File	Simple
new_msaactive	new_MSAA...	MSA Active	Two Options	Simple
new_msaexpirationdate	new_MSAE...	MSA Expiration Date	Date and Time	Simple
new_projecttype	new_Projec...	Project Type	Option Set	Simple
new_sowduedate	new_SOW...	SOW Due Date	Date and Time	Simple
new_statementofworkassista...	new_State...	Statement of Work Assistance Required	Two Options	Simple

Figure 3.29 – New Opportunity fields

Creating these customizations (and any similar customizations you require) will greatly enhance the system, and they will be available to business process flows.

Business process flows

We are now going to modify the business process flow to give your users a guided selling experience through sales stages and process flows.

Using the **Advanced Settings | Settings | Apps** menu, open the Project Operations app in App Designer and select the business process flow to configure **Lead to Opportunity Sales Process**. Select the edit pencil to edit the sales process:

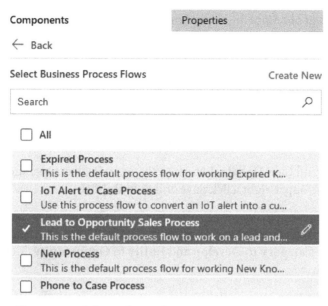

Figure 3.30 – Editing the Lead to Opportunity sales process

As we will see in the rest of this chapter, this is the main business process flow that will outline for you the specific steps (required, recommended, or optional) that will help the Account Manager user perform their tasks.

Some common changes in *Stage 1 – Lead Qualify* are as follows:

1.   Change **Existing Account** to **Existing Client**.

2.   Change **Purchase Timeframe** to **Project Timeframe**.

3.   Change **Purchase Process** to **Decision Process**.

> **Note**
> After each individual change, be sure to click **Apply**!

Some common changes in *Stage 2 – Opportunity Develop* are as follows:

1.   Change **Customer Need** to **Client Project Requirements**.

2.   Add a data step to include the **Project Type** custom field that you just created.

Some common changes in *Stage 3 – Opportunity Propose* are as follows:

1. Change **Identify Sales Team** to **Identify Project Team**.

2. Add a data step to include the **Architect Assistance Required** custom field.

3. Add a data step to include the **Statement of Work Assistance Required** custom field.

4. Add a data step to include the **SOW Due Date** custom field.

Now, click **Validate** and then **Update**. Return to the main Project Operations App Designer page. In the upper right, click **Save** and then **Publish**.

Perform the same types of changes for **Project Service – Opportunity Sales Process**. Also, add a stage between **Qualify** and **Propose** and name it `Opportunity SOW Information`. Set **Category** to **Develop** and **Entity** to **Opportunity**. The end result should look like this:

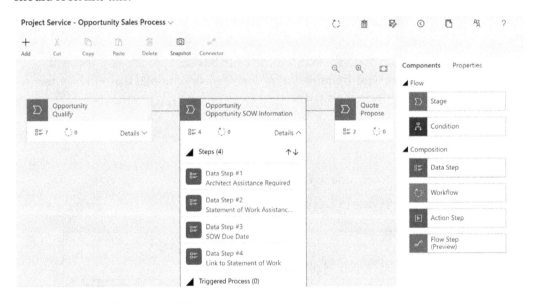

Figure 3.31 – Editing Project Service–Opportunity Sales Process

These are just a few of the customization and configuration changes that you may want to make to further benefit a Project Operations deployment. The intention here has also been to give you an idea of some of the things that you can do in the Project Operations system to make for a much better deployment across the firm.

It is also possible to add steps to the business process flows by clicking the + **Add button** as shown here.

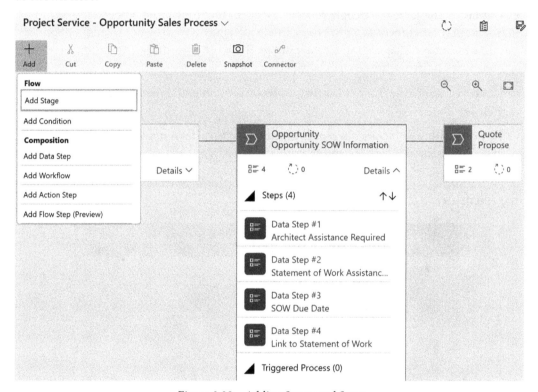

Figure 3.32 – Adding Stages and Steps

The foundation of the system will be the data brought in through your data migration strategy. Therefore, let us look into this further.

Data import

Now that we have set up some users, let's bring in some data to use in the system. The key entities we wish to populate are as follows:

- **Account**: We will customize this to be called **Client**. These are the company records for the companies you do business with.

- **Contacts**: These are the people related to a client record whom you need to maintain contact records with. For example, you may have Bob Smith and a phone number, but you may also track their Skype ID or other forms of communication in their working-from-home environment.

- **Leads**: These are the initial information records of potential new customers of your business.

- **Opportunities**: Typically, these will come in as either open opportunities from your current system or newly created opportunities.

To begin importing data, navigate to the **Advanced Settings | Settings | Data Management** area as shown here:

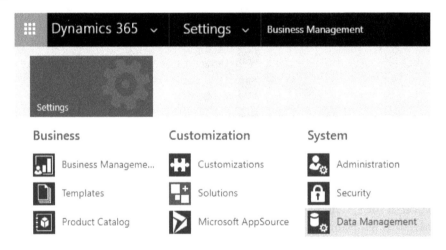

Figure 3.33 – Data Management

Within **Data Management**, select **Templates for Data Import** to create a template for **Clients** and **Contacts**. Select **Client** (note how it has been renamed from Account) and click **Download**. Repeat this for **Contacts**:

Figure 3.34 – Data import template

The files are now in your download folder to save for importing. You can begin by populating the **Client** spreadsheet in Microsoft Excel. Notice as you navigate through that there are prepopulated drop-down fields where there are specific values needed to input. This allows you to easily identify the values needed in the records. Furthermore, each field is named according to its purpose. If you added new fields, the template will be aware of those changes and will populate those fields into the template as well. To use this Excel file, select **File | Save as** and save as a CSV file format. This is the file format Microsoft uses to import.

Some key things to note

If you are populating the CSV file programmatically, be sure to populate the spreadsheet/CSV file as though it was manually input. For example, a client of mine recently entered NULL where there was no data. That is problematic since the import function does not know how to process NULL, and thus we changed the NULLs to blanks… and no values were entered into the fields.

Now we can import the data through the **Imports** process. This wizard-driven process provides you with the necessary, easy-to-follow steps to bring your data into the system.

For our process, we are going to bring in **Clients** first so that when we bring in **Contacts**, we can link to **Clients** directly. So, the first step is to import **Clients**. From the **Imports** screen, choose **Import Data** and follow the prompts from the wizard. During the import, we typically choose and use automatic mapping. Furthermore, at the end of the wizard, you can choose the option to allow or disallow duplicates and select an owner for the records.

Optionally, you can save the options you have chosen as a data map name that can be reused.

Next, import the contacts that link to the clients. Upon completion of these steps, you will have the foundation you need to use Project Operations:

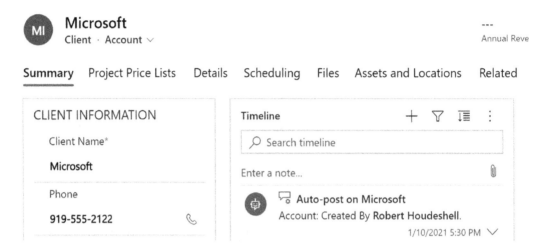

Figure 3.35 – Client information after import

This same process can be followed for both Lead entities and Opportunity entities to bring them in for an initial load. For Lead entities, however, many clients choose to have their frontend marketing lead generation tools integrate directly into the Lead entities so that they can be automatically routed for sales activities and follow-up.

Now that you have a good understanding of some key data import routines, you can use this same approach for anything that you wish to populate in the system. Some of the things that you may run into when importing data are complex lookup requirements when mapping fields in the data import wizard. For example, you may have contacts that you have already imported and you need to look up a contact to set a **Primary Contact** field.

Furthermore, you will definitely want to import a number of records for Project Operations or have them integrated into the system through some other method. These records include, but are not limited to, the following:

- Resources: Your team members.
- Roles: Chargeable and non-chargeable characteristics, which relate to the roles your team members will perform.
- Skills: These are the skills inventory lists that are needed to help find the right people to work on a project using the Schedule Board.
- Client-level price lists: Specific rates for a client.

- Project-level price lists: Specific rates for a project.

- Open project contracts.

- Open projects.

Ongoing data integration is a key need and requirement of any Project Operations implementation. Therefore, let's take a look into this topic.

Integration strategies

There are some areas that will just make sense to integrate through Project Operations. Some of them are on the input side of the system and include the application of sales tax logic, which will affect the invoicing that your client receives. When considering this topic, first search Microsoft's AppSource (https://appsource.microsoft.com/) to determine whether there is an ISV that integrates readily.

A number of clients will also want to integrate their expense entry and reporting system. Some systems, such as Gorilla Expense, Expensify, and Concur, have varying levels of sophistication, but all of them can be integrated into Project Operations. However, look for out-of-the-box integrations first and then build upon that if available. Project Operations integrations with expense systems are typically a multi-directional integration where Project Operations feeds the expense system with projects, tasks, team member information, and other information that is used in the entry of expenses. Then, the resulting approved expense reports integrate back into Project Operations for costing information.

Across ERP systems, Microsoft has two of the most prevalent integration approaches from Project Operations to Finance and Operations for functions such as billing, revenue recognition, project costing, and others.

Microsoft's Data Integrator is a scheduled, asynchronous, one-direction solution that results in duplicated data across the CRM/Project Operations and Finance and Operations system. It works well with bulk data and is change tracking-enabled.

In *Chapter 2, the Using Microsoft Dynamics 365 Framework for Success*, we learned about Dual Write as an integration technology. As an out-of-the-box integration technology for Project Operations, Dual Write is near real time, synchronous, and bi-directional. Although it too results in duplicated data, it is business logic-enabled and single transaction-enabled, which makes it the solution for out-of-the-box integration.

There are a number of different integration tools and technologies, including at the enterprise level, using an enterprise service bus technology that is API-driven and results in a high-volume, high-fidelity data integration platform.

Summary

In this chapter, we learned that there are a number of firm-driven decisions that can result from the questions we asked in the first part of this chapter. One of the key questions we asked was about working with a Microsoft partner who can help drive the success of a deployment. Knowing how to approach the deployment options will be key to the success of your project.

We outlined three different deployment options, ranging from a lite deployment to a resource/non-stocked deployment or a stocked/production deployment. We learned the differences between them and when to use them. Furthermore, we outlined how certain non-Dynamics CRM and ERP components fit into deployment scenarios. We also outlined the upgrade path for customers who have previously used Project Service Automation. Your choice of deployment option will directly impact licensing as well as the full implementation.

We walked through the setup considerations of the Dynamics 365 CE Sales system and then thoroughly reviewed all the elements of Project Operations before tying this together with the high-level steps for implementation. To improve the system for professional services firms, we introduced some customizations and walked through some data migration examples. This should have helped you to understand some key concepts.

Also, we customized the client entity and business process flow, and we identified how to most effectively make Dynamics 365 CE a solution that works for your firm. This will drive user adoption and the success of any implementation.

In the next chapter, we are going to get hands-on with each of the steps needed to configure project selling and outline a path for success in using the system.

Questions

1. Is an Office 365/Azure AD required to use Project Operations?

2. Is Microsoft Dynamics 365 CE – Sales required to use Project Operations?

3. Is Microsoft Dynamics Finance and Operations required to use Project Operations?

4. Which deployment type utilizes only Dynamics 365 CE and Project Operations in the CE environment?

5. Which deployment type provides you with full expense policy management, the ability to scan receipts with OCR, the ability to create customer-facing tax integrated invoices, and revenue recognition?

6. What is the first step in setting up Project Operations?

7. What is the `https://admin.powerplatform.microsoft.com/` site used for in setting up Project Operations?

8. In Dynamics 365 CE – Sales, where do you set up numbering sequences and other advanced settings?

9. Where does a user set up their personal preferences?

10. In Project Operations, where do you set up Project Operations-specific settings?

Further reading

- Read more on specific deployment types at `https://docs.microsoft.com/en-us/dynamics365/project-operations/environment/determine-deployment-type`.

Section 2: Project Sales through Delivery

All projects begin in sales, but how they proceed through the organization depends upon how you organize and plan the sales processes. This section will assist you and help you to define an approach for sales through project opportunities, project contracts, and pricing workflow implementation. This section will also guide you through setting and utilizing direct staffing and centralized staffing models. It section will suggest the best approach from sales to delivery.

This section includes the following chapters:

- *Chapter 4, The Account Manager – Project Selling*
- *Chapter 5, Project Contracts and Pricing*
- *Chapter 6, Practice Manager Functions – We Won the Contract! What Now?*
- *Chapter 7, Resource Manager – Staffing for Success!*

4
The Account Manager – Project Selling

In the previous chapter, we learned how to set up Dynamics 365 CE and Project Operations. In this chapter, we will get into the selling of projects by starting with the lead to opportunity workflow. This will lead us into how to collaborate with our team members and win new business.

All good business begins with sales! Just ask around and you will get that response! Business development, customer acquisition, customer management, and client management. There are many names for the process of bringing new projects into the firm but they all have one thing in common: the client!

Sometimes called the **customer**, the **client** is the lifeblood of the firm. Clients bring in new projects. New projects result in team members facing new challenges and opportunities. Successful completion of tasks and reporting of the work performed results in revenue for the firm and the firm gains a reputation in their industry, geography, or specific client project types.

Empowering the account manager, the name we will give the sales persona for this chapter, is vital to continuing to bring in business to the firm. The account manager persona may work on new business acquisition or existing client fulfillment. They may also work with strategic partnerships and alliances to gain new ground and win new business.

Overall, having the Account Manager in a position to collaborate across the entire firm provides a better solution for the client and improves the firm's reputation. We will also explore the timeline feature of Dynamics 365 as it relates to project selling.

Therefore, in this chapter, you will learn about the following concepts:

- The lead to opportunity workflow
- Maximizing project opportunities to win more business
- Collaboration and document management
- Winning the opportunity

Technical requirements

Please visit the following link to check the CiA videos: `https://bit.ly/3abRHw7`

Understanding the lead to opportunity workflow

Congratulations! You are now ready to begin selling new projects! Note that new projects come from a multitude of sources and work through the project processes as new client projects, existing client projects, project change orders, and a number of other variations.

We will work through the end-to-end processes as they exist in the Dynamics 365 Project Operations system with the configuration and customization changes we have made. We are going to begin with leads in the system. A lead in the system can represent a new business lead for either existing clients or new clients.

The approach we will take will be to create a new client lead for this very reason. A new client lead will qualify and create three different but related records:

- **Client record**: Representing the account information
- **Contact record**: The person you are working with at the client's firm
- **Opportunity record**: Representing the project and monetary opportunity

We will now begin with the creation of a new lead in the Dynamics CE – Sales system.

Creating a new lead

To initiate the creation of information in the CE Sales system, Microsoft has made it easy to input information from either websites through automation, Microsoft Forms through Power Automate, or the *good old-fashioned way* of inputting information from a keyboard. For the sake of the chapter's content, we will assume a keyboard approach to the input of data.

From the **Sales** area of the **Project Operations – Sales** menu group, choose **Leads** and select **+ New** to create a new lead. Input the information that you need to capture in the lead that will create the **Contact**, **Account**, and **Opportunity**.

The following screenshot shows a general set of information input into the lead form. This is pretty basic information and should be understood as such. There is likely to be more information you require for your business processes – this is understood. So, as we progress, you should understand that the information captured in a lead will translate down to a client, contact, and opportunity level, should you wish.

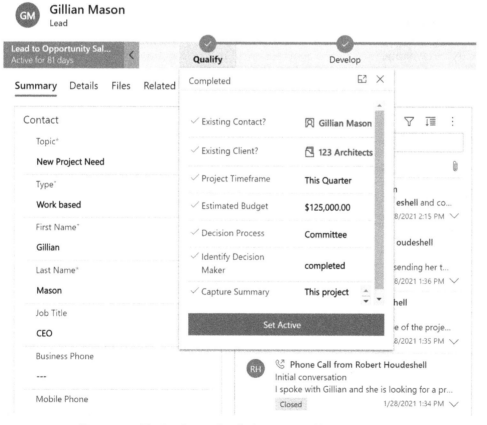

Figure 4.1 – The Lead record with the associated business process

Notice that we are also entering the information being requested in **Lead** to **Opportunity Sales Process – Qualify Stage**. Once we finish entering the information in one stage, we can click the **Next Stage** button to progress the lead through the selling process.

Let's talk about why we are doing this. What is a business process flow? We know we went through and created some changes to the business process flow but why? This all goes back to sales processes and sales stages that are adopted in a firm and result in a standard way in which the firm wins new business.

A sales process is important and, in fact, I can state with confidence that every firm has a sales process whether they have it documented or not. It could be as simple as *go sell something* with one stage and a determined outcome of either a win, a loss, or a no-decision (which is a loss to the competitor of *no decision*).

Within the realm of the sales process is the lead management process. In larger firms, there are major marketing tools such as **Marketo** (now an Adobe solution), which engages clients from marketing automation through email marketing and lead generation. Other firms may choose to use the Microsoft Dynamics 365 Marketing app, which will provide the same functions of marketing automation, email marketing, and lead generation that are natively integrated throughout the Dynamics 365 CE system. This app provides the ability in Dynamics 365 CE to generate email marketing directly out of the app and responses tracked to specific marketing campaigns.

Positive responses to marketing campaigns result in the creation of leads, which must be managed through a process. That is the purpose of the business process flow. It is a way to walk the lead qualification team through standard processes of qualifying a lead. The expected result is to qualify the lead, which results in the qualification of the lead to become an opportunity.

This is why we created the Develop stage to include the client project requirements, proposed solution, and project types as fields that will help build an opportunity in the system.

As a lead is being developed, there are a number of activities that will be done with a lead. In order to facilitate continuity of information across the organization, this information needs to pass onto the next stage of activity. Therefore, all of this information shows in the **Timeline** section of the lead, showing all activities conducted up to this point. The following screen shows these activities linked to the lead.

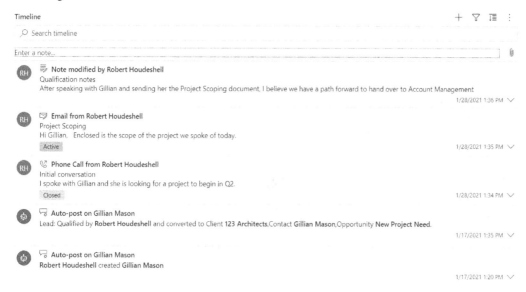

Figure 4.2 – The Timeline within the Lead record

The sales process that is being used will drive the business process flow (the ribbon at the top of the lead) and will logically step the lead qualifier through valuable information-capturing tasks as well as helping the qualifier determine whether a lead is qualified. The following screen shows this lead as it is being qualified.

Figure 4.3 – The business process flow showing the current lead is in the Develop stage

At any point in the process, based upon a number of key questions or considerations in the lead qualification process, the lead may become *qualified*, which means the lead is typically passed onto an account manager (remember, this is our generic name for a project seller). This happens through the clicking of the **Qualify** button at the top of the **Lead** screen.

Upon qualification, this lead will create an account record if the company value is populated with a primary contact if the first name / last name is populated. The qualification will also create an opportunity linked to the account, which we will use in the rest of this sales process.

In the next section, we are going to outline how to use the opportunity record, business process flow, your sales process, and related information to maximize the sales impact of every opportunity.

Maximizing project opportunities

Every opportunity the organization has is a monetary goldmine. Therefore, more than in other industries, collaboration and execution are key to the successful closing of a sale. This means that we need to have a proper plan to close opportunities while also having all of the contractual and other information completed.

Therefore, we will use the business process flow that is built into Project Operations and is also something we customized in *Chapter 3, The How-Tos of Setting Up Project Operations*, to the needs of a professional services firm.

If you recall from the previous section, we qualified a lead that was developed by the marketing team. The result was the creation of a client (account) Contact and Opportunity record in the system. Now let's look at how we can track this through the system.

Business process flow

To provide a unified sales process and guide the selling of an opportunity, we can utilize the business process flow functionality in Project Operations, as shown in the following screenshot.

The following **Opportunity** form is filled out with a general set of information based upon the progression of the business process flow:

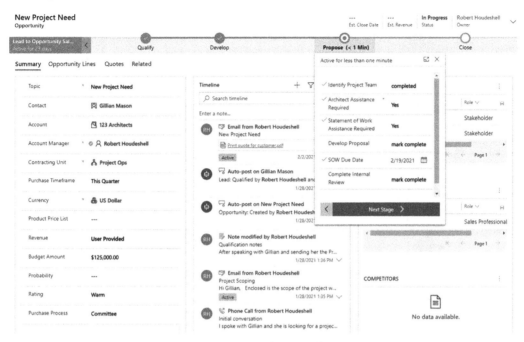

Figure 4.4 – Opportunity as shown in the Propose stage

Notice the **Summary** information in the left-hand pane, the **Timeline** information in the middle (and note that it has been carried across from the lead information) as well as the **STAKEHOLDERS** and **SALES TEAM** information on the right-hand pane. To the furthest right is the current stage in **Lead to Opportunity Business Process Flow**. I purposefully selected the expand icon to move it to the right for readability in the screenshot.

More important than the readability are the fields in the current stage called **Propose**. Here is what is going on behind the scenes. Most of the fields that are part of the **Opportunity** entity are available to be included in the business process flow. The intention of this is to capture a repeatable process that can be utilized to ensure that you capture important data points such as *when is the SOW due*? It can also be used to mark certain items as complete to keep team members on track.

You may ask, what if I have different sales processes that require different business process flows? If that is the case, you can always create multiple business processes and switch to them manually with the **Switch Process** button or automatically if needed.

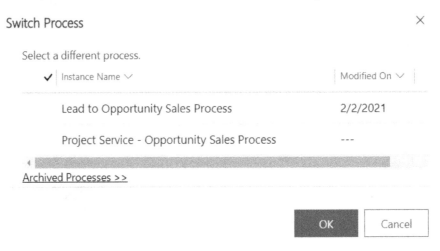

Figure 4.5 – The Switch Process screen

With the current stage we are in, we now need to build a proposal for the client. To do so, we will progress through the **Opportunity Lines** section.

Opportunity Lines

As we continue to have our conversations with the client, we are finding out more about what their needs are and how we can help them.

The following shows a breakout of **Project-based Lines** (top section) and **Product-based Lines** (bottom section):

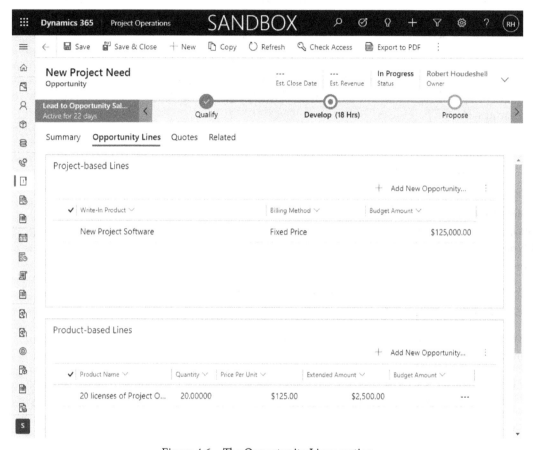

Figure 4.6 – The Opportunity Lines section

The **Opportunity Lines** section contains subsections: **Project-based Lines** and **Product-based Lines**. **Project-based Lines** contains the projects that are being proposed in the opportunity, while **Product-based Lines** contains licenses, products, and other cataloged or non-cataloged items. In this scenario, we have set a project budget of $125,000 and the product-based lines are for 20 licenses of Project Operations on a per user / per month basis.

At this time, you could route this to an approver to review the opportunity by clicking the **Email a Link** button or the **Share** button to share with another team member. Further, you can utilize Flow / Power Automate to automatically route for approval.

Upon approval, you may now want to put a real quote in front of the client for them to approve it.

Collaboration and document management

Collaboration and document management in Dynamics 365 are typically accomplished at a multitude of levels within the system. For example, on every screen that has the timeline included in the screen, we can attach notes as well as documents, emails, and other activities.

When attaching documents to the opportunity, you are saving those documents to the database and making the document available to Dynamics 365 Project Operations or Dynamics 365 CE Sales users only.

> **Note**
> They will not be able to get to the documents unless they have a license!

Alternatives are these: integration with Microsoft SharePoint or Microsoft Teams. Either way, either of these options has been utilized extensively throughout the history of Dynamics 365 CE Sales (from the earliest days of Dynamics CRM). The question of *how* is one that begins with how best you wish to integrate across the platform.

There is some inherent integration with Microsoft Teams at the point of publishing this book. However, it does not quite fit what a professional services firm needs.

Professional services firms need to have really tight control over several key documents – among them are the following:

- **The Master Services Agreement**: Typically a negotiated contract at a client level and best attached to the client record.

- **The Statement of Work**: Typically attached to the project, the SOW is critical and must be accessible to the project team.

- **Change Orders**: Typically attached to the project, Change Orders are critical as an audit trail of authorization of work for additional scope.

- **Other documents**: Other documents such as **Product Orders** and **Subscription Agreements** may also be part of the document management record.

What we typically prescribe for our clients setting up either a Microsoft SharePoint or a Teams document management structure is to do this: set up your folder structure as you would if you have people accessing these documents through SharePoint or Teams directly. That is a great beginning. Ensure you have a logical document management folder structure and the right security around it and you are off and running.

Dynamics 365 CE has native technology to integrate SharePoint into Dynamics 365 CE through setting up document management in the **Advanced Settings | Settings | Document Management** area. To enable SharePoint, you must have it set up and configured with list services installed. When you do, you can set up **Document Management Locations for Client (Account entities)** and other entities in Dynamics 365 CE. Further, within this area, you can set up and enable OneDrive for Business and SharePoint site collections.

To integrate this into Dynamics 365 CE and Project Operations, we typically prescribe building into the **Client** entity. For example, a text field that will link to the SharePoint or Teams document.

For example, the following is a screenshot of a Master Services Agreement link:

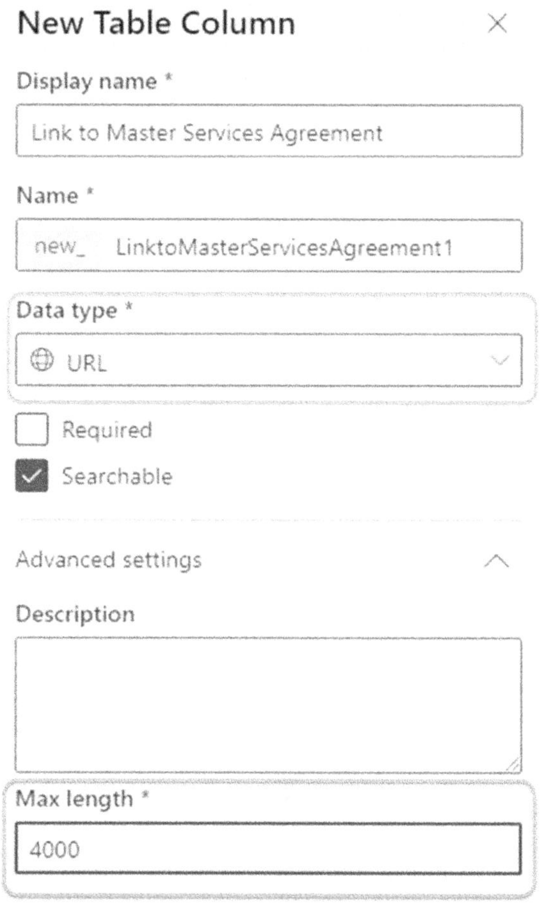

Figure 4.7 – Custom field for the Statement of Work URL

Notice the data type is a single line of text and the format is URL. Also, set the **Max length** field to **4000**.

The next thing is to add this field to the **Client** entity's form as shown in the next screen shot. To add the field on the right from **Field Explorer**, click on the field and then drag the field into its respective area in the **CLIENT INFORMATION** section:

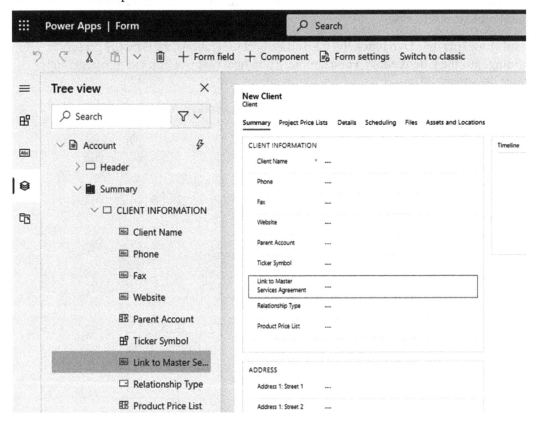

Figure 4.8 – Adding the field to the Client form

The result of the changes made here are shown in the **Client** form as follows:

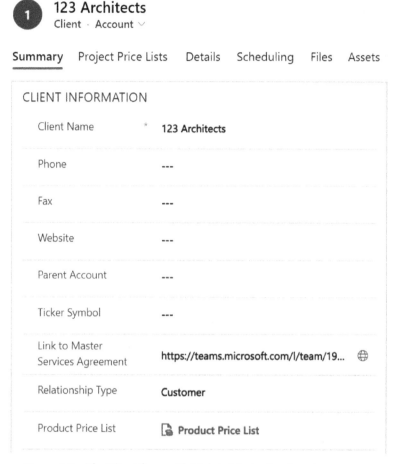

Figure 4.9 – The Client form with Link to Master Services Agreement

We now have successfully customized the system to provide a more familiar environment for our users. Renaming entities, fields, forms, and views will prove very valuable to the overall usability of the system. Now, it's time to have a look at the quoting process.

The quoting process

If the opportunities we create are the monetary representation of the value of the deal, the quoting process is how we fully monetize the deal.

Creating a quote

Moving to the **Quote** section, we now want to create a quote from the **Opportunity Lines** we entered. To do so, select **+ New Quote** and the system will automatically create a quote for you.

The screen the system presents to you next is the **Quote** screen:

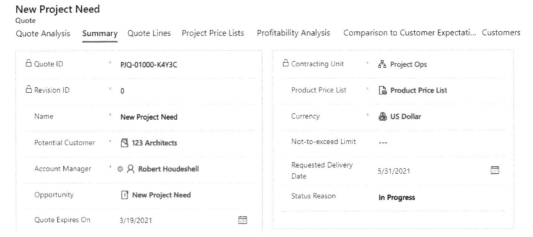

Figure 4.10 – Quote created for this Opportunity

Some key fields to note on this quote are the following:

- **Potential Customer** should be your client record created as part of the lead conversion. However, this could also be an existing client.

- **Account Manager** should be you or whoever the seller is.

- **Quote Expires On** will be when the quote expires for your potential client.

- **Product Price List** is the price list for the products listed in the **Opportunity Lines** section and the **Products** subsection.

- **Requested Delivery Date** is the date your client wants the project delivered to them.

Let's take a look at what we are committing to in this quote by looking at the quote lines.

Quote lines

The **quote lines** are the details that print for a quote when presented to a client. Therefore, you will want to make sure they are accurate and represent the totality of the quoted services and licenses.

The following screenshot shows how the same **Opportunity Lines** for projects and products transfer automatically into the quote:

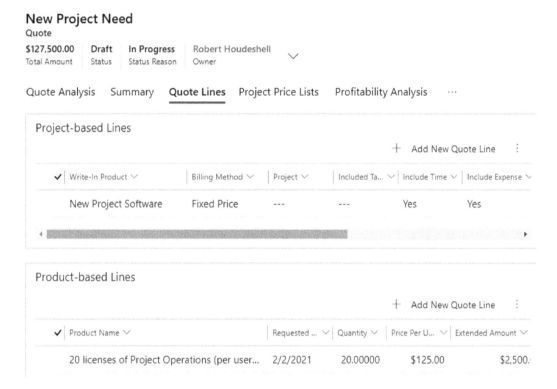

Figure 4.11 – Quote Lines

If you need to add additional quote lines, you can do so directly from this screen in the respective project or product sections.

Project Price Lists

Before we talk about or screenshot what to do in the **Project Price Lists** section, let's talk about the three basic price lists that are part of a Project Operations implementation. They are the labor costs, labor sales price, and product price lists. The following are the three most basic price lists in a Project Operations system:

Active Price Lists ∨

✓	Name ↑ ∨	Currency ∨
	Labor Costs	US Dollar
	Labor Sales Price	US Dollar
	Product Price List	US Dollar

Figure 4.12 – Price lists

These price lists drive all of the costing and selling in the Project Operations system. It is important to realize these price lists are universal and critical decision points for the firm. Therefore, although they can be imported, they would not be decided upon by just one person or team. There will need to be members of accounting, finance, sales, and executives involved in the setup of these price lists.

The **Labor Costs** price list is the blended costs of the roles working on projects. For example, Dynamics 365 architects may have a blended cost of $115 per hour while a Dynamics 365 project manager has a cost of $85 per hour. These are used in a **Time & Materials** contract to provide margin details per project and task. They are also used as the basis for costs in fixed-price projects.

Labor Sales Price is the price list that drives all the selling prices of **Time & Materials** projects as well as the custom pricing per client. The **Labor Sales Price** lists can be modified and associated with a client to create a client-specific price list as well and then used to further refine to a project price list. For example, your firm may charge out a Dynamics 365 architect at $235 per hour – as a standard rate. However, for the 123 Architects client, we may charge out at $225 per hour. However, for a specific project, that rate may be $222 per hour.

Now, back to our **Project Price Lists** section. In this section, we can select **Add New Project Price List** or **Create Custom Pricing**. The difference between the two (as shown in *Figure 4.13*) is that you can either take the Rate Card pricing or create custom pricing that would reflect a different price per role.

New Project Need
Quote

| | $127,500.00 | Won | Won | Robert Houdeshell |
| | Total Amount | Status | Status Reason | Owner |

Quote Analysis   Summary   Quote Lines   **Project Price Lists**   Profitability Analysis   ⋯

↗ Create Custom Pricing   ⋮

✓	Price List ↑ ⌄	Description (Pri... ⌄	Start Date (Pric... ⌄	End Date (Price... ⌄	Currency (Price ... ⌄
	Labor Sales Price	---	---	---	US Dollar

Figure 4.13 – Associated project price list for the quote with Add New Project Price List

The following shows the result of creating a custom price list. The result is the price list is specific to not only this customer but also this project.

New Project Need
Quote

| $127,500.00 | Draft | In Progress | Robert Houdeshell | ⌄ |
| Total Amount | Status | Status Reason | Owner | |

Quote Analysis   Summary   Quote Lines   **Project Price Lists**   Profitability Analysis   ⋯

+ Add New Project Price...   ⋮

✓	Price List ↑ ⌄	Description (P... ⌄	Start Date (Pri... ⌄	End Date (Pri
	Labor Sales Price	---	---	---
	Labor Sales Price - New Project Need - 2/2/2021 10:07:23 PM	---	---	---

Figure 4.14 – Associated project price list with custom pricing – note the difference in the name

When setting up a quote, there are additional sections we have not covered yet but are important to talk through. They are the following:

- **Quote Analysis**, which is the overall profitability and customer expectations **KPI** (**Key Performance Indicator**).

- **Profitability Analysis**, which is another **Key Metrics** data form with cost and revenue graphing.

- The **Comparison to Customer Expectations** section outlines where the quote is coming in compared to what the client's budget was.

Once completed with this quote, you can **Export to PDF** from the top menu. When you do, you will be presented with three options to **Download**, **Email**, or **Save to Dynamics** the quote, as shown in *Figure 4.15*:

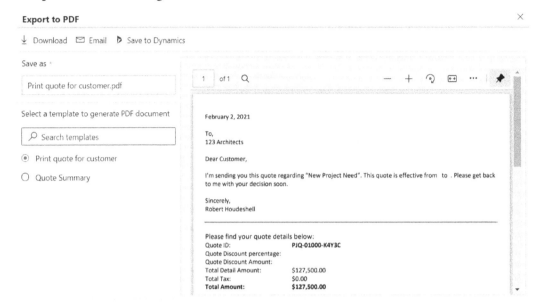

Figure 4.15 – Export to PDF options

When you click on **Download**, you are just simply downloading a PDF. **Email** will send an email to the client through Dynamics CE. **Save to Dynamics** will save the quote to the timeline, as shown here:

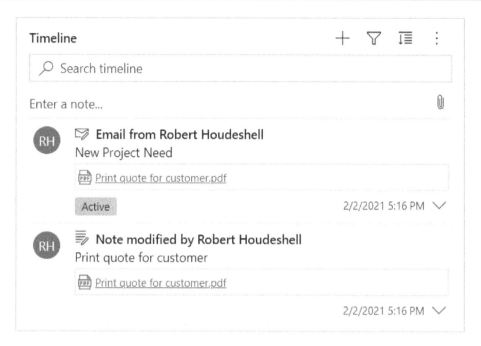

Figure 4.16 – The quote timeline updated with your quote generated as a PDF

Optimistically assuming you deliver this to your customer and they wish to proceed, you can mark this **Closed as Won** from the top menu and call this project **WON**!

Summary

In this chapter, we learned that all good business begins with sales! Although many terms differ from firm to firm, the foundations are the same. Clients bring in new projects, which result in a monetary reward for the firm and great projects for team members.

We worked through the **Lead to Opportunity** workflow and walked through the business process flow. We then turned **Opportunity Lines** into a **Quote** and generated a PDF that saved to the timeline.

We also learned the best ways to integrate Teams and SharePoint links for Master Services Agreements, Statements of Work, Change Orders, and more.

As we enter *Chapter 5*, *Project Contracts and Pricing*, we will get deep into contract creation, pricing, and building out project structures as though we are project architects.

Questions

1. True or False: A lead in Dynamics 365 CE is typically qualified through marketing and becomes an opportunity.

2. A lead that is qualified results in the creation of three records for a new client. Name the three records.

3. What is the name given to the widget in the lead that tracks all the interactions and postings conducted, such as phone calls, emails, and documents?

4. A lead becomes an opportunity when it is _____?

5. This tool provides a guided selling experience where a flow of processes guides sellers through a process. What is its name?

6. What is the lower level of detail in an opportunity that lays out the pricing details for a quote to be generated from?

7. True or False: When storing a document as part of the Timeline in Dynamics 365 CE, anyone in the firm can access that document.

8. True or False: Microsoft Team and SharePoint cannot be integrated into Dynamics 365 CE or Project Operations.

9. To integrate documents in Dynamics 365 Project Operations, which type of field should be used?

10. How do you win an Opportunity or Quote?

5
Project Contracts and Pricing

In the previous chapter, we learned how to create project opportunities through the business process flow and about various other capabilities of the system that will guide an account manager through the processes of selling.

In this chapter, we are going to follow an opportunity through to the contracts and contract types that will drive the billing and revenue recognition of the project we are selling.

This chapter will show you how to set up contracts that will represent the types of work your firm does and build pricing models to support all levels of pricing. Whether your client projects are easy to set up or complex, with mixed line-item types and multidimensional client-pricing models, this chapter will cover it.

In this chapter, you will learn about the following concepts:

- Understanding the workflow from opportunity to project contract
- Implementing project contracts and contract lines
- Contract types (**time and material**; fixed-price; not-to-exceed; retainers)
- Developing price lists and custom price lists
- Exploring roles and role types to control pricing

By the end of this chapter, you will fully understand the opportunity-to-quote-to-contract workflow and its implications for selling. You will be able to implement project contracts, contract lines, relationship-to-price lists, and projects. You will learn to develop standard price lists, custom price lists, roles, and role types to control pricing (chargeable, non-chargeable, and complimentary). The intersectionality of these components will help you to create multidimensional pricing.

Technical requirements

To perform the tasks in this chapter, you will need the following:

- An Microsoft 365 account and an **Azure Active Directory** (**Azure AD**) login
- A Microsoft Dynamics 365 Project Operations **Customer Relationship Management** (**CRM**) license
- A Microsoft Project Plan license

Please visit the following link to check the CiA videos:

```
https://bit.ly/3abRHw7
```

Understanding the workflow from opportunity to project contract

As we saw previously in *Chapter 4, The Account Manager – Project Selling*, our opportunity in the **Customer Engagement** (**CE**) system resulted in a quote and quote lines that mirrored this opportunity. The quote was produced and sent to the customer in **Portable Document Format** (**PDF**) format while simultaneously storing the quote on the timeline so that others who might pick up somewhere in the middle of the process would still be able to see what had been done, each step of the way.

At this point, it is important to talk through the process flow as it relates to the Project Operations system. In the Dynamics 365 CE – Sales system, when we are selling a product, we have a process that is very similar to ours in which we are producing a quote, then a quote becomes an order, and an order becomes an invoice.

The Project Operations process is different—it is a quote to contract invoice(s), meaning multiple invoices for a project. The difference is that a project will produce invoices potentially upon initiation, definitely throughout the project, and at other points in between. This depends greatly upon the contract type. In our example, which we will explore throughout this chapter, we are going to begin with a fixed-fee contract type, which is very simple overall from a billing standpoint. However, from a revenue-recognition standpoint, it can be much more complicated.

Our work example is going to introduce an additional complexity of a time and materials contract for out-of-scope work. Our assumption in the fixed-fee contract is that it is a fixed fee and a fixed scope. Therefore, if there are any items the client wants to have us perform against but that are not part of the scope of the project, we will bill those against the time and materials contract.

We are now going to need to take our project quote and close it as *won* in order to progress through the system. When we do, we are going to work with a project contract that, if you look closely at the system, is a variation of the sales *order* that is used in the product-based scenarios in CRM/CE. This same entity is used for project-based work and has related line items associated. How Microsoft accomplished this is to utilize the Project Operations solution to produce multiple forms and default specific forms in the sitemap in Dynamics 365 CE. This ties together the concepts you worked through in *Chapter 3, The How-Tos of Setting Up Project Operations* (in the *Customizations and configuration* section), and the work with the sitemap for the Project Operations app.

Therefore, let's get started by first closing the quote and marking it as *won*!

Implementing project contracts and contract lines

We now have a project contract in the system that relates to the quote and opportunity we worked with previously. In *Figure 5.1*, you'll notice that these previous documents are easily accessed with a hyperlink click, thus keeping everything front and center for your benefit.

The project contract

The project contract is a grouping of project contract lines, milestones, and roles that result in the financial impact of a project on a firm. Therefore, as shown in the following screenshot, this project contract drives all further financial activity in the system:

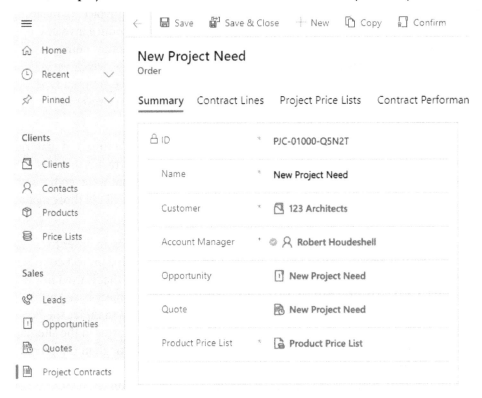

Figure 5.1 – The project contract header showing key fields

There are a lot of additional details that you may want to complete. Remember that you can add fields through customizations and configuration, or update existing field definitions as per your business requirements.

Project contract lines

Project contract lines are used to provide additional line-item detail for contracts.

When navigating to the project contract lines section, we get a view of both the project contract and the product lines on one screen. By opening the **New Project Need** project contract line we created, we now have the ability to tie this together with other assets in the system—namely, the project we will manage. We will further set up invoice schedules and define our billing around this project.

First, from the contract line (order line), let's create a project to link this contract with, as shown in the following screenshot:

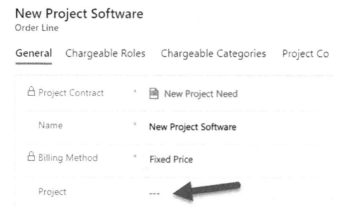

Figure 5.2 – The project contract line: Project link

As shown in the preceding screenshot, click into the **Project** field and select **+ New Project**, which will initiate the new project **Quick Create** screen, as illustrated in the following screenshot:

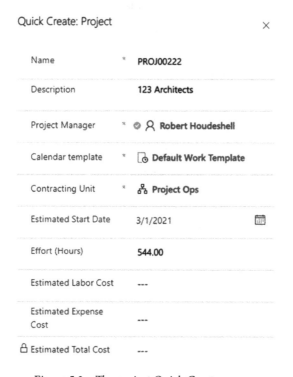

Figure 5.3 – The project Quick Create screen

> **Note**
> The contract line and project combination must be unique. Duplicate combinations are not allowed.

Although for this first contract line we are using a billing method of **Fixed Price**, we can also use the **Time and Material** billing method on another, distinct contract line. We are going to review this scenario shortly.

The billing method drives the contract types that are available within Project Operations. The contract types are as follows:

- **Time and Material**: A contract type where you bill out time at an agreed-upon rate and bill out materials or expenses at agreed-upon rates.

- **Time and Material Not to exceed**: This allows you to place a not-to-exceed limit or a cap on a project.

- **Fixed-Price Lump Sum Billings**: A **specific scope** and price for a project set contractually with the client.

- **Fixed-Price Milestone Billings**: An **invoice schedule** produces **milestone billings**, which allow you to bill out according to milestones specified in the contract.

- **Fixed-Price Date Based Billing**: **Invoice schedules** allow you to bill out *based on an agreed-upon schedule*.

- **Fixed-Price Retainers**: Project contract line details give you the ability to bill out *retainer fees and expenses*.

Additional considerations for the project contract line are outlined here:

- **Chargeable roles**: Identifying roles we are going to bill for on the contract

- **Chargeable categories**: Identifying which expense categories (along with **Fixed Price – Contract Line Details**) will be billed

In the **Project** field, either enter the project (which may already be defined) or create a new project to use as the management tool. The result should be a project that looks like this:

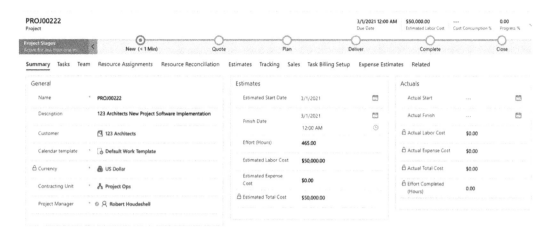

Figure 5.4 – The project that is linked to the contract line

The reason we need the project is to have something to enter the time against, as we have team members working on the project.

Next, we need to create an invoice schedule from the contract line. For this type of project, we are going to have three invoices, two for $50,000 and one for $25,000, representing the entirety of your milestones. Now, you may wonder: *why milestones*? Typically, a milestone project is designed to have either a date or a deliverable become the milestone or marker within the project, to say we are going to conduct a billing event.

> **Note**
> Milestones of the ancient kind could be found across the former Roman Empire and have recently been unearthed in construction projects. Milestones such as mile markers on our modern roadways marked the distance traveled on a road. Our milestones are a little more modern!

Our billing schedule is set up to reflect the initial billing being conducted in March and the final billing being conducted in May. In all instances, the billing is generated on the seventh day of the respective months, and that was set up within the **Invoice Frequency** setting. The invoicing frequency drives the monthly billings of the project.

You can see the **Invoice Frequency** setting in the following screenshot:

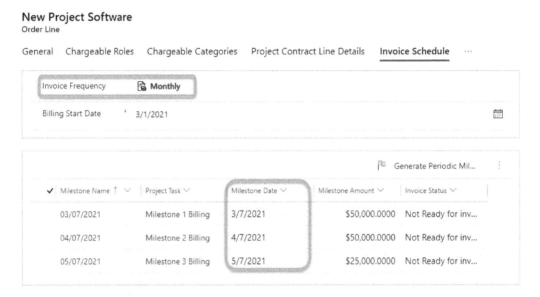

Figure 5.5 – The billing milestones

This project is running off a **Monthly** invoicing frequency. You can have different invoicing frequencies representing different business requirements. An example may be where you are billing a subscription on a specific day of the month but labor on a different day. You may also have different business units billing on different days. The **Invoice Frequency** setting provides you with this capability.

Since we have three milestones, we are keeping our tasks simple as well. When we are working on a project that is fixed-fee, we still have chargeability concerns regarding the tasks. We will get into chargeability more as we explore roles a little later on.

For now, though, note that since you added a project task to the **Invoice Schedule**, there are respective **Chargeable Tasks** that are being used in this contract line, as shown in the following screenshot:

New Project Software
Order Line

General   **Chargeable Tasks**   Chargeable Roles   Chargeable Categories   Project Contract Line Details   Invoice Schedule   Cust

Chargeable Tasks

✓	Task ∨	Parent Task (Task) ∨	Billing Type ∨	Effort (Task) ∨	
	Milestone 1 Billing	---	Chargeable	176.00	
	Milestone 2 Billing	---	Chargeable	176.00	
	Milestone 3 Billing	---	Chargeable	88.00	

Figure 5.6 – Chargeable Tasks

Then, there are **Chargeable Roles**, which show the different types of roles included in this contract line that will be used for chargeability. Chargeability is driven by the roles, and the roles have a selling price and costs that directly impact the project profitability.

The following screenshot shows the roles that, if placed on a project, will have costs and selling rates associated with them that apply to the project:

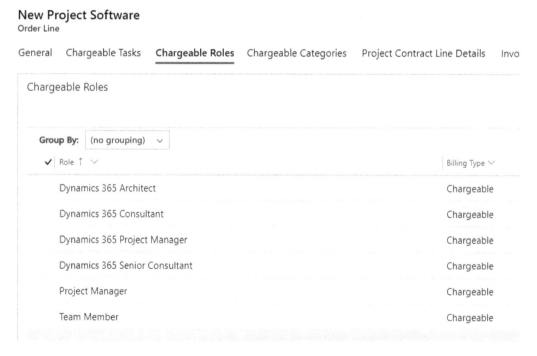

Figure 5.7 – Chargeable Roles

Chargeable Categories are expenses chargeable to the project. Most of the time, expenses become billable and become part of the client's invoice for things such as travel and expenses. Here's what the **Chargeable Categories** tab looks like to bill out expenses to the client:

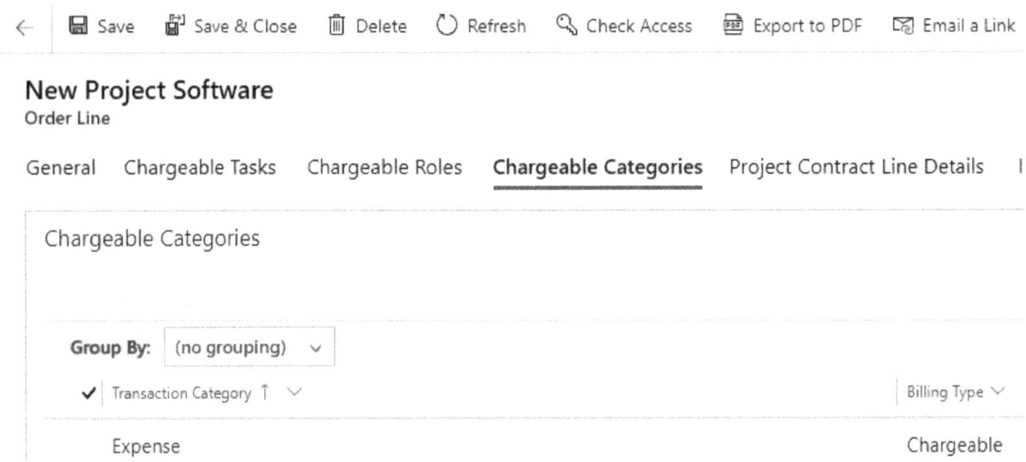

Figure 5.8 – Chargeable Categories

> **Important note**
>
> Many a time, people often get confused with the terms *chargeability* and *billability*. For your understanding in this book and for the *Project Operations* book, chargeability will reflect the fact that the time or expense entered against a project will be chargeable against it, meaning that for every dollar chargeable, a dollar will be reduced from the project's profit. However, billability means that the resulting charges will be marked up (as in a time and materials contract) or will be passed through (as in an expense for travel).

In this scenario, the charges result in a billable invoice line that makes it to the customer.

Why is this important? A firm's financial lifeblood is the profit derived from the work performed. If we as a firm miss out on billing expenses, the impact on profit is significant. Consider, if you will, a straightforward example of a contract that has the following rebill scenario:

Revenue Expected	$1,000
Expected Cost	($500)
Expenses Rebilled	$100
Expense Cost	**($100)**
Gross Margin	$500

Table 5.1 – Proper expense rebill scenario

What happens if we do not bill out our expenses? Well, it looks something like this:

Revenue Expected	$1,000
Expected Cost	($500)
Expense Cost	**($100)**
Gross Margin	$400

Table 5.2 – Gross margin impact

Thus, that $100 that we do not rebill immediately gets deducted from the gross margin. If your typical gross margin is 33% of revenue, that means you have really taken away $300 in revenue impact.

Not-to-exceed limit

There are some exciting capabilities with Project Operations that allow for more flexibility on a contract. For example, our contract with our client is for a $125,000 fixed fee. As we know, nothing goes as planned, right? Therefore, the client has agreed to a contingency fee equal to 20% of the overall contract.

Therefore, we have added a contract line for $25,000 as a time and material line item with a not-to-exceed limit of $25,000. Not-to-exceed contract limits are best used in a scenario such as this, where you are providing equal contractual protection for both the client and your firm by agreeing to a contingency but not allowing the out-of-scope task to take on a life of its own.

The following screenshot shows how to produce a not-to-exceed contract line:

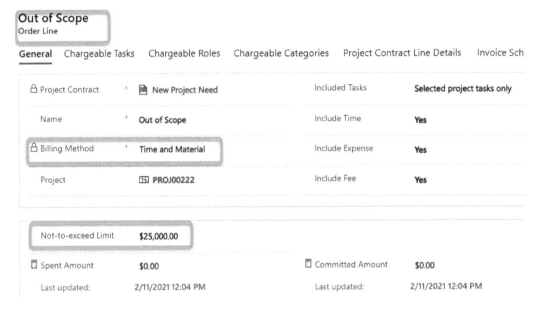

Figure 5.9 – Out of Scope contract lines

The process shown in *Figure 5.9* shows that we are setting up a new order line with a name that outlines this is for out-of-scope work. The billing method is **Time and Material** and, when chosen, this then allows you to place in the **Not-to-exceed Limit** monetary amount. The subsequent fields are for tracking purposes.

This concludes the contract components for the project we are working with. In this section, we have identified the various contract types we have for our project. We have set up fixed-price contract lines and billings for the main work we will perform. We have also set up a time and material line for any out-of-scope work. On that line, we also set the out-of-scope work to **Not-to-exceed Limit**, as per the contract with the client.

There are still some additional pricing and costing considerations that we will explore in the next section.

Developing price lists and custom price lists

Multidimensional pricing is a feature of Project Operations that provides a professional services firm with the functionality it require to meet the firm's—and the client's—needs. Professional services firms typically have rates they have defined for roles within a firm. There are typically two rate types: selling and costing. Let's have a quick rundown on each.

Selling rates

Selling rates are most typically spoken of as a *rate card*, coming from the historical, physically printed rate card that was carried by partners of a firm to communicate the hourly price of a particular role within the firm. As you may expect, though, clients expect preferential pricing, especially if they are larger clients of a firm. Furthermore, if a preferential client is taking on a large project, they might even expect further price concessions.

A firm is typically going to protect its rates at various levels as much as possible. The rate card represents its first line of defense. This sets a price within the firm and one outside the firm, for roles. The client rate sets the expectation of pricing for the client, while the project rate sets the pricing for a project.

Let's take a look at each. From the Project Operations app menu, go to the **Sales** area under the **Customers** section and navigate to the **Price Lists** menu. From here, you will see the three price lists that we have created, as shown in the following screenshot:

Active Price Lists ∨

✓	Name ↑ ∨	Currency ∨
	Labor Costs	US Dollar
	Labor Sales Price	US Dollar
	Product Price List	US Dollar

Figure 5.10 – Three common price lists

In the preceding screenshot, the three price lists shown are common for any firm. The **Labor Costs** and **Labor Sales Price** lists drive sales and labor cost pricing for Project Operations. The **Product Price List** list is used to drive the sale of products in the system.

For the selling rates, click on the **Labor Sales Price** list. This price list is date-respective, meaning that you can make your rates date-effective; so, you can have a 2021 rate, a 2022 rate, and so on. The rates are also currency-respective, so you can utilize multiple currencies. You will further notice the **Time Unit** listing, which identifies what you are selling— typically an **Hour** unit.

Let's explore, though, the actual rates associated with our roles. In our firm, we have four roles working in Dynamics 365. They have selling rates (rate-card rates) that are *published*. When a rate card is published, this is generally based upon the firm's history and tradition. Sometimes, a firm will reevaluate its rates on an annual basis and adjust accordingly. This helps the firm to readjust its rates to accommodate team member raises in salary.

The following screenshot shows the labor rates for the four Dynamics 365 roles we set up in the system:

Labor Sales Price
Price List

General	**Role prices**	Role price markups	Category prices	Price List Items	Territory Relationships	Related

✓	Role ↑ ∨	Resourcing Unit ∨	Unit ∨	Price ∨		Currency ∨
	Dynamics 365 Architect	Project Ops	Hour	$235.00		US Dollar
	Dynamics 365 Consultant	Project Ops	Hour	$205.00		US Dollar
	Dynamics 365 Project Manager	Project Ops	Hour	$215.00		US Dollar
	Dynamics 365 Senior Consultant	Project Ops	Hour	$215.00		US Dollar

Figure 5.11 – A firm's rate card

To set up a client-specific price list, navigate to the client record in Project Operations and choose the **Project Price Lists** section. Next, select the **Add New Project Price List** button and add a named price list for the client, and then select the **Labor Sales Price** list. This will create a client-specific price list, but you now need to open this price list and modify the role prices for the client's pricing.

The following screenshot shows the process of creating a custom price list for the client:

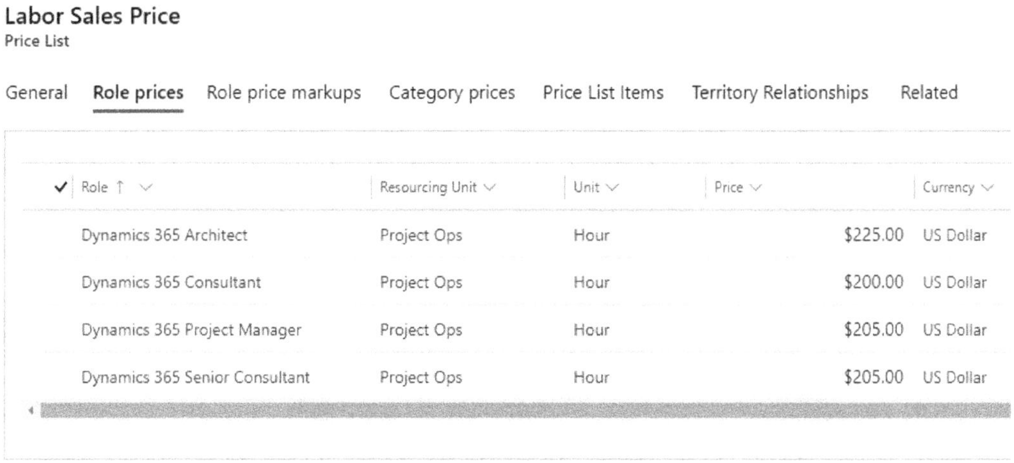

Labor Sales Price
Price List

General   **Role prices**   Role price markups   Category prices   Price List Items   Territory Relationships   Related

✓	Role ↑ ∨	Resourcing Unit ∨	Unit ∨	Price ∨		Currency ∨
	Dynamics 365 Architect	Project Ops	Hour	$225.00		US Dollar
	Dynamics 365 Consultant	Project Ops	Hour	$200.00		US Dollar
	Dynamics 365 Project Manager	Project Ops	Hour	$205.00		US Dollar
	Dynamics 365 Senior Consultant	Project Ops	Hour	$205.00		US Dollar

Figure 5.12 – The client's rate card

Notice how the rates for each role are discounted. As a real-life application, notice that none of our rates has been reduced below $200 per hour. Keeping your rates above a numerical threshold has an impact on the rates' value.

For our project, however, our client is requesting even further discounts on their rates. To accommodate this, we now need to navigate back to the project contract. From the **Project Price Lists** section, choose **Create Custom Pricing** and select the record you created. Notice that as you pulled this in, it pulled in the client's price list as a baseline. This is quite convenient because you can then be assured that you are working with the specific pricing for your client, and you can now modify the rates to the terms of the contract.

The following screenshot shows the process of creating a custom price list for a project:

Labor Sales Price - New Project Need - 2/11/2021 6:24:47 PM
Price List

General   **Role prices**   Role price markups   Category prices   Price List Items   Territory Relationships   Related

✓	Role ↑ ∨	Resourcing Unit ∨	Unit ∨	Price ∨		Currency ∨
	Dynamics 365 Architect	Project Ops	Hour	$220.00		US Dollar
	Dynamics 365 Consultant	Project Ops	Hour	$200.00		US Dollar
	Dynamics 365 Project Manager	Project Ops	Hour	$200.00		US Dollar
	Dynamics 365 Senior Consultant	Project Ops	Hour	$200.00		US Dollar

Figure 5.13 – The project's rate card

We have successfully used multidimensional sales pricing to create a rate card for a firm and have used custom pricing for the client, as well as project-specific pricing. All of these price lists are within the *sales context*, meaning they are all customer-facing prices.

However, there is a costing component to Project Operations as well that will, when combined, provide the ability to perform project profitability reporting.

Costing rates

Role-based costing is also part of the Project Operations system. For example, our rate card for a Dynamics 365 Architect is a $235-per-hour selling price. However, that is not our cost per hour for that role.

Costing rates are generally set up as a blended rate, derived from the following factors:

- **Salary**: The average or blended salary of team members in this role
- **Benefits, overhead, and burden**: The average factor above and beyond the salary to account for additional costs per role
- **Other costs**: Firm-specific costs per role
- Utilization expectations such as 50% utilization or 80% utilization

Therefore, if you have a blended team cost of $150,000 per year, with a burden rate of 30% and a utilization expectation of 80%, then the formula looks like this:

$$\$150,000 \ x \ 1.30 \ / \ .80 \ = \ \$243,750 \ per \ year \ cost$$

To transform this into an hourly rate, you must divide your number of workable hours per year. Your workable hours will be custom to your firm. For our example, we will use a 260-day year minus 10 days for holidays and 10 days for paid time off. Multiply this by an 8-hour day and you get 1,920 hours billable. The result is $126.95, or roughly a $127-per-hour cost.

This is one example, and for your firm this may be vastly different from the calculations and factors you use. However, the results end up the same, which is a blended rate per hour for the cost of a role.

Some additional notes about costing. Some firms call blended costing *standard costing*. Regardless of the name one main concept remains, and this is vitally important. It is not *actual costing*.

Actual costing is something potentially concerning for a firm if you try to do this in a Project Operations system. For example, our preceding calculations would not be used but, instead, the average cost of a role would simply be divided by the number of hours, and team members could derive from this that one person's role makes much more money than a different role. Thus, this could cause some unwanted problems for firms.

Furthermore, even though the costing information for a blended cost is much more padded with other costs, as you can see from the following screenshot, there are still some assertions to be made about salary and roles:

Labor Costs
Price List

| General | **Role prices** | Role price markups | Category prices | Price List Items | Territory Relationships | Related |

✓	Role ↑ ∨	Resourcing Unit ∨	Unit ∨	Price ∨		Currency ∨
	Dynamics 365 Architect	Project Ops	Hour		$115.00	US Dollar
	Dynamics 365 Consultant	Project Ops	Hour		$75.00	US Dollar
	Dynamics 365 Project Manager	Project Ops	Hour		$85.00	US Dollar
	Dynamics 365 Senior Consultant	Project Ops	Hour		$85.00	US Dollar

Figure 5.14 – Labor Costs price list

The costing of projects is significantly important to a firm so that the right costs are associated with a project.

Additional labor-costing considerations

There are instances where you may have offshore, nearshore, and domestic developers with different rates. Each of these can have costing effective to each of their scenarios, with currency effectiveness as well.

There is one really critical thing you will need to do, or your costs will not come through on a project: set up your version of Project Operations! Setting up Project Operations relies on the **Cost Price Lists** functionality of the **Organizational Unit** to create costing. The following screenshot outlines the most critical costing link in the system:

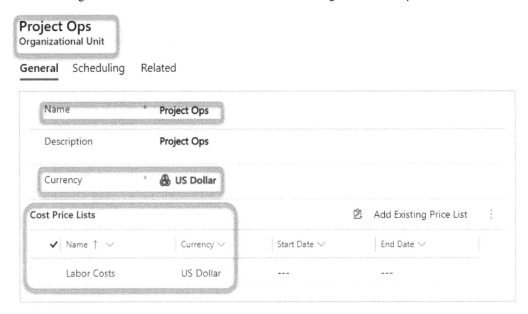

Figure 5.15 – Organization-level Labor Costs price list

Without the cost price list at the organizational unit level, when you approve timecards (time) each hour billed would have a selling price (since the project has a contract) but would not have a costing price.

Therefore, the combination of cost price lists and the organizational unit can allow for different cost rates and bill rates per organizational unit. The following table outlines this:

Role	Organizational Unit	Bill rate	Cost rate
Consultant	US Division	$205	$115
Consultant	Fr Division	€185	€95
Consultant	Offshore Division	$95	$45

Table 5.3 – Organizational unit costing

Whether you are a large tech firm or a small company delivering services across the country, these principles of price lists will drive revenue and costing, thus resulting in profitability for your firm.

There are additional factors that need to be discussed around roles and pricing, so let's get into that next.

Exploring roles and role types to control pricing

In Project Operations, we now have the ability to perform task-level chargeability, as we saw in our contract lines setup section. This flexibility gives you the best ability to meet the needs of your clients, as well as account for those needs organizationally.

We will now discuss how to set up roles that, when combined with all the project contract lines, will provide the necessary pricing structure for your clients.

Non-chargeable roles

We will create a contract administration that needs to be added to the project. We can do so in the contract lines, as shown in the following screenshot:

New Project Software
Order Line

General   **Chargeable Tasks**   Chargeable Roles   Chargeable Categories   Project Contract Line Details   Invoice Schedule   Cus

Chargeable Tasks

✓	Task ∨	Parent Task (Task) ∨	Billing Type ∨	Effort (Task) ∨
	Milestone 1 Billing	---	Chargeable	176.00
	Milestone 2 Billing	---	Chargeable	176.00
	Milestone 3 Billing	---	Chargeable	88.00
	Admin Task	---	Non Chargeable	20.00

Figure 5.16 – Tasks list showing the Admin – Non Chargeable tasks

However, there are also times where a particular role within a firm is always non-chargeable. An example of this may be a pre-sales role.

This scenario sometimes plays out where a firm may want to have a deep understanding of its sales (customer/client acquisition) costs. Many times, a firm is thrilled to have new business come its way, and the project may even appear to be profitable—that is, until they look at the 300-plus hours of pre-sales time that was spent to get the deal. Some firms will then track the entire sales team's time spent on a pursuit, to further analyze and evaluate what the true cost of client acquisition is. This helps them to then further determine what their rates should be and which deals they ought to pursue.

To set up a non-chargeable role in Project Operations, navigate to **Projects | Roles Add a new role**, as shown next:

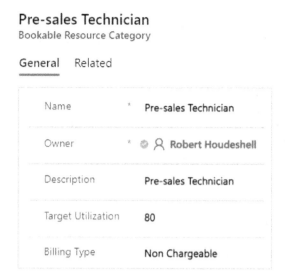

Pre-sales Technician
Bookable Resource Category

General   Related

Name	* **Pre-sales Technician**
Owner	* ⊘ ᚛ **Robert Houdeshell**
Description	**Pre-sales Technician**
Target Utilization	80
Billing Type	**Non Chargeable**

Figure 5.17 – Non-chargeable roles

Setting up this role type and linking this to a team member who performs that role will provide the team member with a way to input their timecard against the sales pursuits they have, while providing a way for a firm to account for their time but not bill the customer.

Nothing special needs to be done for the team member to input their time. However, how you use this data will be key. To have some meaningful data to pursue, you may want to set up a labor cost for the **Pre-sales Technician** role, as shown in the following screenshot:

Labor Costs
Price List

General   **Role prices**   Role price markups   Category prices   Price List Items   Territory Relationships   Related

✓	Role ↑ ∨	Resourcing Unit ∨	Unit ∨	Price ∨	Currency ∨
	Dynamics 365 Architect	Project Ops	Hour	$115.00	US Dollar
	Dynamics 365 Consultant	Project Ops	Hour	$75.00	US Dollar
	Dynamics 365 Project Manag	Project Ops	Hour	$85.00	US Dollar
	Dynamics 365 Senior Consul	Project Ops	Hour	$85.00	US Dollar
	Pre-sales Technician	Project Ops	Hour	$75.00	US Dollar

Figure 5.18 – Non-chargeable role with a cost associated

The preceding scenario will provide data for each team member assigned to the **Pre-sales Technician** role who enters a time to calculate their total costs as they are posted into the **Actuals** records in Project Operations.

Complimentary roles

There is one more category of role that may be appropriate to capture in your Project Operations deployment. In many firms, there are Practice Managers, Practice Directors, or—sometimes—Customer/Client Relationship Managers who work on projects to keep them progressing forward.

Therefore, the following setup will allow for a complimentary service that can be accounted for on a project as well:

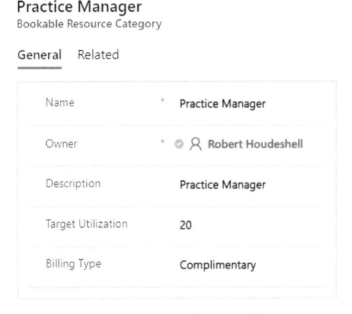

Figure 5.19 – A complimentary role

Similar to the **Pre-sales Technician** role, we can cost this role as well, for the same reasons. The following is the labor cost setup for a **Practice Manager** role:

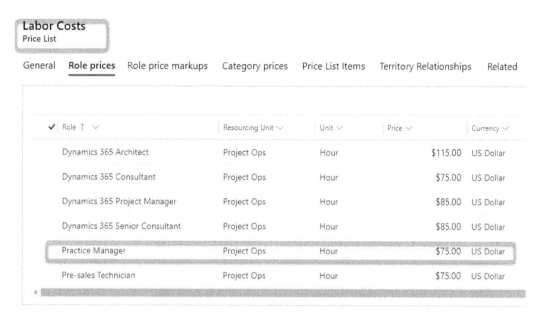

Figure 5.20 – A complimentary role with labor costs

Let's summarize the costing conversation. You may sometimes encounter costing issues where you might run into resistance when trying to set up some of the costing scenarios listed previously.

For example, a firm may not want to expose any level of costing information to users of the system. This is a reasonable objection. What I have done previously to overcome this objection is one of the following two things:

- The first option is to use field-level security and only allow practice managers or other elevated roles to see the costing fields that come as standard in Microsoft.

- The second option is to create a new form based on the **Project** form, using customization and solutions. In this new form, you can assign it to a specific group, such as the **Project Manager Security Role** group, then remove all the fields that relate to cost from that form. You can also change views and assign them to the **Project Manager Security Role** group.

Other things you may run into are that project managers and other staff in a firm may not want to see all of the invisible costs (admin, pre-sales, practice managers) on the costs of the project. This is a decision point that will need to be made.

Overall, come to a consensus with your team on which factors and formulas you wish to use, and you will have a mutually agreeable solution for your firm.

Summary

In this chapter, we followed the sales process from the opportunity through to the project contracts and associated price lists. We took a quote and turned it into a project contract. The project contract has the line-level detail that sets up the billing types and allows you to link to a task level within a project.

We set up an example project that has a fixed-fee contract line and a time and material line. The time and material line was set up with a not-to-exceed contract limit. The skills learned here will provide you with the ability to meet the contractual needs of the client and the company.

The sales price lists are important to all of this, specifically when working with time and material contracts, since the price list will drive the hourly rate that factors out to the billable amount. The cost price lists are important to all other aspects of a contract, since all the costs associated with a team member and their role will factor into the costs of the project.

As we enter into the next chapter, we will work through the project director and project manager roles as they relate to the Project Operations system.

Questions

1. In the Project Operations system, what is a record called when it changes from a quote to *won*?

2. True or False: The Project Operations system only allows one invoice per project.

3. What type of billing can be used to set up billing on a periodic basis?

4. True or False: You can relate multiple contract lines to a contract.

5. True or False: Contract lines can only be of one type per project/contract combination.

6. What function does the **Invoice Frequency** setting perform?

7. Selling rates or billable rates are applicable to which type of contract: fixed-price or time and materials?

8. What are the three levels of multidimensional pricing?

9. True or False: Labor cost rates only apply to time and materials contracts.

10. True or False: Project costing is simply a matter of populating the labor cost rate tables and assigning them to the appropriate roles.

6
Practice Manager Functions – We Won the Contract! What Now?

In the previous chapter, we learned how to set up the project contracts and pricing. This chapter will take us through the next steps and talk through the work a practice manager will do in Project Operations. As a practice manager, you will undoubtedly have the challenges and pressures of finding people to staff projects directly. Furthermore, you will have to understand the cost and quality implications of your decisions. This chapter is designed to provide you with a level of confidence that enables you to confidently forecast and track utilization across your teams.

Therefore, in this chapter, you will learn about the following concepts:

- Understanding direct staffing models and how they work
- Understanding centralized staffing models and how they generate bookings for team members
- Direct versus centralized staffing models

- Using resource forecasting
- Using revenue forecasting
- Resource utilization tracking

By the end of this chapter, you will have learned how to set up, perform operations on, and utilize **direct staffing models** and a **centralized staffing model**. Additionally, you will be able to utilize resource forecasting to balance workloads, and track and manage performance.

Technical requirements

To perform the tasks in this chapter, you will need the following:

- An Microsoft 365 account and an **Azure Active Directory** (**Azure AD**) login
- A Microsoft Dynamics 365 Project Operations **Customer Relationship Management** (**CRM**) license
- A Microsoft Project Plan license
- A practice manager security role

Please visit the following link to check the CiA videos:

```
https://bit.ly/3abRHw7
```

Understanding direct staffing models

When handled through a **resource management office (RMO)** or a resource manager, you typically have a designated person, or people, handling resource requests that come into the system. The handling of these requests is generally very process-driven and is controlled by demand, supply, and data.

However, there are firms that are maybe smaller in size whose practice management is more directly involved in assigning people to projects. If your firm falls into this category, this section is for you and will also include some suggestions that can help you and your resource managers as well.

For this section, a practice manager is responsible for keeping new business coming in, staffing the right team members, forecasting utilization, and tracking billability. They typically perform these functions with disparate systems and a lack of visibility. This is where the functionality of Project Operations can be helpful.

Working with backlog tracking

First things first… what is your backlog and when can you consume it? A backlog is work that has been booked through the sales process and that requires signed statements of work to be performed. Furthermore, there are different types of backlog that you will want to manage.

A backlog can be tracked by different types of work, different types of projects, or different contract types. Some examples that we will work through are fixed-price and time and material projects. In either example, though, work needs to be assigned to team members.

Other types of backlog tracking may be across product lines, service lines, or other delineations of the types of work being performed.

For example, you have a project that has been booked for a $125,000 fixed price plus $25,000 out-of-scope time and material. That is great, but who can do the work on the project? What skills are needed and who is available? Furthermore, are there any pauses in starting the project? Any delays from within the project? Any issues that may cause the project to go on pause? Magnify this by the many various projects and the stage they are at in the project pipeline, and you'll see the challenges that a practice manager may have in managing backlogs.

To solve this problem, we need to get the right people booked onto the project and get the project started. Let's begin by looking at a project's work breakdown structure. An example is given in the following screenshot:

Grid   Board   Timeline

	Name ∨	Assigned to ∨	Duration ∨	Effort ∨
1	∨ Milestone 1 Billing - Define and Design		15 days	180 hours
2	Architect Hours	G Generic - Dynamics 365 Architect	3 weeks	80 hours
3	Project Manager Hours	G Generic - Dynamics 365 Project Manager	3 weeks	40 hours
4	Consultant Hours	G Generic - Dynamics 365 Consultant	3 weeks	60 hours
5	Milestone 2 Billing	Robert Houdeshell	180 hours	176 hours
6	Milestone 3 Billing	Robert Houdeshell	90 hours	88 hours
7	Out of Scope Time & Materials	Robert Houdeshell	3 months	80 hours
8	Admin Task		1 day	20 hours

Figure 6.1 – Project work breakdown structure

As we can see in *Figure 6.1*, our work breakdown structure has three milestones we are going to bill out. The first milestone, though—the **Define and Design** milestone—needs to have an architect, a project manager, and a consultant all working together to pull together the system requirements, epics, user stories, and story points for the next sprint cycles.

In our example, we need to identify team members who have the skills to do the work outlined in *Figure 6.1*. As a practice manager of a reasonably sized firm, I know that I want to assign **William Michaels** to the **Architect role**, **Ruvika Marisamy** to the **Project Manager** role, and **Louisa Hernandez** to the **Consultant** role.

Therefore, for each of the respective lines I will substitute each generic assignment with the respective team member (resource), as shown in the following screenshot:

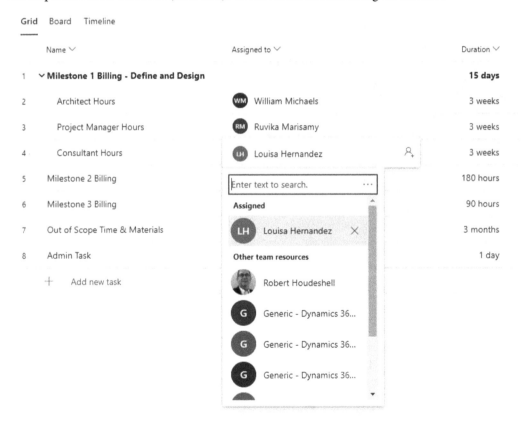

Figure 6.2 – Direct resource assignment

At this point, as Ruvika, Louisa, and William are entering their time into Project Operations, they will see their assignments show up as available to enter time against. To prove this, you can enter a timecard for one of the resources. Incidentally, as a practice manager, you may need to know this. This is also how you will input time into the system if you need to do so on behalf of an absent team member, maybe due to emergency leave of absence or other reasons.

To exemplify this, we first need to make a minor change to the **Create Time Entry** form, as follows:

1. Using the same logic applied in *Chapter 3, The How-Tos of Setting Up Project Operations*, in the *Dynamics 365 CE – Sales customizations* section, open your customization solution and add the **Time Entry** form. Then, start to modify the **Create Time Entry** form, which is shown in the following screenshot:

Figure 6.3 – Create Time Entry form to customize

2. Once the **Create Time Entry** form is opened, from the **Field Explorer** on the right, choose to add the **Bookable Resource** field wherever you wish. Note that we can lock this down too with field-level security so that only practice managers can perform this task. The following screenshot shows the **Bookable Resource** field added to the form:

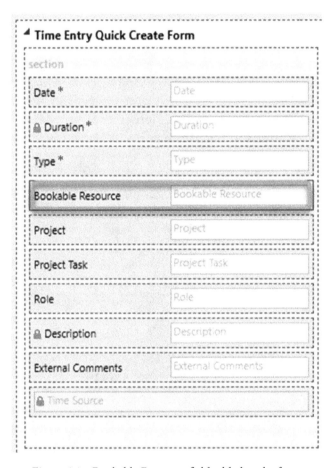

Figure 6.4 – Bookable Resource field added to the form

3. Once you complete *Step 2*, you will get the following result:

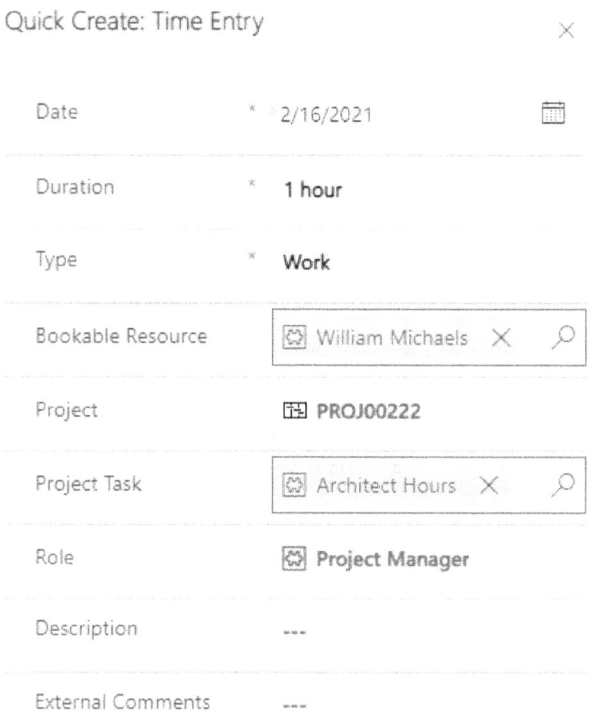

Quick Create: Time Entry   ×

Date	* 2/16/2021
Duration	* 1 hour
Type	* **Work**
Bookable Resource	William Michaels × 🔍
Project	PROJ00222
Project Task	Architect Hours × 🔍
Role	**Project Manager**
Description	---
External Comments	---

Figure 6.5 – Time booked to a team member (delegated time entry)

Here, you can see that we have booked a time to a team member.

Let's now explore how resources and roles can be functionally utilized to generate the best results for the performance of a project.

Building resources and roles

Building resources and roles is vitally important for the overall success of your projects since these will directly impact the billing, costing, and profitability of the overall project.

Resources and roles are of critical importance to the overall Project Operations system. Resources and roles are accessible from the lower-left **Areas** menu (lower-left portion of **Project Operations**), through the **Resources** area.

Resources are team members and are thus the most important part of a professional services firm. Some resources can be internal (user resources), which consume a Dynamics license, while other resources may be external or partner resources (account or contact resources).

Resources have roles that they can perform—for example, a team member may be able to perform architect and project manager roles. Therefore, you may assign them to one project as an architect and another project as a project manager. This is a common practice.

Roles are also going to drive your billing rates for time and material projects—as well as your costing rates—across the board. Some scenarios that complicate a professional services firm generally center on the costing rates for the same role.

For example, you may have a Dynamics 365 consultant that has an internal rate per hour of $75. However, that same role fulfilled externally with a partner may cost $95 per hour. When you try to enter a duplicate role price to the **Labor costs** price list, the system will not allow a duplicate record.

To solve this, there are a couple of different approaches. The first approach is to potentially create a new Organizational unit for the partner organization you are working with and assign a role to that Organizational unit. This would solve the need to not have duplicate records.

Another approach is to create a similar role—with either a suffix or some other identification to show that the role is a partner role (primarily for your users to work with) —that states something such as **Dynamics 365 Consultant – External/Partner**, and then cost this role at $95 per hour. There are other ways as well to solve this issue.

Now that the resources and roles are structured, we will fill out the details of the resource member's capabilities.

Skills and certifications

Skills and certifications are of key importance to practice managers since, after all, they are the reason team members succeed! Skills are accessible through the **Resources** area. As of the point of publication, skills are named **Characteristics** in the system, and the reason behind that is that skills and certifications are two sides of the same coin. As the following screenshot shows, you can have almost identically named skills and certifications but they mean different things technically:

Figure 6.6 – Certifications and skills shown as two different types

Figure 6.6 shows **Dynamics 365 CE** as a skill that the team member possesses, demonstrating that they are proficient with Dynamics 365 CE. The **Dynamics 365 CE – Foundation** certification is an actual certification, assigned through the process of taking an exam and meeting certain criteria.

For skills, there is a rating system available that can rate a team member as **Level 1**, **Level 2**, **Level 3**, or something else such as **Standard**, **Advanced**, or **Expert** in some other considerations.

There are contracts that a firm may have that require certifications to be active in order to perform work on the account. This expands beyond technical certifications and may also be used for tracking licenses in the engineering field or other licensure requirements. There is a typical need that clients have expressed over the years, and that is for the addition of licensing expiration dates. Adding this through customization provides you with the ability to report on and create workflows around the license expiration date.

Therefore, with plenty of lead time, you can notify a team member of their license renewals, as well as report on this as the expiration date approaches.

With this understanding of the baselines of resources, roles, skills, and certifications, let's take a look at how this all becomes important in the system.

Understanding centralized staffing models

A **centralized staffing model** requires a firm to have a solid identification of their resources, roles, skills, and certifications. Over time, resource managers learn who is skilled where, and there is a considerable amount of internal knowledge that builds up.

However, even resource managers take time off! When they do, replacing *their skills* is not easy! In larger firms, knowing who to assign a project to becomes difficult (if not totally untenable) without a solid foundation of data-driven tools.

Let's take a look at the characteristics (skills and certifications) for **William Michaels**. William can do a multitude of things for the firm, as we see in the following screenshot:

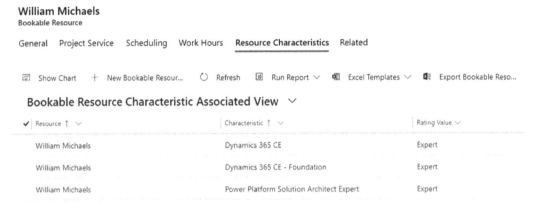

Figure 6.7 – Team member characteristics

William also works in two roles, with two different billing rates for customers, as illustrated in the following screenshot:

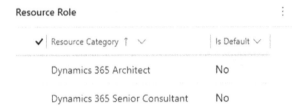

Figure 6.8 – Team member roles

These factors drive the centralized resource scheduling dashboard. The **Schedule Board** has multiple filters that include the following:

- **Characteristics** (with **Ratings**)—This allows you to choose from not just a list of skills but also ratings. This applies to skills and certifications.

- **Roles**—This includes each of the roles outlined in the system.

- **Territories**—This includes geographic locations.

- **Organizational Units**—This can be used if you are using Organizational units for cross-practice functionality or potentially using them for external partners and costing.

- **Resource Types** – This most commonly refers to users (internal resources) or contacts (partner/external resources).

- **Pool Types**—This includes **All Accounts/Contacts** and other filters.

- **Teams**—This can be used if you are using Microsoft Teams. You can filter on the team you wish to see.

- **Business Units**—This includes an organization's business units.

As a practice manager, this **Schedule Board** is going to be your main source of information for future resource forecasting.

The importance of these decisions will drive the efficiency of your firm. You can further utilize these decision points as a catalyst to driving discussion and potential change within an organization.

Let's now explore direct and centralized staffing models and how they relate to each other.

Direct versus centralized staffing models

As a practice manager, director, program manager, operations manager, or operations officer, you are undoubtedly going to have interaction with the Project Operations system. Depending upon your resourcing models, you may get directly involved in resourcing, or this may be handled through a resource manager. Following are some key differences:

Differences	Direct staffing	Centralized staffing
Type of organization	A direct staffing model of project management is quite common. The characteristics of a direct staffing model reflect typically the size, culture, and structure of the company performing the staffing. Direct staffing typically indicates a very close knowledge of a project's resourcing needs.	Centralized staffing models may typically be used in larger companies, but they can also be used in small or mid-sized companies, for many of the same reasons as previously discussed.
Reason	The reasons for this can be wide and varied. Sometimes, it is because of the size of the team or the project. This indicates that a person—such as a practice manager—knows the project, the team, and the team member availability.	The most common reasons include the need to assign work to team members based upon specific roles, skills, or other characteristics.
Involvement	As such, direct staffing decisions are made and managed through direct involvement of the practice manager. Other reasons behind direct staffing may be due to specific knowledge of a team member or the desire of a client to have a specific person on a project.	In both models, we are placing team members on a project to perform work. In a direct model, this is performed through institutional knowledge of a person or people. In a centralized model, this is performed with systems, databases, and team member recommendations. For either approach, we will need to review the overall governance related to staffing.

Table 6.1 – Differences between direct staffing and centralized staffing model.

In both models, we are placing team members on a project to perform work. In a direct model, this is performed through institutional knowledge of a person or people. In a centralized model, this is performed with systems, databases, and team member recommendations. For either approach, we will need to review the overall governance related to staffing.

Using resource forecasting

Resource forecasting is the forward view of your practice utilization. It is not a firm prediction of what exactly a team member will work on, but is instead is a plan of what they should work through in the next timeframe.

As you may recall, team members have roles and skills assigned to them that provide you with the ability to assign them to a project based upon those filters. Once a team member is booked, their calendars and work week should reflect bookings that have been made. Therefore, based upon their utilization goals, you should be able to view the proper utilization of your team members.

The following screenshot shows the utilization of our team members across a monthly timeline:

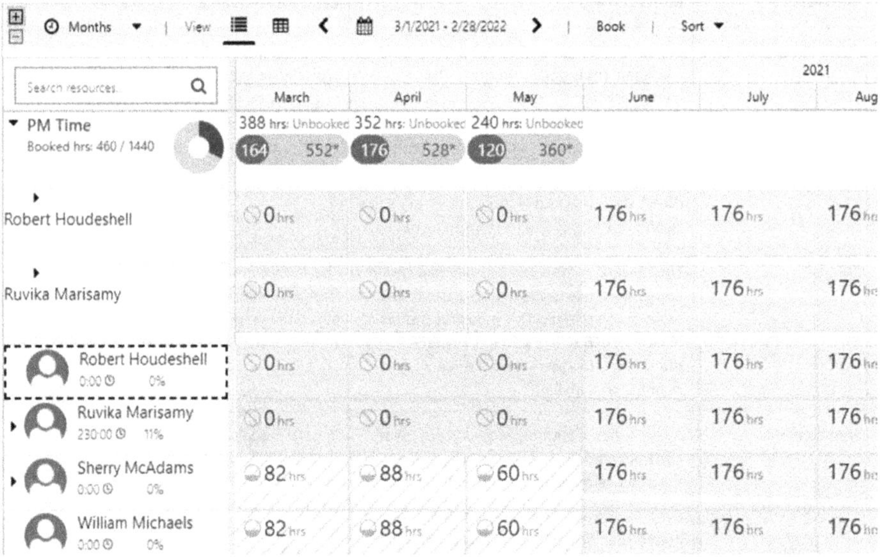

Figure 6.9 – Schedule board forecasting

The schedule board forecast shown in *Figure 6.9* is purely an hours-driven view of the forecasted utilization of your team. The implications of this forecast drive revenue, whether working a time and material or a fixed-price contract. For fixed-price contracts, hours worked turn into recognized revenue.

This also drives the productivity of team members who rely on having a well-constructed flow of project work assigned to them. As you see in *Figure 6.9*, for the months of **March**, **April**, and **May**, **Robert Houdeshell** and **Ruvika Marisamy** are booked solid, while **Sherry McAdams** and **William Michaels** have **82**, **88**, and **60** hours available through the respective months.

As we see at the top of *Figure 6.9*, this project still has a requirement of **PM Time** that has **552**, **528**, and **360** hours respectively across the months to find resources for. Therefore, this means as a practice manager that you can see the demands of the project numerically and get the insight you need to find additional resources, if needed.

All of this information should give you, the practice manager, a series of data points that you can use to drive the productivity of your team. Furthermore, your resource managers should have these same tools to provide them with the ability to balance workload and match the right people to the right projects, to bring projects to a successful conclusion.

Using revenue forecasting

As we discussed (or hinted at) in the *Using resource forecasting* section, time equals money. I think we have heard this before, right? Time is money, though regardless of the type of contract being worked on in the professional services firm. To accentuate this, let's look at a few contract types and talk about the *time equals money* axiom. Some typical contract types are outlined here:

- **Time and Material contracts**: When billed after conducting the work, each hour worked turns into an hour billed. There are variations for tracking **Work in Progress** (**WIP**) that help a firm attain **Generally Accepted Accounting Principles** (**GAAP**)-compliant financial reporting. Furthermore, revenue may or may not be recognized right away, depending upon other accounting factors. However, you can be assured that over time, time will equal money.

- **Fixed-price contracts**: When billed out, a fixed-price contract may have revenue billed upfront and/or billed in milestones throughout a project. Time equals money when the contractual obligations of the statement of work are met and milestones are accepted. Furthermore, revenue may be recognized on a percent-completion basis. As the contract concludes, you can be assured that time will equal money, even if that money means costs overrun due to unavoidable resource costs impacting the profitability of a project.

- **Not-to-exceed contracts**: These are much like a time and material contract but with a cap on billings to the client. Just as the cost of a fixed-price contract overruns, this type of contract's cost will directly impact the profit.

So, how is a practice manager to forecast these variations of projects across their practices? The answer is: through the practical application of forecasting logic across the revenue stream's list, as outlined previously.

For a time and material contract, you can look at a project's **Estimates** tab and see the costs that are predicted across the various timescales of the project, as shown in the following screenshot:

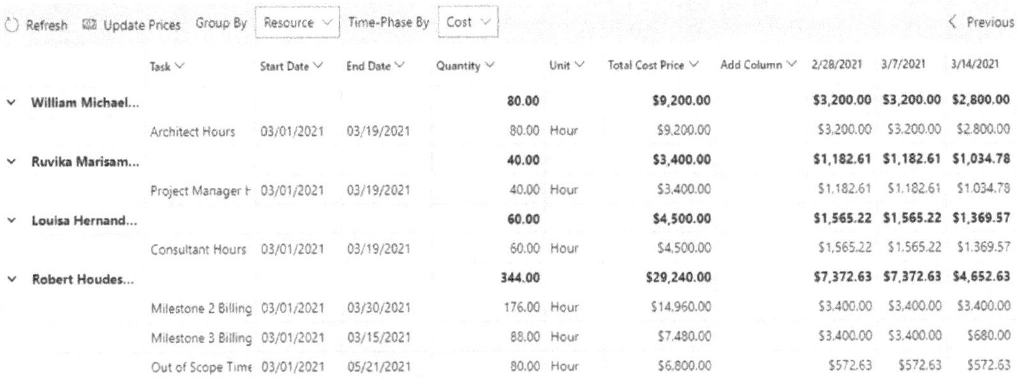
Refresh | Update Prices | Group By: Resource | Time-Phase By: Cost | < Previous

	Task	Start Date	End Date	Quantity	Unit	Total Cost Price	Add Column	2/28/2021	3/7/2021	3/14/2021
William Michael...				**80.00**		**$9,200.00**		**$3,200.00**	**$3,200.00**	**$2,800.00**
	Architect Hours	03/01/2021	03/19/2021	80.00	Hour	$9,200.00		$3,200.00	$3,200.00	$2,800.00
Ruvika Marisam...				**40.00**		**$3,400.00**		**$1,182.61**	**$1,182.61**	**$1,034.78**
	Project Manager H	03/01/2021	03/19/2021	40.00	Hour	$3,400.00		$1,182.61	$1,182.61	$1,034.78
Louisa Hernand...				**60.00**		**$4,500.00**		**$1,565.22**	**$1,565.22**	**$1,369.57**
	Consultant Hours	03/01/2021	03/19/2021	60.00	Hour	$4,500.00		$1,565.22	$1,565.22	$1,369.57
Robert Houdes...				**344.00**		**$29,240.00**		**$7,372.63**	**$7,372.63**	**$4,652.63**
	Milestone 2 Billing	03/01/2021	03/30/2021	176.00	Hour	$14,960.00		$3,400.00	$3,400.00	$3,400.00
	Milestone 3 Billing	03/01/2021	03/15/2021	88.00	Hour	$7,480.00		$3,400.00	$3,400.00	$680.00
	Out of Scope Time	03/01/2021	05/21/2021	80.00	Hour	$6,800.00		$572.63	$572.63	$572.63

Figure 6.10 – Project estimates: Cost view

The **Sales** view of this same information can be seen in the following screenshot. We can see this same information but from a **Sales/Billing** view:

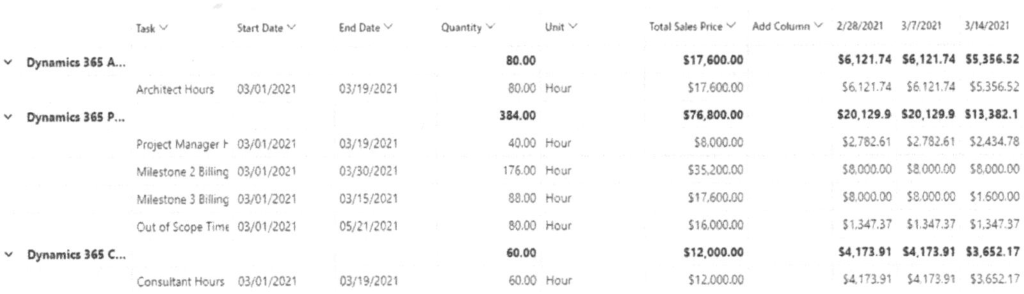

	Task	Start Date	End Date	Quantity	Unit	Total Sales Price	Add Column	2/28/2021	3/7/2021	3/14/2021
Dynamics 365 A...				**80.00**		**$17,600.00**		**$6,121.74**	**$6,121.74**	**$5,356.52**
	Architect Hours	03/01/2021	03/19/2021	80.00	Hour	$17,600.00		$6,121.74	$6,121.74	$5,356.52
Dynamics 365 P...				**384.00**		**$76,800.00**		**$20,129.9**	**$20,129.9**	**$13,382.1**
	Project Manager H	03/01/2021	03/19/2021	40.00	Hour	$8,000.00		$2,782.61	$2,782.61	$2,434.78
	Milestone 2 Billing	03/01/2021	03/30/2021	176.00	Hour	$35,200.00		$8,000.00	$8,000.00	$8,000.00
	Milestone 3 Billing	03/01/2021	03/15/2021	88.00	Hour	$17,600.00		$8,000.00	$8,000.00	$1,600.00
	Out of Scope Time	03/01/2021	05/21/2021	80.00	Hour	$16,000.00		$1,347.37	$1,347.37	$1,347.37
Dynamics 365 C...				**60.00**		**$12,000.00**		**$4,173.91**	**$4,173.91**	**$3,652.17**
	Consultant Hours	03/01/2021	03/19/2021	60.00	Hour	$12,000.00		$4,173.91	$4,173.91	$3,652.17

Figure 6.11 – Project estimates – Sales view

The information in the preceding screenshot provides you with a complete view into the revenue and cost projections for a project. As a practice manager, you may use this information to make project staffing changes or other decisions.

The milestone view of your projects shows a different picture, but there is some relationship to the previous two: *Figure 6.10 – Project estimates – Cost view* and *Figure 6.11 – Project estimates – Sales view*. The loose relationship is this: for a milestone-based project, you are going to bill a project out according to the schedule shown in the following screenshot:

Chargeable Tasks

	Task ∨	Parent Task (Task) ∨	Billing Type ∨	Effort ... ∨	Start (Task) ∨	Finish (Task) ∨	
	Milestone 1 Billing - Defir	---	Chargeable	171.96	3/1/2021	3/31/2021	
	Architect Hours	Milestone 1 Billing - Define and Design	Chargeable	80.00	3/1/2021	3/19/2021	
	Project Manager Hours	Milestone 1 Billing - Define and Design	Chargeable	40.00	3/1/2021	3/31/2021	
	Consultant Hours	Milestone 1 Billing - Define and Design	Chargeable	51.96	3/1/2021	3/26/2021	
	Milestone 2 Billing	---	Chargeable	176.00	4/1/2021	5/3/2021	
	Milestone 3 Billing	---	Chargeable	88.00	5/3/2021	5/21/2021	
	Admin Task	---	Non Chargea...	20.00	3/1/2021	5/21/2021	

+ New Project Contract ...   ⟳ Refresh   ⋮

Figure 6.12 – Project Contract Line Tasks/Milestone billings

We can also see the billing schedule, as follows:

Invoice Frequency   📄 Monthly

Billing Start Date   ˙ 3/1/2021

Generate Periodic

	Milestone Name ↑ ∨	Project Task ∨	Milestone Date ∨	Milestone Amount ∨	Invoice Status ∨	
	03/07/2021	Milestone 1 Billing - Define and Design	3/7/2021	$50,000.0000	Customer invoice posted	
	04/07/2021	Milestone 2 Billing	4/7/2021	$50,000.0000	Not Ready for invoicing	
	05/07/2021	Milestone 3 Billing	5/7/2021	$25,000.0000	Not Ready for invoicing	

Figure 6.13 – Project invoice schedule

For a fixed-price project, the invoice schedule is going to drive billings that go out to the client, whereby your client gets an invoice from your firm and pays it based upon the terms outlined in your contracts. Even when receiving the payment in an accrual accounting system, you may not have revenue recognized yet due to contractual terms. *Figure 6.12* shows how you might see each task unfold on a date-driven basis. But more accurately, *Figure 6.10* and *Figure 6.11* show how resources are planned and therefore may be consumed against a project. This can loosely correlate to your anticipated revenue recognized over the lifetime of a project, based upon the consumption of resources across a timeline.

The following screenshot shows a revenue-forecasting spreadsheet with combined contract and revenue types and demonstrates how they factor into a forecast across a timeline:

Contract Type	Revenue Type	Forecasted Hours	Contract Value	Hourly Rate	Month 1 Forecast	Month 2 Forecast	Month 3 Forecast
Time and Materials	Labor	200	$ 55,000.00	$ 275.00	$ 25,000.00	$ -	$ 10,000.00
Time and Materials	Labor	2673	$ 735,075.00	$ 275.00	$ 25,000.00	$ 50,000.00	$ 75,000.00
Fixed Price	Milestone	1818	$ 500,000.00	$ 275.00	$ -	$ 250,000.00	$ -
Time and Materials	Labor	182	$ 50,050.00	$ 275.00	$ -	$ 50,000.00	
Fixed Price	Percent Compl	2636	$ 725,000.00	$ 275.00	$ 25,000.00	$ 175,000.00	$ 150,000.00
Time and Materials	Labor	200	$ 45,000.00	$ 225.00	$ 10,000.00	$ 20,000.00	$ 30,000.00
Time and Materials	Labor	1218	$ 334,950.00	$ 275.00	$ 10,000.00	$ 25,000.00	$ 50,000.00
Fixed Price	Milestone	2545	$ 699,875.00	$ 275.00	$ 150,000.00	$ -	$ 250,000.00
TOTAL REVENUE FORECAST					$ 245,000.00	$ 570,000.00	$ 565,000.00

Figure 6.14 – Overall revenue forecasting

The view we have in *Figure 6.14* is built from data that is in the system (forecast data for team members and milestone billings for milestone contracts). Although it is not a standard report in the system today, it is something that can be built using *Power BI* as a modern reporting tool, as follows:

Project ID	Revenue Type	Contract Type	Contract Value	Hourly Rate	Month 1 Forecast	Month 2 Forecast	Month 3 Forecast	Month 4 Forecast	Month 5 Forecast	Month 6 Forecast
		TOTAL REVENUE FORECAST			326400	575,928.42	558,873.68	600000	405000	150000
PROJ0022	Labor	Time and Materials	125000	215	106400	5,928.42	3,873.68	0	0	
PROJ0024	Labor	Time and Materials	735075	275	25000	50,000.00	75,000.00	75000	75000	75000
PROJ0026	Milestone	Fixed Price	500000	275	0	250,000.00	0.00	250000	0	0
PROJ0027	Labor	Time and Materials	50050	275	0	50,000.00				
PROJ0028	Percent Complete	Fixed Price	725000	275	25000	175,000.00	150,000.00	200000		
PROJ0029	Labor	Time and Materials	45000	225	10000	20,000.00	30,000.00	25000	30000	25000
PROJ0030	Labor	Time and Materials	334950	275	10000	25,000.00	50,000.00	50000	50000	50000
PROJ0031	Milestone	Fixed Price	699875	275	150000	0.00	250,000.00	0	250000	0
Total			3214950		652800	1,151,856.84	1,117,747.36	1200000	810000	300000

Figure 6.15 – Power BI forecasting report

This information can be utilized by a practice manager to make staffing, recruiting, and hiring decisions, as well as overall projections for executive teams to predict revenue. This information provides you with the data to support your business.

Looking forward is important for the prediction of what *will be*, while resource utilization tracking is a look backward at the performance of team members.

Resource utilization tracking

Resource utilization tracking is a historical look at the time entered into the system and approved for your team members. As team members receive their project assignments, they will count on these assignments to translate to time-entry capabilities in the system.

When a team member enters their time in the system, it will go through the process of entry, submission, and approval by the project manager. When the project manager approves the time, the hours will show in the **Resource Utilization** screen available from the **Resources** or **Projects** areas of the system. In the following screenshot, you can see an example of missing time entries, which may help you identify who needs to have a reminder of time-entry policies:

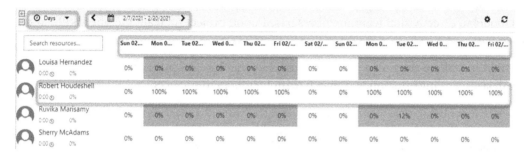

Figure 6.16 – Resource utilization chart

Note that this view is available to be included or not included in the **Security** section, so you can keep this information confidential.

The view shown in *Figure 6.16* has been highlighted (manually). In the upper left, we see the timescale of **Days** versus **Weeks** or **Months**. You can change this as you wish, and the screen refreshes. The dates highlighted show the timescale in the display. The calendar days are shown across the header.

The team members are listed below the header, and one team member is highlighted as entering **100%** of the time for that timeframe. The other two are highlighted as not having entered their timecards (thus missing time for the 2 weeks). Thus, we can use this information to drive the completion of a timecard for these team members.

Looking backward, we can also look forward to ensure that whatever impediments are keeping team members from being successful can be removed, and their success improved.

Summary

In this chapter, we engaged with the practice management needs of the Project Operations system by first taking a look at staffing models and how they are constructed. There are a number of decision points within this chapter that will drive the overall productivity of the system.

As we look into direct staffing models, we see that a practice manager will typically use this model to directly staff team members based upon project fit, team member skills, and experience.

Centralized staffing requires a lot more setup, but enables a resource management office to take data-driven information and match team members to projects.

Resource forecasting provides a practice manager with a forward-looking view of the team's performance. Resource forecasting allows a practice manager to see which problems may come up in the future. It also allows a resource manager to see the same problems, and provides a forum to drive resource matching.

Resource utilization shows how to view the past performance of team members. This can also provide insight into missing timecards or other impediments to team members' success.

As we enter into *Chapter 7, Resource Manager – Staffing for Success!*, we will drill deeper into the resource manager's job in the Project Operations system.

Questions

1. In the Project Operations system, which staffing model involves practice managers or others directly assigning work to team members?

2. True or False: Backlog is the total work under contract (booked work) to be worked and billed.

3. Team member _____ and _____ result in a team member (resource) being scheduled to work on a project.

4. True or False: Currently, Project Operations does not provide for delegated time entry.

5. Roles in the Project Operations system drive which three major functions?

6. Skills and certifications are both stored in which Dynamics 365 CE entity?

7. Which filter is NOT part of the **Schedule Board**?

    a) **Roles**

    b) **Characteristics**

    c) **Quality of Work**

    d) **Territory**

8. What type of forecast is resource forecasting?

9. This type of forecasting combines contract types to give you information to drive the practice.

10. Resource _____ tracking provides you with a historical look at hours entered and approved, as well as an awareness of potential issues.

7
Resource Manager – Staffing for Success!

In the previous chapter, we learned the foundational concepts of resourcing through the experience of the practice manager.

In this chapter, we are going to bring these foundational concepts to a centralized model and identify how a resource manager (and the **Resource Management Offices**) (**RMOs**) can create a schedule more effectively. As a result, you will be able to work with the **Schedule** board to optimize scheduling.

Therefore, in this chapter, you will learn about the following concepts:

- Staffing projects for success
- Generating bookings
- Maximizing the **Schedule** board
- Resource utilization management

By the end of this chapter, you will be able to lead the RMO and its function to improve the overall staffing and efficiency of a project's execution.

Technical requirements

To perform the tasks in this chapter, you will need the following:

- An Microsoft 365 account and an **Azure Active Directory** (**Azure AD**) login
- A Microsoft Dynamics 365 Project Operations **Customer Relationship Management** (**CRM**) license
- A Microsoft Project Plan license
- A Resource Manager security role

Please visit the following link to check the CiA videos: `https://bit.ly/3abRHw7`

Staffing projects for success

As a resource manager or a member of the RMO, it is your priority to match the right team members to the right projects and tasks. You are responsible for forming project teams with the proper skills to meet project demands. In this section, we will learn to build a team to take us on a path to success. We will begin with generic resources.

Generic resources

To perform this function, you will generally begin with a project that has been constructed with generic resources, representing the roles needed in a project.

Our **work breakdown structure** (**WBS**) has tasks assigned to the generic resources that represent the types of roles we want on our project. These also show up in the **Teams** tab on the **Project** form in Project Operations.

For example, in our project, we are implementing Project Operations at *123 Architects*, and therefore we need to have Dynamics 365-qualified team members working on the project. In addition, we need to have an admin available to help keep some contractual obligations. The following screenshot shows what we see in the **Teams** tab of our project:

✓ Bookable Resource ↑ ∨	Role ∨	Resourcing Unit ∨	Position Name ∨	Start ∨	Finish ∨	Required Hours ∨	Hard Book... ∨	Total Effort (Ho... ∨
> Generic Resource	Project Manager	Project Ops	Project Manager 2	3/1/2021	5/21/2021	---	---	0.00
> Generic Resource	Dynamics 365 Project Manager	Project Ops	Dynamics 365 Project Manager 1	3/1/2021	5/21/2021	490.83	---	490.84
> Generic Resource	Dynamics 365 Consultant	Project Ops	Dynamics 365 Consultant 1	3/1/2021	3/19/2021	120.00	---	120.00
> Generic Resource	Admin	Project Ops	Admin 1	---	---	---	---	---
> Generic Resource	Dynamics 365 Architect	Project Ops	Dynamics 365 Architect 1	3/1/2021	3/19/2021	83.47	---	83.48

All Team Members ∨   + New   ↻ Refresh   Excel Templates ∨

Figure 7.1 – Generic resources in a project

Each of these roles will need to be supported by the scheduling requirements. As we proceed with matching team members to projects, there are other considerations to take into account.

At the highest level is the role. The role will drive the broad-brush capabilities a team member can perform. Note that a team member may be qualified to perform multiple roles in a project. For example, as a Dynamics 365 Architect, a team member may also be able to perform a Dynamics 365 Project Manager role. This may apply when you are resource-constrained in terms of a role.

Specific patterns

Time constraints are the most common constraints a resource manager will face in the scheduling of a project. It is common for a client to want a project to begin the day they sign the contract. However, unless you have team members *on the bench* (that is to say, not working on a project), then you need to find out what a reasonable starting point will be with a project. This is where we will begin: with the generation of a resource requirement for a role. The following screenshot shows the ability to specify a pattern for a role:

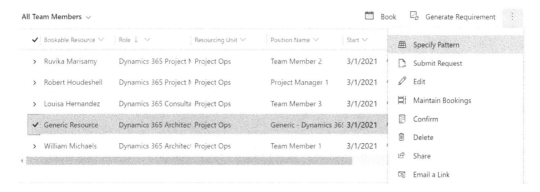

Figure 7.2 – With the role highlighted, you can specify the hours needed on a project

Since our project is beginning quickly, we need to get a team member engaged upfront to begin the work. We have inquired and found out that we have a Dynamics 365 Architect that we can have start on **Monday**, but she only has **2** hours a day available until **Thursday**, at which time she can begin working 8 hours a day. Therefore, we can get to the level of specificity shown in the following screenshot:

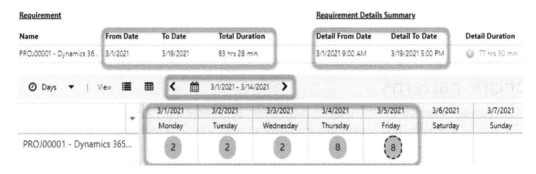

Figure 7.3 – Hours specific to a role per day

Figure 7.3 reflects the requirement shown from **3/1/2021** to **3/19/2021** of 83.5 hours. However, across this 2-week time period, we have shortened **Monday**, **Tuesday**, and **Wednesday** to **2** hours a day, thus reducing the duration of the role for this first week. However, because we are increasing our hours to 8 hours a day thereafter, we do not have quite as much of a deficit as we could have had.

Generating requirements

Now that we have specified how we can begin the project with a Dynamics 365 Architect, we will generate the requirement that can be used by the **Schedule** board to determine availability. From the same **Team** tab, with the **Generic Resource – Dynamics 365 Architect** role highlighted, click on the upper right of the pane shown in the following screenshot and select **Generate Requirement**, as highlighted:

	Bookable Resource ↑ ∨	Role ∨	Resourcing Unit ∨	Position Name ∨	Start ∨	Finish ∨	Required Hours ∨	Ha	
>	Generic Resource	Project Manager	Project Ops	Project Manager 2	3/1/2021	5/21/2021	---	---	0.00 Not Pe
>	Generic Resource	Dynamics 365 Project Manager	Project Ops	Dynamics 365 Project Manager 1	3/1/2021	5/21/2021	490.83	---	490.84 Not Pe
>	Generic Resource	Dynamics 365 Consultant	Project Ops	Dynamics 365 Consultant 1	3/1/2021	3/19/2021	120.00	---	120.00 Not Pe
>	Generic Resource	Admin	Project Ops	Admin 1	---	---	---	---	--- Not Pe
✓	Generic Resource	Dynamics 365 Architect	Project Ops	Dynamics 365 Architect 1	3/1/2021	3/19/2021	83.47	---	83.48 Not Pe

Figure 7.4 – Generating the requirement for a centralized scheduling model

Upon generating the requirement, what this is doing is creating demand on the **Schedule** board that can be met by finding a team member with the roles, skills, and other factors necessary. Upon generating the requirement, you will be able to view the open requirements in the **Schedule board**, which we will discuss later in this chapter.

To view all outstanding requirements, we should now go into the **Resources** area and select the **Requirements** menu. Find the requirement that you have generated and open it. You can now add some additional detail to the requirement in order to communicate most effectively.

Note that generating the requirement puts the requirement on the **Schedule board** as well as in the **Requirements** menu. When on the **Schedule board**, this requirement is available to book at that point. However, you may also have a request that has been generated from the requirement as well. Therefore, think about how you may work through the workflow in your company when you are both generating a requirement and submitting a request.

The following screenshot shows more specificity added to the **Skills** and **Resource Preferences** sections:

Figure 7.5 – Resource Requirement – additional details

Some of the key fields highlighted in *Figure 7.5* are outlined here:

- **Resource Type**: We have chosen **Contact** and **User**, meaning that we could use a partner resource (contact) or a user (internal team member).
- **Skills**: We have chosen to add a skill, such as certification in Dynamics 365 Solution Architecture.
- **Roles**: Defaults to the role that is associated with this requirement.

- **Resource Preferences**: We have chosen **William Michaels** as a resource as we know he could potentially work on this project, but this needs to be validated.

- **Preferred Organization Units**: Defaults to our current organizational unit but can also be set to some other organizational unit to choose from a different resource pool.

There are some additional scheduling options you can specify as well, as shown in the following screenshot:

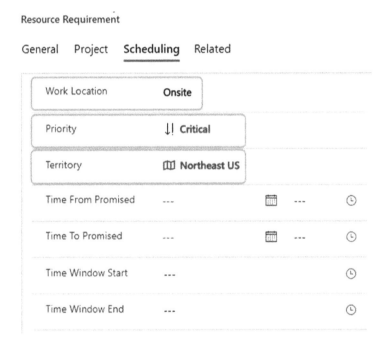

Figure 7.6 – Resource Requirement – Scheduling tab

As you can see, you can specify the work location, priority, and territory when these criteria are needed to perform the proper scheduling. When scheduling on-site work this becomes even more helpful, as you can find resources matching the territories involved.

When we add these criteria, they immediately filter into the **Schedule Assistant Filter** in the **Schedule board** to find the right resources, as shown in the following screenshot:

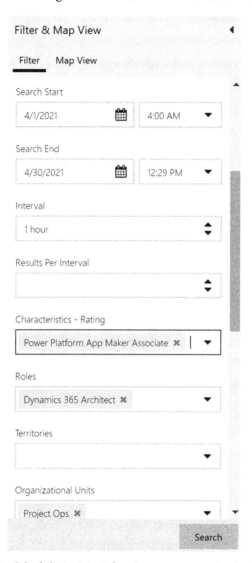

Figure 7.7 – Schedule Assistant showing your parameters in the filters

The preceding work completes the requirement for the resource and provides us with more details for the Resource Manager.

Submitting a request

Once you have your details outlined, you can submit this requirement, which means this: the requirement becomes a request that can be viewed and approved within a requests queue.

The purpose behind this in a centralized scheduling scenario is that you will utilize this to provide the resource manager with the ability to assign resources to a project. After a resource request is fulfilled, then the generic resource that was in the WBS's task is replaced with a named resource.

Therefore, there are a couple of ways in which demand (requirements) meets supply (team members). Let's take a look at the role bookings play in this situation as well.

Generating bookings

Generating bookings is an efficient way of assigning work to team members to benefit the time entry of these team members.

Bookings relate to the core assignment of a team member to a project, a task, and a timeline. Bookings have a variety of booking statuses and allocation methods that drive bookings for a team member.

Bookings are important since they are most likely going to be the basis of many management decisions. Some of the decisions may include the following:

- What is our forecasted utilization?
- Do we have enough team members to meet the demand of our clients?
- Do we have team members who are underutilized?
- What is our finance forecast based on bookings?
- What other constraints do we have in our business?
- How are our team members performing against their bookings?
- Are team members working the assigned number of hours?

There is also the potential to book directly from the **Bookings** screen. Let's take a look at it further.

Direct bookings

Bookings can be created manually by performing the booking process from the requirement. From the **Team** tab on a project, you can also directly book a team member onto a project by selecting the **Book** button, as shown in the following screenshot:

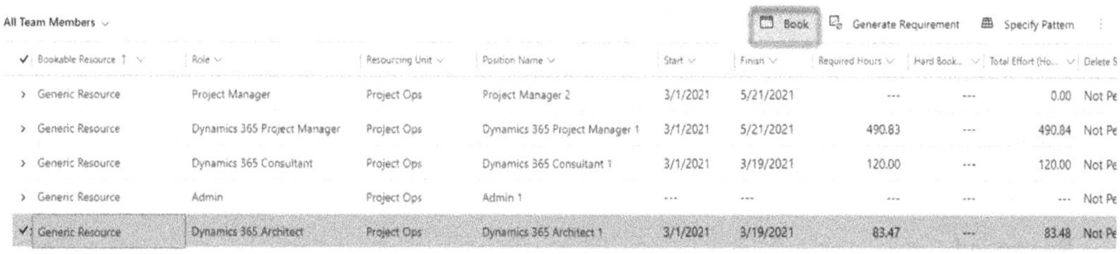

✓	Bookable Resource ↑ ∨	Role ∨	Resourcing Unit ∨	Position Name ∨	Start ∨	Finish ∨	Required Hours ∨	Hard Book... ∨	Total Effort (Ho... ∨	Delete S
>	Generic Resource	Project Manager	Project Ops	Project Manager 2	3/1/2021	5/21/2021	---	---	0.00	Not Pe
>	Generic Resource	Dynamics 365 Project Manager	Project Ops	Dynamics 365 Project Manager 1	3/1/2021	5/21/2021	490.83	---	490.84	Not Pe
>	Generic Resource	Dynamics 365 Consultant	Project Ops	Dynamics 365 Consultant 1	3/1/2021	3/19/2021	120.00	---	120.00	Not Pe
>	Generic Resource	Admin	Project Ops	Admin 1	---	---	---	---	---	Not Pe
✓	Generic Resource	Dynamics 365 Architect	Project Ops	Dynamics 365 Architect 1	3/1/2021	3/19/2021	83.47	---	83.48	Not Pe

Figure 7.8 – Direct booking for a direct scheduling model

As we perform bookings, it is important to know that there are different elements within the bookings to be fully aware of.

Booking types

Bookings are generally broken up into hard and soft bookings when companies talk about how a team member is staffed.

Many times, when a project is coming onboard, the practice manager or other leaders in the company will begin sketching out who can work on the project. Some of this may come from team member assignments within the tasks that are in the WBS. Alternatively, though, team members can be booked onto a project in what is called a **soft booking**. This generally results in a booking that a team member may even put their time against as part of their timecard entry. However, since it is a soft booking, there may still be some contractual paperwork to be fulfilled.

A **hard booking** is a booking type that factors directly into a resource's time entry as well as resource reconciliation. Only hard bookings are considered when reconciling bookings against assignments.

Note that the terminology around booking types varies from company to company. Some may call soft bookings *unconfirmed bookings*. Other terms abound. Therefore, this is a field that you can customize to your company's terminology.

There are multiple ways of looking at a booking status as well.

Booking statuses

Booking statuses can be as detailed or summarized as you need them to be. They are set up within the **Resources** area | **Settings** | **Booking Statuses**. Depending upon how you look at your implementation, some of this may be duplicative.

Out of the box, the statuses are shown here:

- **Cancelled**
- **Committed**
- **Hard**
- **Proposed**
- **Soft**

You can modify this list, and each of the statuses (regardless of what you call them) map to the standard three system statuses of **Proposed**, **Committed**, and **Cancelled**. These should be pretty self-explanatory but if you need more details, you can refer to the Microsoft online documentation.

Booking statuses should be used as a way to communicate organizationally the status of work being allocated to a project. This manifests itself in the words we use, such as *We have soft booked that project for now*, or *Rachael, we have hard booked you on this project to task # 3*.

Bookings are created on a daily basis in the system and therefore show as daily entries in the **Active Bookable Resource Bookings** view, shown in the following screenshot:

Active Bookable Resource Bookings ∨

✓	Resource ∨	Start Time ↓ ∨	End Time ∨	Duration ∨	Booking Type ∨	Booking Status ∨
	Sherry McAdams	5/21/2021 9:00 AM	5/21/2021 5:00 PM	8 hours	Hard	Canceled
	Ruvika Marisamy	5/21/2021 9:00 AM	5/21/2021 1:00 PM	4 hours	Hard	Hard
	Robert Houdeshell	5/21/2021 9:00 AM	5/21/2021 1:00 PM	4 hours	Hard	Soft
	Sherry McAdams	5/20/2021 9:00 AM	5/20/2021 5:00 PM	8 hours	Hard	Proposed
	Ruvika Marisamy	5/20/2021 9:00 AM	5/20/2021 1:00 PM	4 hours	Hard	Hard

Figure 7.9 – Booking statuses

The preceding booking statuses represent a common mix that a team may see across their work schedule. You may notice a structured duration of 4 or 8 hours, matching a full or half day of a booking. This potentially happens with the **Specify Pattern** option shown earlier in this chapter. It also happens with the allocation methods in the bookings.

Booking allocation methods

When booking resources, there are a number of factors that come into the equation. At the highest level is the work calendar of the team member. The calendar is going to determine—for example—the holiday schedule for the company, which will factor in global days off.

Secondarily, each team member has a work schedule such as **Monday** through **Friday** from **9:00 A.M.** to **5:00 P.M.**, equating to 8 hours a day, 5 days a week, for 40 total hours. One thing to note here, though, is this: set up the team member's work calendar so that it runs from 9:00 A.M. to 5:00 P.M., or 8 hours a day. If you set it up to run from 8:00 A.M. to 5:00 P.M., assuming an hour off for lunch, the system does not factor that in. The system will calculate 9 hours per day or 45 hours a week, which will throw your scheduling off.

With that as a backdrop, we now may have a team member who works 40 hours a week but is already booked on a project for 20 hours a week. When we are booking our project to this team member, how are we going to consume the remaining 20 hours a week? This is where allocation methods come into play.

There are six booking allocation methods in Project Operations. Taking the preceding paragraph's example, let's assume the team member is working 20 hours a week for the next 2 weeks. Furthermore, we have 80 hours of work to book for the next 2 weeks. We can use one of the following booking allocation methods to do this:

- **Full capacity**: This booking allocation method will book 40 hours each week, regardless of any previous bookings. What this does is book an additional 40 hours to the first and second week, resulting in total bookings of 60 hours per week for the next 2 weeks. This may not be desirable, but be aware that this is the result.

- **Remaining capacity**: This booking allocation method will be available from the **Schedule** board and will result in a neatly scheduled team member. What this does is take the 20 hours already booked and allocate 20 hours per week for the new booking for the next 2 weeks. The result is that in the third week and beyond, you still have another 40 hours to book. If the team member's schedule frees up, then the remaining capacity is used up in future weeks.

- **Percentage capacity**: This booking allocation method will allocate based upon a percentage. If, in our example, we choose **75%** allocation (or 30 hours per week), this will result in our team member having their original 20 hours per week plus the **75%** or 30 hours, meaning that they will be expected to work 50 hours for the next 2 weeks. The remaining hours in the booking will need to be consumed in the weeks subsequent to our 2-week booking.

- **Evenly distribute hours**: This booking allocation method will allocate an even amount, such as 20 hours per week, as 4 hours per day. Should this method be used, it can be powerful in fully allocating a team member's schedule, but it can also result in overbookings.

- **Front load hours**: This booking allocation method will perform all the math to front-load all the bookable hours upfront to fill all the remaining capacity. However, if the team member is already fully booked, an error message may be displayed.

- **None**: This is the default setting for the project manager role that gets assigned when a project is created. You may be that project manager and wonder: *How do I get my time booked against capacity?* You can resolve this by making modifications in the **Teams** tab on the project or by using the **Extend Booking** setting in the **Resource Reconciliation** tab.

In the preceding outlined scenarios, the **Full**, **Percentage**, and **Even Distribution** allocations can potentially overbook resources. This will be important to factor into your business processes, especially if you are tracking team member performance against their bookings.

Looking at a booking in more detail, there are a few other considerations to include. They can be viewed in the bookings themselves, through the **Scheduling** tab. In here, you will see some other information that may be helpful, such as travel and location information.

All of this factors into the **Schedule board**, as we will see next.

Maximizing the Schedule board

As we begin talking about the **Schedule** board, let's first understand what the **Schedule** board is and what it does. The **Unified Schedule Board**, as it is sometimes called, is a resource that is used extensively across both the **Field Service** and **Project Operations** solutions. The **Schedule** board has these dual functions, but for the purposes of this chapter and book, we will focus only on the scheduling of resources to projects.

To begin with, we will look at the **Schedule** board and its various elements. A key thing to know about the **Schedule** board is that it is configurable, meaning that you can make it look the way you want through the settings. It is also customizable, meaning that you can extend it through additional fields. It also has a variety of areas that we will point out in the following overview.

The following screenshot shows the **Schedule** board with the **Weekly view** default setting:

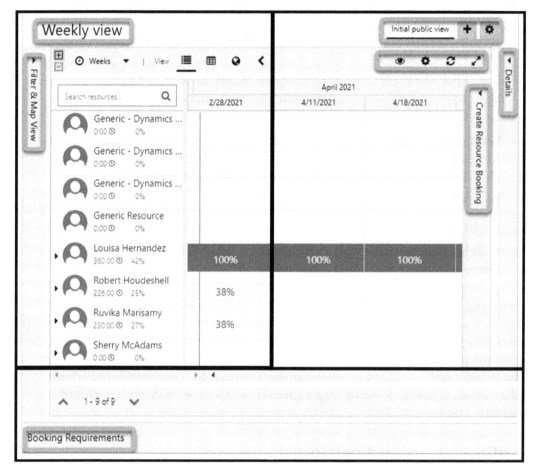

Figure 7.10 – The Schedule board

> **Note**
> The preceding screenshot has been edited to provide a clear view of the
> options.

For this section, we are going to review each of the following areas that are highlighted in the preceding screenshot, beginning in the upper-left corner and rotating clockwise:

- **Weekly view**: This is the title of the view, which changes upon altering the view from **Weeks** to **Months** or **Days**.

- **Initial public view**: This is where the system begins the view you initially see. However, with the settings and the ability to create your own views, you can capitalize on this to create a view that is unique to how you plan your projects.

- **Settings area**: This is where we set the accessibility mode and the **Settings** button, which allows you to modify what you see and how you view your own personal view. This also allows you to expand the view to fill the screen.

- **Details**: Provides you with the booking detail.

- **Create Resource Booking**: Creates a resource booking for a booking requirement.

- **Booking Requirements**: This shows all outstanding booking requirements generated through the project creation.

- **Filter & Map View**: This is where your requirement's specifics filter to the most qualified candidates.

Now, at this point, it is probably becoming very clear to you that you may need an upgrade to your monitor to be able to take all of this detail into account. The screenshots we are going to cover will represent a different monitor size from ones you will likely work with. In the case of the **Schedule** board, bigger curved monitors work well when dedicated as a secondary monitor.

Configuration and settings changes

To work through a practical example, we will first make some changes to our display. To do so, next to the **Settings** area, click on the settings gear to open the **Settings** view, shown in the following screenshot:

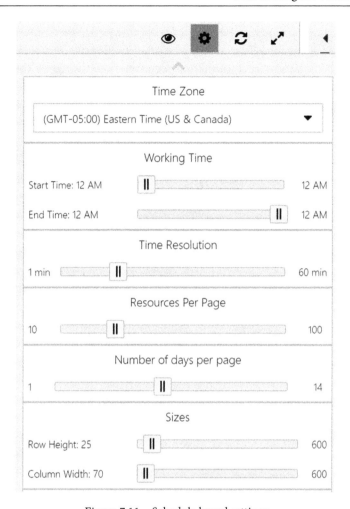

Figure 7.11 – Schedule board settings

Some common changes here include changing the **Resources Per Page** setting and the **Number of Weeks Per Page** setting. This basically defines the timeline in which you are scheduling. For more daily scenarios such as **Field Service**, this is down to the daily level (working in minutes and hours) versus project operations, where it may involve weekly or monthly scheduling, and working time is in hours and days.

A change I like to make is to the row height and column width. I generally change these to be more visible in the monitor I am using. The other fields are pretty well named, thus I will not go through explaining each of them. I recommend clicking on **Tab Settings**, to arrive at the following screen:

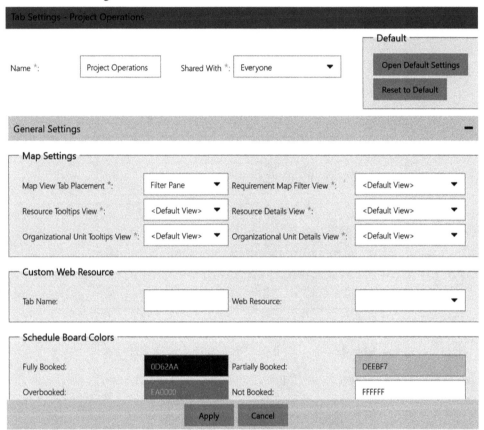

Figure 7.12 – Schedule board: Tab Settings

The **Tab Settings** functionality allows you to create your own **Schedule** board that will provide you with custom elements and configuration settings for your company. In the upper level, you can name this whatever you want it to be named. Furthermore, the **Schedule** board can be shared with everyone or be private/shared with specific people. In the **Default** area, rest assured that if you make some hideous changes, you can reset to the default setting.

Without going into every detail, suffice it to say that you can change views from their **<Default View>** setting to very specific views created in the Project Operations system. You can add your own custom web resources, as well as modify the **Schedule** board colors to be more meaningful to your company.

In the **Schedule Assistant** area, you can make modifications to the **Schedule Assistant**, which drives who can be seen in the **Schedule** board. Let's now take a look at this in practice.

Requirement for bookings

Reflecting on the generation of project requirements, we now have a number of requirements that were created from generic roles attached to the project. Furthermore, some requirements had some additional specificity relative to skills and certifications, as well as territory requirements.

From the **Schedule board** in the **Booking Requirements** section, click the expander to view the booking requirements we created. In here, we are going to select the requirement we created that resulted in a Dynamics 365 Architect being required from the Project Operations Organizational Unit that is either a user (an internal team member) or a contact (which is a partner resource). This is the scenario shown in the following screenshot:

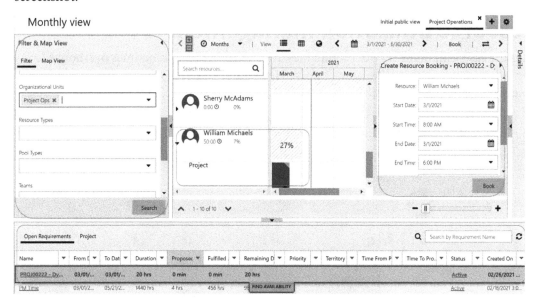

Figure 7.13 – Schedule board resource bookings (screenshot cropped to show detail)

In the preceding example, we have all of the filtering that has come from our specific requirements and that now drives the Schedule Assistant.

In the middle section, we have the timeline in which we are searching, showing that **William Michaels** is available and can be assigned to the project beginning in March and continuing through April and May.

In the right section, we see the specific booking that occurred for **William Michaels**, and will reflect this in his work schedule.

The end result of this is that we have generated project requirements that have the roles, the duration, and additional requirements, and all information needed has been submitted to a centralized resource management function.

Upon generation, these requirements—along with all other requirements—can be reviewed and matched with team members (either internal or partner team members) who meet the needs of the project.

Upon completion, William now has work booked throughout May for this project.

We will now take a look at how to manage resource usage.

Resource utilization management

As is the case with many services companies, team members are sometimes overbooked. The following screenshot shows how **Louisa Hernandez** has been overbooked for the first 3 weeks of the month of March:

Figure 7.14 – Schedule board showing an overbooking for Louisa

There are options here that resource managers know they can take advantage of, including moving the work to **Ruvika Marisamy**, who has some availability during the required timeframe. Furthermore, this work can be pushed out to the month of May to enable **Louisa Hernandez** to be the assigned team member, as shown in the following screenshot (with the Schedule board, this is a drag and drop of the booking to the new date):

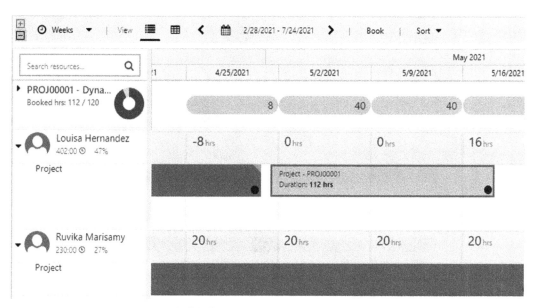

Figure 7.15 – Schedule board showing the booking reassigned for May

From a 30,000-foot view, a resource manager can see the overall usage of their resources, open requirements, and team availability in one screen—the same screen we have been working in. The **Schedule** board is a powerful tool to use to do this, as can be seen in the following screenshot:

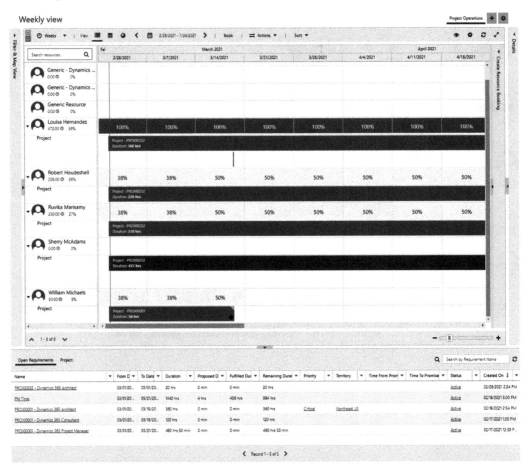

Figure 7.16 – Schedule board 30,000-foot view

Resource management, through all its various approaches, is a vital part of a service company's functions. A resource manager is responsible for making sure the right team members are staffed to projects they will succeed in. Furthermore, the productivity and optimization of a team will enhance a company's bottom line.

Summary

In this chapter, we built upon the preceding knowledge of finding the right team members to staff our projects. This is important since this will drive the success of projects, productivity of the team, and profitability of the company.

When staffing projects, we learned how important roles are to the overall staffing model. We built upon that by identifying specific patterns of scheduling and adding specifics to each requirement. The value of this is to improve communication for the people responsible for scheduling.

We then were able to generate requirements and submit requests to be processed through the **Schedule** board. This provides a company with the management tools to keep team members assigned to the right tasks.

Building upon the concepts of booking types, statuses, and allocation methods, we reviewed how to maximize the **Schedule** board and improve the overall productivity of a company.

As we enter into *Chapter 8*, *Managing a Project to Success*, we will see how we can utilize out-of-the-box project management functionality, combined with Microsoft Teams collaboration and delivery of time-entry functions in Microsoft Outlook.

Questions

1. A generic resource is a role that provides which function in the Project Operations system?

2. Generic resources are utilized in the WBS or _____ _____ _____ to define the required hours per team member type.

3. What is the function that allows you to outline the specific hours per week or day a team member role is needed?

4. True or False: Generating requirements shows the requirement on the **Schedule** board.

5. What is the purpose of resource requests?

6. True or False: **Resource Requirement**—additional details do not filter through to the resource requirement.

7. True or False: From the **Team** tab on a project, using the **Book** button you can book a resource directly.

8. Hard and soft bookings drive which function within the resourcing of team members?

9. Which three allocation methods may result in overbookings?

10. Where can a resource manager view a 30,000-foot view of resource utilization?

Section 3: Project Delivery through Operations

Now that we have the project staffed, we will identify how to deliver and bill the project based upon the requirements of your customers. In this chapter, you will gain practical knowledge of project timeline management, pricing management, resource assignments, and modifications, and it will enable you to manage project changes confidently. Toward the final chapters, you will learn to use Project Operations effectively for project accounting and finance.

In this section, there are the following chapters:

- *Chapter 8, Managing the Project to Success*
- *Chapter 9, Team Member Activities*
- *Chapter 10, Approvals and Exceptions*
- *Chapter 11, Project Accounting and Operations*

8
Managing the Project to Success!

In this chapter, we will review how to best manage the timelines and activities within a project. We will review cost and selling price implications and why you may make changes to a project. We will further set up collaboration capabilities that will help in the overall usage of the system. The value of collaboration is in project execution, which means meeting project goals while managing a project smoothly.

Therefore, in this chapter, you will learn about the following concepts:

- Managing the project timeline and activities
- Substituting resources
- Changing project contracts, costs, and selling prices
- Managing risks, status reports, and change orders
- Collaborating through Microsoft Teams and Outlook
- Time entry considerations

By the end of this chapter, you will be able to manage a project, team members, and all other aspects of a project to a successful conclusion. It is unrealistic to think that a project will always go as planned. In fact, I do not know of any past projects I've been involved in that ever have.

Therefore, we must be prepared for the technical, people, budgetary, and time challenges that will arise.

Technical requirements

To perform the tasks in this chapter, you will need the following:

- An Microsoft 365 account and an **Azure Active Directory** (**Azure AD**) login
- A Microsoft Dynamics 365 Project Operations license
- A Microsoft Project Plan license
- A project manager security role

Please visit the following link to check the CiA videos:

```
https://bit.ly/3abRHw7
```

Managing the project timeline and activities

As a project manager, you may have been involved in some of the previous steps of setting up a project for your company. You may have been involved in the process of setting up a project's **work breakdown structure** (**WBS**). You may have contributed to or set up generic resources and roles that apply to a project. We are now at a point where we need to review a project's completion in detail before we begin having team members book time to it.

This includes completing the project's **Summary** tab and **Tasks** section. The **Summary** tab is going to have key information that will drive downstream processes. The **Tasks** section provides **Task**, **Timeline**, and **Grid** views to support your project timeline and planning needs. Therefore, let's take a look at a project's **Summary** tab.

Project Summary tab

A project's **Summary** tab shows you an overall project at a glance and gives you the highest level of information about the project. The following screenshot provides an example of what the **Summary** tab looks like:

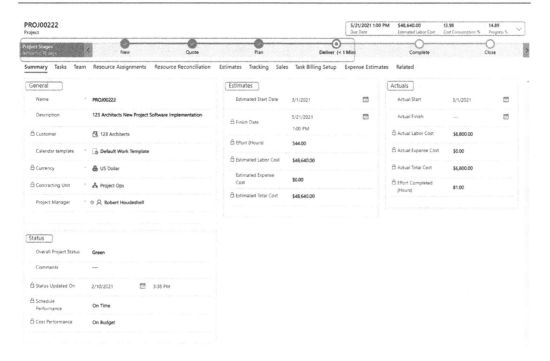

Figure 8.1 – The project Summary tab

Let's look at the highlighted areas in *Figure 8.1*, as follows:

- In the upper left and progressing across the screen to the right is the business process flow shown in the preceding screenshot as **Project Stages**. This business process flow provides a system-configurable set of stages and checklists that can guide a project professional through a project. This is important since it will provide a consistent and uniform approach to working through a project successfully. Within this section, you can include requirements for team members to review the statement of work, along with any specific project details, policies, and other required steps for the project.

- In the upper right, we have a snapshot of the project deadline or due date, the estimated labor costs, the cost consumption percentage, and the progress as a percentage of the project.

- In the **General** section, we have the project's name, description, and other valuable fields. The project name—or, potentially, the project number—are going to be really important if you are integrating to an external accounting system and using this field as a key field. In the example screenshot in *Figure 8.1*, the **Name** field is shown as PROJ00222, which is more like a project number. In an external accounting scenario, the project **Name** field may be the primary key for the integration. Although with Project Operations you can change this field out of the box, in an integrated environment this would be undesirable. Therefore, consider that if you are using this as a key field, you may need to add some logic behind the handling of this field and set it to **Read-Only**.

  The **Customer** field is also something unique to an integrated environment. This field will require a valid customer that is in the Dynamics 365 **Customer Engagement** (**CE**) database that integrates with the accounting system. This customer record must be set up in the accounting system as a customer with credit terms and valid contracts on file, and with all the company's processes and policies followed.

- Also notable in this section is the **Calendar template**, which is important for scheduling. **Currency** is important for transactions that result from the work performed, while the **Contracting Unit** is critical for the costing of the project.

> **Reminder**
> The **Contracting Unit** must have a cost price list or you will not get the costing information you need. Lastly, a project manager will be responsible for owning the project and approving transactions.

- The **Estimates** section presents a calculated summary of the effort in hours, labor costs, expense estimates, and estimated total cost, as well as estimated start and end dates.

- The **Actuals** section presents the actual start date (input by the project manager) and the actual labor, expense, and total costs and hours, as well as actual start and end dates.

- The **Status** section provides you with the overall status of a project. This section is designed to have a user-entered **Overall Project Status** field and comments, combined with system-generated status information. The **Status Updated On** field tracks when a project manager has last updated the status. Additionally, you can add additional fields using the **Customization** functionality in the **Advanced Settings** area.

The **Timeline** and **Tasks** are a major part of the project management world. They are the heart and soul of project management and are handled with Project Operations the web capabilities of Microsoft 365.

Tasks tab

For a project manager, the **Tasks** tab is the heart and soul of a project. The **Tasks** tab in Project Operations is built upon Microsoft Project for the web. This means that you will be consuming a Microsoft Project license and will also have access to Project for the Web and Project Online (the SharePoint Project Web App). The following screenshot shows the work breakdown structure of the project we have created:

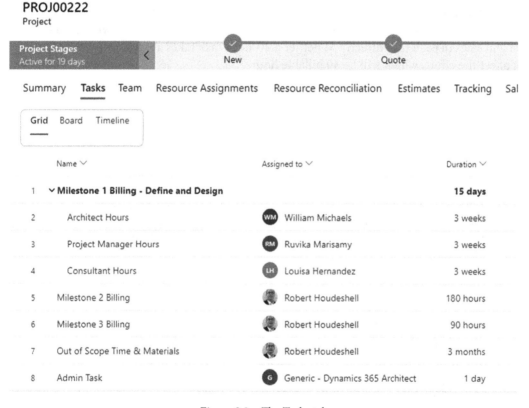

Figure 8.2 – The Tasks tab

The task structure we create contains the same data that will be used for all elements of the project task structure.

Grid view

The **Tasks** tab defaults to the **Grid** view of the tasks outlined in the project. *Figure 8.2* has can be configured to show the fields you want to see for this project, such as **% complete**, **Effort completed**, **Effort remaining**, **Estimate at completion**, and others.

The example we have built out lends itself to more of a waterfall look of a project. This means that, as we see in *Figure 8.2*, the **Architect**, **Project Manager**, and **Consultant** hours are indented as child tasks to **Milestone 1 Billing – Define and Design**.

The assignments in *Figure 8.2* are specific to people. However, when we began building this project out, this is where they were assigned to generic resources.

Duration and **Effort** are two interdependent—but independent—fields. **Duration** is the amount of elapsed time that will occur between a task's start and end dates. The **Effort** field is quite important as this is the number of hours for each task, which will impact the cost and sales of each task directly. Whether a 40-hour task takes a week or 3 weeks does not affect the effort, which will be 40 billable hours.

The **Effort completed** and **Remaining hours** fields will show the amount of time entered and remaining for these tasks. The effort estimated at completion is a calculated field showing how much your effort (or billable hours) will be at completion. Finally, we have our start and end dates.

Note

When changing the start or end date, you are going to affect the duration of the project. This will affect the effort of the project as the system tries to reflect the change in the timeline. Thus, remember this so that your budgets are unaffected.

Board view

The **Board** view provides you with a Kanban view of the project where you can manage a Scrum board of tasks. Although you use a different view you are using the same data, which is highly beneficial to the overall integrity of a project.

The following **Board** view shows how you can use the **Bucket** feature to plan and manage in an agile methodology:

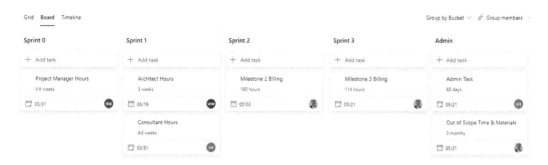

Figure 8.3 – The Board view

In the preceding view, we can take our project management hours and place them in **Sprint 0** while assigning our other tasks to **Sprint 1**, **Sprint 2**, and **Sprint 3**. We further have the **Admin** bucket that is set up for **Admin Task** and an **Out of Scope Time & Materials** task.

A more traditional bucket view may be a simple **To Do**, **In Progress**, and **Completed** task or any number of other bucketed views. The power of it is that this is totally up to you how you use this **Board** view and how you track and measure your projects.

Timeline view

The **Timeline** view allows us to view a robust timeline control that includes drag and drop dependency creation, very much like you have used in Microsoft Project. The following **Timeline** view shows how we can manage tasks across an interrelated timeline:

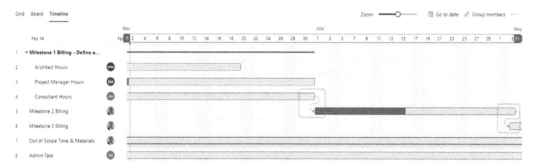

Figure 8.4 – The Timeline view

The highlighted connectors in the preceding screenshot are dependencies between tasks that allow you to connect one task to another, creating predecessor relationships. You can also slide a task to shorten or lengthen its duration, with the same caveats noted previously about changes to the effort or budget.

While working with the project timeline, you may find yourself switching between these views many times. This is expected, and since you are using the same data it is beneficial to be able to work with team members in an Agile methodology while presenting the project plan to the client as more of a timeline, with the timeline showing completion of tasks.

Now that you have control of your project and its tasks, boards, and timeline, we will next take a look at the resource side of a project.

Substituting resources

Some projects will have a static team that will deliver a project from start to finish. Other projects—and maybe a majority in your project world—will have changes throughout the project. Some of these changes will be due to the skills and talent needed to fulfill the project's requirements. Others will be potentially due to changes in the workforce, or people leaving the company or the project.

The **Team** tab is how we add team members to a project. This can be seen in the following screenshot:

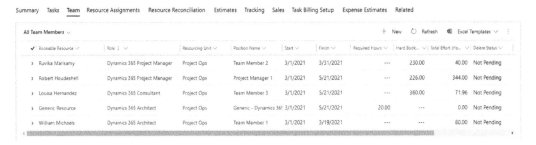

Figure 8.5 – The Team tab

The **Team** tab shows not only the team members on the project but also their roles, resourcing units, required hours, hard booked hours, and total effort. To add team members to a project, select the **+ New** button and add a new position to the project.

After being added to the project team, you will want to go back to the **Tasks** tab, in **Grid** view, and add the team member as a resource to the task. (An important note to keep in mind is that adding a new resource to a task may also split the hours across additional team members.) To manage a task detail, you can use the vertical ellipsis and select **Open details** to open the task details, as shown in the following screenshot:

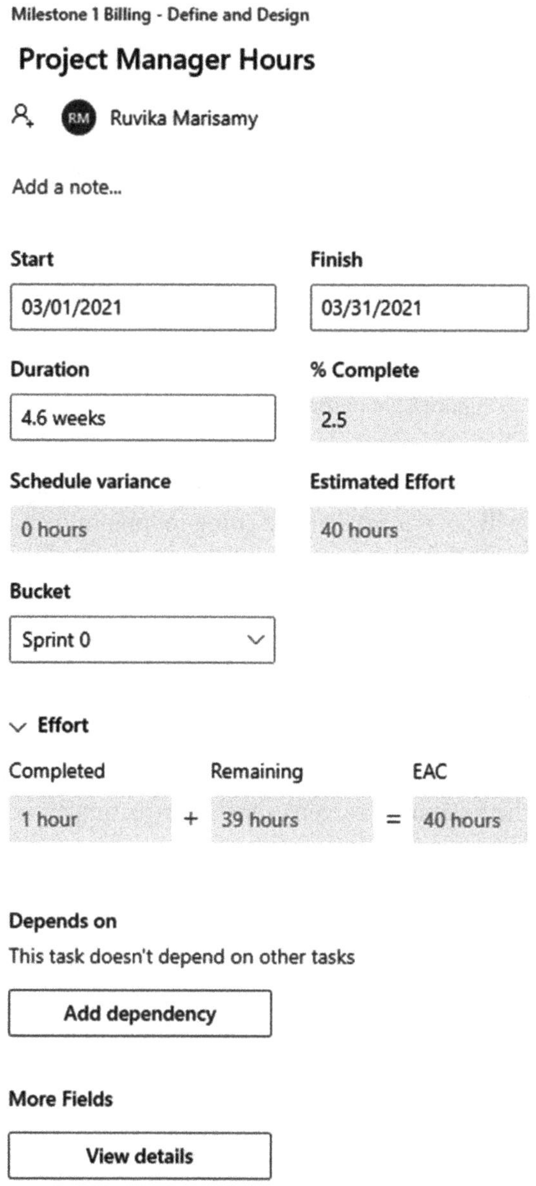

Figure 8.6 – Task details

Project managers over time have learned to rely on a numerical view of their resource assignments, and Project Operations supports this as well with the **Resource Assignments** tab. The following screenshot shows the resource assignments grouped by **Resource**. Alternatively, you can group by **Role**:

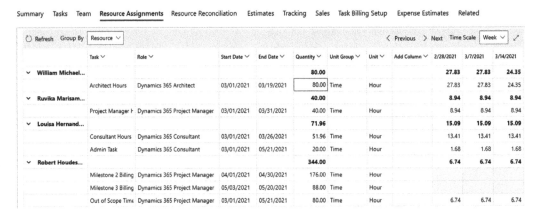

Figure 8.7 – Resource Assignments tab

Some changes will also come to pass due to costing considerations. Consider that some work can potentially be performed offshore and accomplished through a different costing structure This is what we will cover next. We are going to look into change orders, costing, and selling, and how to change some key elements of a project in flight. Resource assignments can be viewed in daily, weekly, monthly, or yearly allocations.

Changing orders to costs and selling price

Making changes to the costing of a project is a process of changing out the resources you have currently staffed with offshore resources from a different organizational unit. The following screenshot (of the **Estimates** screen) shows the costing associated with the project as we have it outlined currently:

Summary Tasks Team Resource Assignments Resource Reconciliation **Estimates** Tracking Sales Task Billing Setup Expense Estimates Related

	Task ∨	Start Date ∨	End Date ∨	Quantity ∨	Total Cost Price ∨	Add Column ∨	2/28/2021	3/7/2021	3/14/2021	3/21/2021	3/28/2021	4/4/2021	4/11/2021
∨ William Michael...				80.00	$9,200.00		$3,200.00	$3,200.00	$2,800.00				
	Architect Hours	03/01/2021	03/19/2021	80.00	$9,200.00		$3,200.00	$3,200.00	$2,800.00				
∨ Ruvika Marisam...				40.00	$3,400.00		$759.78	$759.78	$759.78	$759.78	$360.89		
	Project Manager H	03/01/2021	03/31/2021	40.00	$3,400.00		$759.78	$759.78	$759.78	$759.78	$360.89		
∨ Louisa Hernand...				71.96	$5,397.00		$1,131.90	$1,131.90	$1,131.90	$1,006.20	$126.32	$126.32	$126.32
	Consultant Hours	03/01/2021	03/26/2021	51.96	$3,897.00		$1,005.59	$1,005.59	$1,005.59	$879.89			
	Admin Task	03/01/2021	05/21/2021	20.00	$1,500.00		$126.32	$126.32	$126.32	$126.32	$126.32	$126.32	$126.32
∨ Robert Houdes...				344.00	$29,240.00		$572.63	$572.63	$572.63	$572.63	$1,932.63	$3,972.63	$3,972.63
	Milestone 2 Billing	04/01/2021	04/30/2021	176.00	$14,960.00						$1,360.00	$3,400.00	$3,400.00
	Milestone 3 Billing	05/03/2021	05/20/2021	88.00	$7,480.00								
	Out of Scope Time	03/01/2021	05/21/2021	80.00	$6,800.00		$572.63	$572.63	$572.63	$572.63	$572.63	$572.63	$572.63

Figure 8.8 – Estimates

When adding a team member from a different resourcing unit, remember that you need to set up a cost price list to the role and the organizational unit. Without this, your costs will be missing from the estimates and this will affect your billings.

The following screenshot shows how we can add a new team member to a project. This is performed by opening the **Team** tab and selecting **+ New Team Member**:

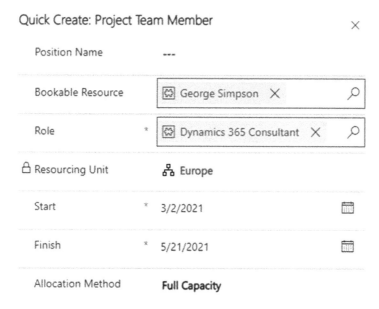

Figure 8.9 – Adding an offshore team member

As a project manager, you may also need to validate that billing is set up properly in a project. To view this information, you can use the **Task Billing Setup** tab. The following screenshot shows a specific task called **Out of Scope Time & Materials** that, when managing a project, may cause a project manager to question whether this is set up correctly:

Figure 8.10 – Task Billing Setup tab

By clicking the right chevron > and looking into the details, we can see for sure that the task is set up as **Time and Material**.

Additional expenses on a project can be estimated with the **Expense Estimates** tab, as follows:

Figure 8.11 – Expense Estimates tab

Figure 8.11 shows how you would set up **5** days of expenses to deploy a project at a client site. The expenses set up here show which task these expenses are billed to, and then the quantity and unit prices associated with each line item. This can get as detailed or as be as summarized as a project manager requires.

As a project continues, we will now manage our risks, produce status reporting, and change orders.

Managing risks, status reports, and change orders

Managing risks, change orders, and status reporting is one of the key elements of a project manager's job. Depending upon the project management methodology employed, there are things that may be beneficial to use to manage a project internally as well as communicate the project status externally.

One of the key areas a project manager will focus on is the resourcing area. This is natural, as labor costs are the primary costs that will affect a project. The **Resource Reconciliation** screen will provide a project manager with not only what the resources bookings are short of or in excess of but will also give them the ability to extend bookings. The following screenshot shows the **Resource Reconciliation** screen, and what we see here are the hours that have been assigned and booked for each of our resources:

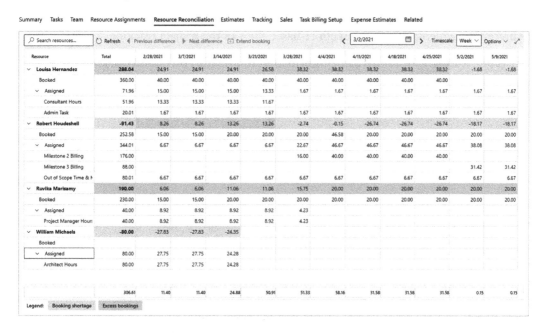

Figure 8.12 – Resource Reconciliation screen

On a larger project, we may see this screen full of resources, so you have the ability to search within this screen as well. You can further change the timescale and the weeks within which you are working.

Furthermore, project managers will also want to see, at a summary level, how a project is progressing task by task. To see this information, a project manager can utilize the **Tracking** tab, as illustrated in the following screenshot:

Refresh Tracking Effort

	Name	Effort	Effort remaining	% complete	Effort completed	Effort Estimate At Complete	Schedule Variance
	PROJ00222	535.96	454.96	15.11 %	81.00	535.96	0.00
1	Milestone 1 Billing - Define and Design	171.96	170.96	0.58 %	1.00	171.96	0.00
2	Architect Hours	80.00	80.00	0.00 %	0.00	80.00	0.00
3	Project Manager Hours	40.00	39.00	2.50 %	1.00	40.00	0.00
4	Consultant Hours	51.96	51.96	0.00 %	0.00	51.96	0.00
5	Milestone 2 Billing	176.00	96.00	45.45 %	80.00	176.00	0.00
6	Milestone 3 Billing	88.00	88.00	0.00 %	0.00	88.00	0.00
7	Out of Scope Time & Materials	80.00	80.00	0.00 %	0.00	80.00	0.00
8	Admin Task	20.00	20.00	0.00 %	0.00	20.00	0.00

Figure 8.13 – Tracking tab: Effort view

The preceding screenshot shows an effort-based view of the project tracking.

There is also a **Cost** view of this same information to provide cost-based tracking, as shown in the following screenshot:

Refresh Tracking Cost Use Cost Rate

	Name	Planned Cost	Remaining Cost	Cost Estimate At Complete	Actual Cost	Cost Consumption %	Cost Variance
	PROJ00222	$47,237.00	$40,437.00	$47,237.00	$6,800.00	14.40 %	$0.00
1	Milestone 1 Billing - Define and Design	$16,497.00	$16,497.00	$16,497.00	$0.00	0.00 %	$0.00
2	Architect Hours	$9,200.00	$9,200.00	$9,200.00	$0.00	0.00 %	$0.00
3	Project Manager Hours	$3,400.00	$3,400.00	$3,400.00	$0.00	0.00 %	$0.00
4	Consultant Hours	$3,897.00	$3,897.00	$3,897.00	$0.00	0.00 %	$0.00
5	Milestone 2 Billing	$14,960.00	$8,160.00	$14,960.00	$6,800.00	45.45 %	$0.00
6	Milestone 3 Billing	$7,480.00	$7,480.00	$7,480.00	$0.00	0.00 %	$0.00
7	Out of Scope Time & Materials	$6,800.00	$6,800.00	$6,800.00	$0.00	0.00 %	$0.00
8	Admin Task	$1,500.00	$1,500.00	$1,500.00	$0.00	0.00 %	$0.00

Figure 8.14 – Tracking tab: Cost view

Some projects and the management of these projects will require more of a cost-based view. This is particularly important within governmental contracts where cost is a key determinant in the project billings.

There is no doubt that a business delivering projects will have changes to the projects they have. Therefore, we need to identify how to manage *change orders* effectively. Some businesses will call these change requests or call them by another name. For our purposes, we will call them change orders. We will now cover change orders and how to most effectively manage them.

Change orders

Managing change orders is a critical factor in the project management process. Each **project management office** (**PMO**) will have its own preferences as to how to best manage these change orders.

Some approaches to change orders involve having all processes handled outside the system. A change order is created by the project manager and is then presented to the client. This is the paperwork that generates the authorization to change the budget. Once the change order is complete (signed by the client), the result is generally a new task that adds to the budget of the project.

Additional approaches have also involved the creation of a change order entity (currently not in Project Operations). With a change order entity, you can build a business process flow around it, as well as include a timeline to track all notes, documents, and supporting material for the change order.

Whichever approach you choose or even if you do something totally different, the recommendation is this: work within your PMO to understand what your contractual requirements are that need to be met for your clients.

There is a lot of compliance and governance that can be set up within Project Operations. However, there is also a lot of collaboration that can be set up in Microsoft Teams and Outlook.

Collaborating through Microsoft Teams and Outlook

Microsoft Teams is undoubtedly one of the most powerful tools to come out of Microsoft. Teams gives us the ability to talk to our colleagues on a regular basis and communicate effectively across multiple teams and multiple channels. We can run meetings and save documents in Teams, giving us unlimited capabilities to manage a project across a whole organization. Therefore, it is worthwhile outlining how we can best integrate our project into Microsoft Teams so as to keep our users from context switching throughout their day. **Context switching** refers to the process of a user needing to sign in to a specific application to perform a function on such a periodic basis that it is disruptive and detracts from productivity during the working day.

Utilizing Microsoft Teams to perform some functions such as project overview and time entry keeps context switching to a minimum. This results in less multitasking, resulting in your team members being able to log in to one application and perform the majority of their workday tasks.

The following screenshot shows how you can set up a project team for **PROJ00222** and integrate the project within this team:

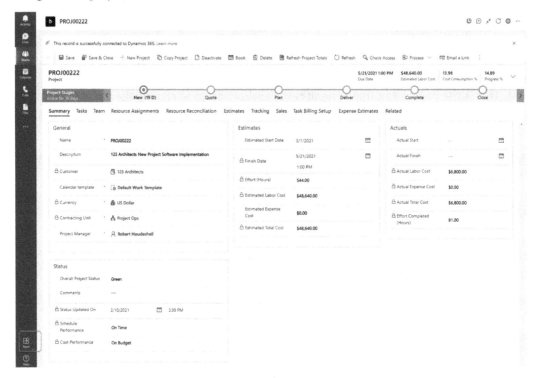

Figure 8.15 – Project Operations integrated with Microsoft Teams

This allows you to keep all pertinent communications, files, and information relating to the project team.

To set this up, let's follow these steps:

1. In *Figure 8.15*, you will notice that we have the ability to add apps, as shown in the lower left of the screen. To launch this process, click on the **Apps** icon and look for **Dynamics 365**, shown as follows:

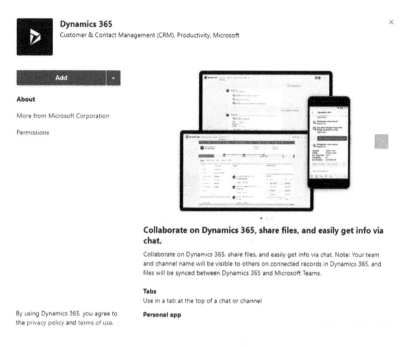

Figure 8.16 – The Dynamics 365 customer relationship management (CRM) app for Teams

2. Next, choose the Dynamics 365 environment (**org**) and the Dynamics 365 app (**Project Operations**), as illustrated in the following screenshot:

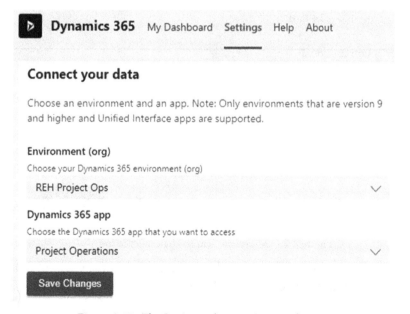

Figure 8.17 –The Settings tab: organization chooser

3. Create a team for the project, as follows:

Figure 8.18 –Microsoft Teams: Team creation screen

4. Next, from the team created in the preceding step, create a channel for the **Projects** team, as illustrated in the following screenshot:

Create a channel for "Projects" team

Channel name

123 Architects - PROJ00222

Description (optional)

Help others find the right channel by providing a description

Privacy

Standard - Accessible to everyone on the team

☑ Automatically show this channel in everyone's channel list

Cancel   Add

Figure 8.19 –Microsoft Teams: channel creation

5. We are almost there! From the channel you created, select the **General** channel and click + to add a tab for the channel for Dynamics 365. Some example app tabs are shown in the following screenshot:

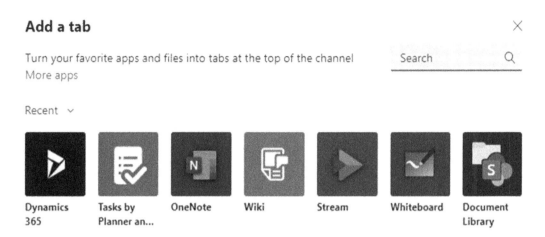

Figure 8.20 – Microsoft Teams: Dynamics 365 tab selection

6.   Select the entity you wish to add, as shown in the following screenshot:

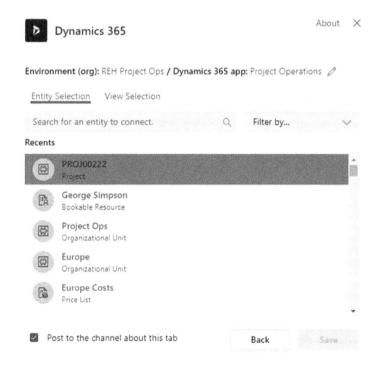

Figure 8.21 – Selection of the entity you wish to present in Microsoft Teams

This will provide you with a Microsoft Teams channel that is specifically dialed into your project. Building this out, you can fully involve all team members into the project life cycle.

Arguably, the more you make the system work for you, your company, and your teams, the less you will have to mitigate risks and handle unnecessary complications.

One of the areas to be mindful of is time entry. Where you have maybe 5 to 10 project managers, you may have 200 to 300 team members all using time entry. So, let's take a look at some considerations relating to this.

Time entry considerations

In this chapter, among the topics most important in a project manager's world and in managing a project to success, we cannot ignore the importance of time entry. As we all understand, labor is the biggest part of our project costs.

Therefore, one of the key considerations we need to make is what kind of timeframe we capture time in. Do we work on a Sunday-through-Saturday week or according to some other calendar? These are all pertinent details inside of the project setup that will drive the success of the time entry.

It is further important to realize that the time entries that are put into Project Operations appear to be entered on a weekly basis, but the result of the time entries will be daily records representing the hours entered in the **Weekly** view. This is important as you follow the downstream effects of time entry.

When it comes to getting time into the system, it is important to capture project costs quickly and efficiently. However, how do we do this in the context of a very large and diverse audience? One of the ways is to set up a variety of channels.

As we will see in *Chapter 9*, *Team Member Activities*, team members will have a traditional web-based **user interface** (**UI**) to input their time. What we can cover here in the project manager world is more about the impact of providing additional time entry channels.

Using the same steps as we followed for setting up a Teams channel, we can also set up a **Time Entry** Teams channel that can make time entry more *upfront* for a Teams user.

The following screenshot shows how we can use the same approach we used for the project to add **Time Entry** into Teams as well, thus keeping a well-unified environment:

Figure 8.22 – Teams apps: adding Time Entry channel

Another way to get team members to input their time is to make it happen within the confines of Microsoft Outlook. Very similar to inputting through Teams, the Outlook approach is designed to provide a team member with the easiest way to get time into the system.

To accomplish this, the first thing that you need to do is configure the Outlook app for your team members. This is performed in the following steps:

1. In **Settings | Email Configuration**, select the mailboxes to set up.

2. Select **Test & Enable Mailbox** and **Activate**.

3. Next, select **Settings | Dynamics 365 App for Outlook**.

4. Add the app for all eligible users.

5. Click **Save**.

This adds the **Microsoft Dynamics 365 App for Outlook** package for the users processed previously. This means that in Outlook, the team member will have a Dynamics 365 icon in the ribbon bar for their instance of Dynamics 365. In the following screenshot, you can see a team member's ability to enter their time spent on this meeting with **123 Architects** directly into **Time Entry** without logging in to Project Operations:

Figure 8.23 – Dynamics 365 App for Outlook

This app is exactly like all the other apps in Dynamics 365—it can be configured in the **App Designer**, as shown here:

Figure 8.24 – Configuring Dynamics 365 App for Outlook

To enable the **Time Entry** entity for **Dynamics 365 App for Outlook**, you will want to add that entity to the sitemap, save, and publish.

This is really powerful as you can configure this app to show precisely what you want to show to the user community! For example, you can create custom entities that are exposed through **Dynamics 365 App for Outlook**. This reduces context switching or multitasking so that team members can stay in one app to do all their work. Further, the training involved to enable use of the Outlook app takes less time than training a team member how to log in to a specific app in a browser. You are in the driver's seat!

Summary

In this chapter, we gained an understanding of how to manage our projects. We began with the work breakdown structure and the tasks that are created. As we reviewed the various views of the tasks, we discussed how this helps a project manager work through tasks such as a budgetary item; a Kanban board as an agile type of management approach; and a **Timeline** view where you can generate dependencies and move the timeline. All of this supports the modern project manager's need to deliver projects successfully.

We then reviewed the resourcing, costs, and selling aspects of the project and the tabs that drive these factors. We learned how to add and remove team members from a project and how to set up offshore resources with different cost rates, organizational units, and currencies. This allows us to make real-time personnel adjustments, resulting in better costing and profitability of our projects.

While learning how to manage risks, change orders, and status reports, we also learned how to review and leverage each team member's bookings and time allocated to a project. This provides us with the ability to manage the uncertainties of a project in real time.

Finally, we set up collaboration capabilities for our team members so that they can use Microsoft Teams or Outlook as their main gateway into Project Operations.

As we enter into *Chapter 9, Team Member Activities*, we will leverage the setup performed in this chapter to efficiently perform team member activities.

Questions

1. What function does the business process flow provide in the context of a project?
2. In an integrated environment with an accounting system, what kind of importance does a **Project** field become to the integration of a project?
3. True or false: The **Customer** field is important for integration with accounting.
4. What are the three views available in the **Tasks** tab?
5. Which **Task** view is suitable for an agile environment?
6. Which tab is used to substitute resources?
7. Where can I view the cost of the resources on my project?
8. True or false: Change order management functionality comes out of the box with Project Operations.
9. True or false: Microsoft Teams has an app to show Dynamics 365 CE entities, meaning you can use Teams to deliver Project Operations functionality.
10. Which app allows you to input time through Microsoft Outlook?

9
Team Member Activities

In the previous chapter, we learned about the project processes that need to be performed to keep a project on time and within budget through the use of built-in tools and technologies. The Project Operations solution provides a sophisticated solution that also includes time and expense entry. The previous chapter covered time and expense entry from a setup perspective.

This chapter will identify the user processes that team members will need to do to input information into the Project Operations system. These input points will be most important as they will drive the project cost, selling, and profitability. As a team member, you are part of the largest pool of users the Project Operations system will have. As such, it is critical that we meet the requirements of the team members well.

For the purposes of this chapter, we will work with the Dynamics 365 **Customer Engagement** (**CE**) Project Operations app rather than the Microsoft Dynamics 365 for **Finance and Operations** app.

In this chapter, you will learn about the following concepts:

- Entering time
- Using Teams and Outlook time entry
- Entering expenses
- Submitting and recalling time and expenses

By the end of this chapter, you will be able to process time and expenses in the Project Operations system effectively. You will be able to enter time and expenses into the system through the browser, Microsoft Teams, or the Microsoft Outlook app. This chapter should give you the knowledge you need to produce your time and expenses records as well as recall them.

Technical requirements

To perform the tasks in this chapter, you will need the following:

- An Microsoft 365 account and Azure **Active Directory** (**AD**) login
- A Microsoft Dynamics 365 Project Operations (C) license
- A Microsoft Project Plan license
- The Team Member security role

Please visit the following link to check the CiA videos:

```
https://bit.ly/3abRHw7
```

Entering time

As a team member, entering time is something that you may typically do weekly. This process is carried out across millions of team members all doing the same thing: accounting for the time spent working in the last week. For some team members, this may be performed using a spreadsheet. For others, this involves using a browser-based system or a mobile app.

For Project Operations, time can be entered daily or weekly and submitted line by line to give the most flexibility to the system. As you are entering your time weekly, there are options that are going to help everyone's job down the line.

Requirements of time entry

For a team member to enter time, they must be set up as a resource in Project Operations. This is more than just setting up a resource, as there are costing implications related to the roles these team members are set up with.

Therefore, ensure that your team members (resources) are most minimally set up with their resource record and an associated role for the proper organizational unit in order for time to be costed and sold properly. While you are setting up team members, you should also give consideration to setting up their skills and certifications as well, since this will benefit the resource management function.

To enable a team member to enter time against a project, they will need to be added to the team of the project through the **Teams** tab, as outlined in *Chapter 7, Resource Manager – Staffing for Success!.*

To enable a team member to enter time against a task, they will need to be assigned to that task through the **Tasks** tab in the **Grid** view.

As with a good time entry system, there are a variety of ways in which you can input information into Project Operations. We will cover each of these entry methods in the subsequent sections.

Time entry – line entry mode

The **line entry mode** of time entry is probably the most common user interface most team members are familiar with. It involves a team member logging into Project Operations and inputting a project and a task, which will result in a weekly view of time to enter, as we see in *Figure 9.1.* There are other modes that will automate time entry, which we will cover in the *Time entry – import* section:

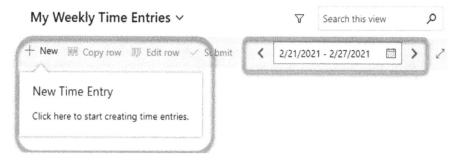

Figure 9.1 – The time entry screen

There are two major elements to this screen, the **+ New** section and the week selector highlighted in the upper right. The week selector function allows you to browse through week by week where you will enter time. The **+ New** section will open a right rail entry screen as shown in *Figure 9.2*. This process begins the time entry line item for the day you choose. Once a single row is enabled, you are able to tab through the additional days and enter your time for each of the days:

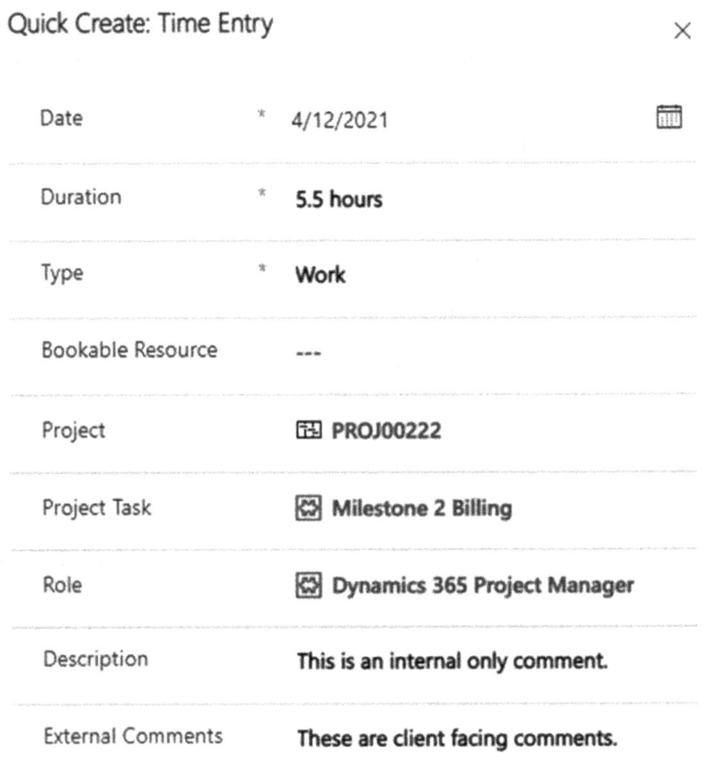

Quick Create: Time Entry   ✕

Date	* 4/12/2021	📅
Duration	* **5.5 hours**	
Type	* **Work**	
Bookable Resource	---	
Project	🔳 **PROJ00222**	
Project Task	🔲 **Milestone 2 Billing**	
Role	🔲 **Dynamics 365 Project Manager**	
Description	**This is an internal only comment.**	
External Comments	**These are client facing comments.**	

Figure 9.2 – Quick Create: Time Entry

The **Quick Create** form shown in *Figure 9.2* is a completely customizable form that starts the line item entry. It is a form in which you can configure or customize to meet your company's needs. Furthermore, you can create a plugin to perform specific validations on these fields.

The fields in *Figure 9.2* are relatively self-explanatory, but there are some notations to make. The first notation is the **Bookable Resource** field. When left blank, this results in a time entry for only yourself. When the field is enabled and visible, you may enter a different bookable resource, that is, a team member is chosen, then you have the ability to perform time entry for another team member. This is delegation of time entry, also called **delegated time entry**, which you can perform with this customization. A recommendation for this is to wrap security around this form, where only project managers or line managers can see this field.

The **Description** and **External Comments** fields are very important fields needed for the billing processes. The description field is typically renamed **Internal Comments** or something like that. The **External Comments** field is typically renamed **Billing Notes** or **Invoice Comments** since these comments flow through the invoicing.

Once completed, what you have accomplished is the creation of a time entry line that is tied to a project, task, role, duration of time, and internal and external notes. Now that you have a line item, let's explore the buttons that drive the rest of the timecard functionality. This is really cool because you can use these functions to minimize your time entry effort and save time overall for the firm.

Time entry control buttons

Going from the **+ New** button clockwise, there are a number of other beneficial buttons to know about, which can be seen in the following figure. We will look at how to use these buttons shortly:

Figure 9.3 – Time entry – key buttons

The checkbox to the left of the highlighted row is important. This selects the row that is highlighted so that you can perform functions upon that row. For example, you can see how these buttons automate the data entry:

- **Copy row**: Allows you to copy the highlighted row and create a new row
- **Edit row**: Allows you to change the project, task, or role for the highlighted row
- **Submit**: Submits this row (as highlighted) or all highlighted rows for approval by the project manager of the project
- **Recall**: If submitted in error, you can recall your time entry

- **Delete**: Self-explanatory
- **Refresh**: Refreshes the grid
- **Copy week**: Copies a previous week's entries, thus reducing the time it takes to enter a timecard
- **Import**: Imports and automates the entry of time based upon a few factors that we will explain in the following subsections

Time entry – import resource assignments

When working on a project, you will be assigned tasks to perform. In order to quickly import these assignments by date and time, you can use the **Import Resource Assignments** process from the **Import** button, which is located to the right of the **Copy week** button. This automates the previous steps of having to perform the right-railed **Quick Create** by automatically populating your timecard for you.

Navigate from **Import** to choose **Resource Assignments** and the following screen will appear:

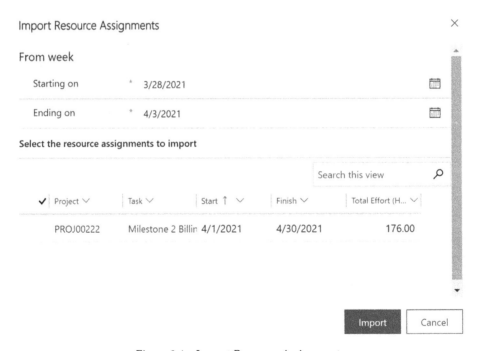

Figure 9.4 – Import Resource Assignments

Once we perform this function, we can see a list of entries. We can keep or remove the entries we want before the system enters them. The system is presenting a list of potential entries shown in *Figure 9.5* in which you can select the entries you wish to delete from your time entry:

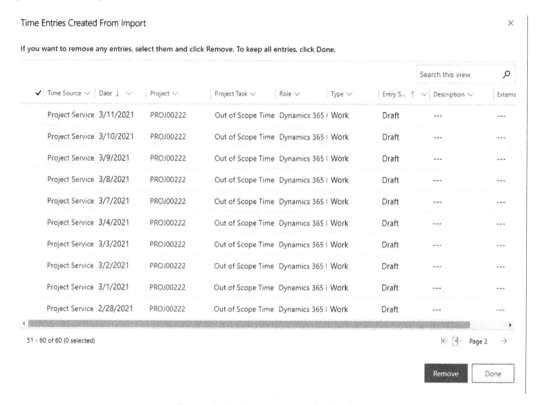

Figure 9.5 – Import – record selection

Click **Remove** to remove any entries or accept the entries presented and select **Done** to finish the process. This process will bring in the expected work schedule based on the allocation method used. Therefore, sometimes the work comes in as odd hour amounts. This can be updated in the time entry screen.

Time entry – import resource bookings

For team members who have bookings for their projects, the **Import Resource Bookings** functionality will import this time for them. *Figure 9.6* shows the list of bookings for a team member entering time, wherein they can select which lines they wish to import:

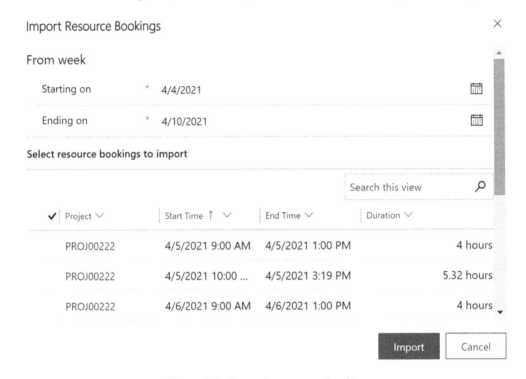

Figure 9.6 – Importing resource bookings

Similar to *Figure 9.5*, you can select the records you wish to remove from the import.

The result for both of these import processes from resource assignments or from resource bookings is bringing in time that has been assigned to you by other people (project or resource managers). However, you can input data from your Outlook calendar directly through the use of **Import Exchange Appointments**, which will bring in your Outlook/Exchange calendar meetings.

Time entry – Import Exchange Appointments

We have the ability in **Project Operations** to import from Exchange and bring in calendar items as time entries. How this works is that you select **Import | Exchange appointments**. Let's have a look at how to do it in a detailed manner:

1. Import the time:

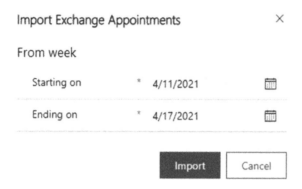

Figure 9.7 – Import Exchange Appointments

2. The filtering process is similar to *Figure 9.5,* but notably different in this respect. A team member's calendar may have appointments on it that are not necessarily project-related, such as the highlighted row in *Figure 9.8*. This process allows you to remove these non-project-related entries before they are imported:

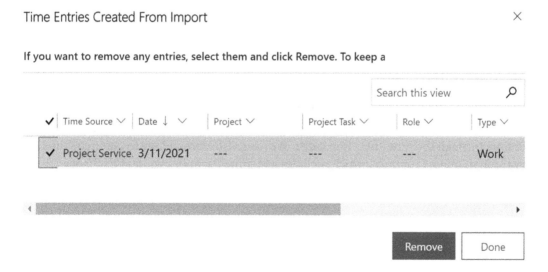

Figure 9.8 – Import – record selection

3. While reviewing your time, notice that **Project**, **Task**, and **Role** are blank and therefore will need to be filled in. A completed example showing how this translates to a timesheet is shown in *Figure 9.9*:

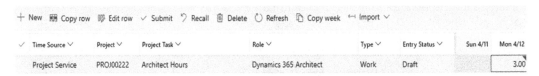

Figure 9.9 – Time entry from an import of Exchange calendar items

4. If you edit the entry for Monday, you will see that the description from the calendar item is imported into the **Description** (remember the internal comments) field as shown in *Figure 9.10*:

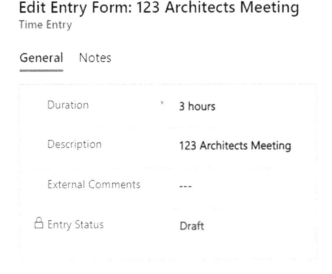

Figure 9.10 – General information imported from the calendar

We know through the preceding examples that there is a simple line-entry way to enter time through the time entry line items. We have also learned how to automate time entry through import routines, which includes assignments, bookings, and Exchange calendar items.

Team members who do not wish to input their time into the Project Operations screens through a browser as we have shown thus far can also input their time using the Dynamics 365 app for Outlook. We will discuss this in detail in the following section.

Using Teams and Outlook time entry

There is more than one way to accomplish time entry for team members who may not be generally inclined to log in to a browser and navigate through Project Operations. Here are a couple of options you can explore.

Time entry – Outlook

To input time from your **Outlook** calendar will require the administrator to set up the Dynamics 365 app for Outlook as outlined in *Chapter 8*, *Managing the Project to Success*. From the Outlook calendar item, you need to select the **Dynamics 365** app add-on as shown in *Figure 9.11*:

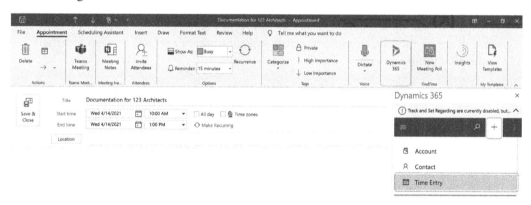

Figure 9.11 – Using the Dynamics 365 app for Outlook

Once you select **Time Entry**, enter your time into the **Quick Entry** screen for just this one-time transaction.

Furthermore, some team members may work from Microsoft Teams primarily and wish to have their time entry performed through this common interface.

Time entry – Teams

Utilizing the same Dynamics 365 app that we set up in *Chapter 8*, *Managing the Project to Success*, we have the ability to set up a new Teams site and channel. This can be used by team members who are part of this team to enter their time in more of a grid fashion, as shown in *Figure 9.12*:

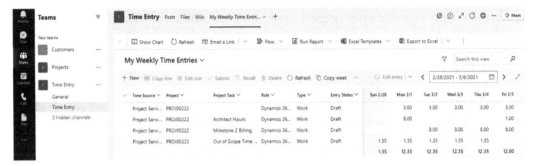

Figure 9.12 – Using Microsoft Teams to enter time

Since we are now looking at the same familiar time entry screen on *Figure 9.11*, we will not go into detail on this. The same time entry and submission processes covered earlier apply to the rest of the process.

It is important to recognize that this is yet another way in which a team member can enter their time, thus giving the most flexibility to team members working on projects.

In this section, we have covered a lot of different ways in which you can enter time as team members. This is important because not every team member works the same. This flexibility gives you the tools you need to do your job exceptionally well. When you do that, it adds to the value of the project and you deliver the most value to the company. In the next section, we will discuss how to enter expenses.

Entering expenses

Project Operations provides for a Dynamics CE entry point of expenses into the system. This expense entry is generally very similar to the time entry functionality. It begins with navigating to the **Expenses** menu and selecting **+ New**. The **Quick Create** form for expenses is structured very much like the time entry form and may also be configured or customized.

The out-of-the-box expense entry for our PROJ00222 for an airfare is shown in *Figure 9.13*:

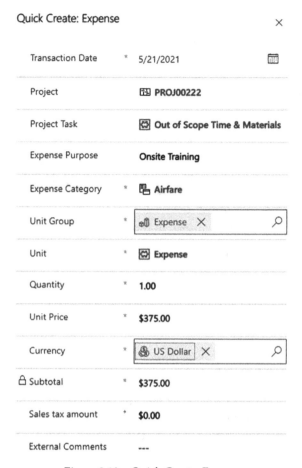

Figure 9.13 – Quick Create: Expense

The result of the expense entry is very much the same as for the time entry. The expenses are entered into a grid view as shown in *Figure 9.14*:

Transacti... ↓ ∨	Expense Purpose ∨	Quantity ∨	Unit ∨	Subtotal ∨	Unit Price ∨	Project ∨	Project Task ∨	Expense Ca...
5/21/2021	Onsite Training	1.00	Expe...	$1,375.00	$1,375.00	PROJ00222	Out of Sco...	Airfare

Figure 9.14 – Expense entry – grid view

Expenses are sometimes entered through other apps that are commercially available and utilized throughout the industry. Some examples are **Concur**, **Gorilla**, and **Expensify**. When these applications are being used, the primary concern becomes how to integrate the resulting approved expenses into Project Operations.

This will depend upon how detailed you wish to track your expenses. One thing to consider is whether you are concerned mostly with the expenses hitting the project ledger or seeing all the details? If you want to see all the details, you may end up mirroring a lot of the out-of-the-box functionality to get this result. If it is just the expense amounts, then a more summarized approach will be advised.

In order for Project Operations time and expense to be billed to the client, they must first be approved. We will discuss this next.

Submitting and recalling time and expenses

Submitting time and expenses is almost identical in terms of process. It begins with a completed time or expense entry, as shown in the following figure:

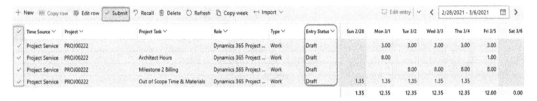

Figure 9.15 – Submitting time for approval

Two significant elements to submitting time are the record selector on the left side of each row (highlighted in *Figure 9.15*) and the **Submit** button (also highlighted). With the record selected, you can submit one of, a variety of, or all of the records on the page. When you do, **Entry Status** will change to **Submitted**.

After this point, the project manager will be responsible for approvals and further processing. You now know how to submit the time and expenses for approval as well.

If, at some point, you wish to recall your timecard (meaning that you made a mistake that you wish to correct after submission), this is performed with a similar process to what you used to submit a time entry. Select the record you wish to recall and select the recall button to the right of the submit button.

As we finish our submission of time, we hand our time entries to project management and approvers for further processing. Therefore, it is always important to ensure that you have quality in mind when producing your time entries.

Summary

In this chapter, you have learned how to enter time through a variety of methods, including native time entry in Project Operations and time entry through the automated importing of information from assignments, bookings, and calendar entries. You also learned why this is useful, in that it provides team members with the ability to make their time entry process match their work style.

You also saw how you do not necessarily need to enter into Project Operations to enter time. You also learned how to enter time through the Dynamics 365 app for Outlook, which allows you to enter time from your calendar directly into your timesheet.

Furthermore, you performed the same kind of functionality through Microsoft Teams. Both approaches give you further avenues to enter time and expenses.

The final thing you learned about in this chapter was submitting time to the project manager. You now can enter time and expenses through Project Operations as well as Outlook and Teams, and then submit time and expenses to your project managers.

All of this will provide quality data that will result in better financial performance for your business, resulting in benefits for each of the team contributors.

As we enter into *Chapter 10*, *Approvals and Exceptions*, we will follow through with the project manager approval processes and exception handling.

Questions

1. True or false: Time entry in Project Operations is a weekly process.
2. What are the requirements to set up a team member for time entry?
3. Which field in the **Quick Create: Time Entry** form is the client-facing field?
4. To repeat the same entries from a previous week into this timesheet, what function is used?
5. Which import function will result in importing a team member's calendar information?
6. True or false: When importing time, the system always gives you a validation screen.

7. What is the app that is used to input time through Outlook?

8. True or false: While it would be nice, you cannot enter time through Microsoft Teams.

9. True or false: Only Project Operations expenses can be used to determine expense costs.

10. When submitting time or expenses, what needs to be done?

10
Approvals and Exceptions

Building on top of the previous activities, we know that it is necessary to process approvals as well as perform exception handling within Project Operations.

In order to meet the needs of exceptions, this chapter is going to identify several ways in which approvals and actuals are processed.

In this chapter, you will learn about the following concepts:

- Understanding the approvals and actuals process
- Recalling time and expense
- Using time corrections and exception handling

By the end of this chapter, you will be able to approve and handle exceptions in the time and expenses entered into Project Operations. The benefit of this is the increased capability of team members, project managers, and administrators to manage complex project exceptions while maintaining integrity in the data.

Technical requirements

To perform the tasks in this chapter, you will need the following:

- An Office 365 account and **Azure Active Directory** (**Azure AD**) login

- A Microsoft Dynamics 365 Project Operations **Customer Relationship Management** (**CRM**) license

- A Microsoft Project Plan license

- A project manager security role

Please visit the following link to check the CiA videos: `https://bit.ly/3abRHw7`

Understanding the approvals and actuals process

The time- or expense-approval process begins with submitted entries, as outlined in *Chapter 9, Team Member Activities*. The approval process is generally performed by the project manager of a project. However, for the purposes of the Project Operations app, it should be noted that whoever the project manager is designated as on the **Summary** tab of a project is the person who will be responsible for approvals.

Approvals are important since they are the validation of quality data going into the Project Operations system. With this quality step, a project manager is able to validate the project and task information as well as the quality of customer-facing information. This results in better accounting and billing data.

The approval process is important for the validation of the quality of data, which becomes the quality of financial transactions. The quality of this data will literally result in either better cash flow—due to no errors in invoicing—or bad data and reduced money coming into the business. We will elaborate more on this in the next section.

The approval process

Knowing about the approval process is important, and we should also talk about who a project's approvers are. A project approver is, most generally, the project manager of a project. However, in some instances, there may be a separate project approver from a project manager, for the following reason. There may be times when a project manager is validating the hours being charged to a project while a separate project approver does a final **Quality Assurance** (**QA**) pass on the time entered, as well as billing notes. To view the project transactions to approve, we use the **Approvals** menu. Note that the **Approvals** menu view selector can be changed to include other types of approvals beyond time approvals.

From the **Project Operations | Projects** area, choose the **Approvals** menu. When you do, you will be presented with the **Time Entries for Approval** screen, shown as follows:

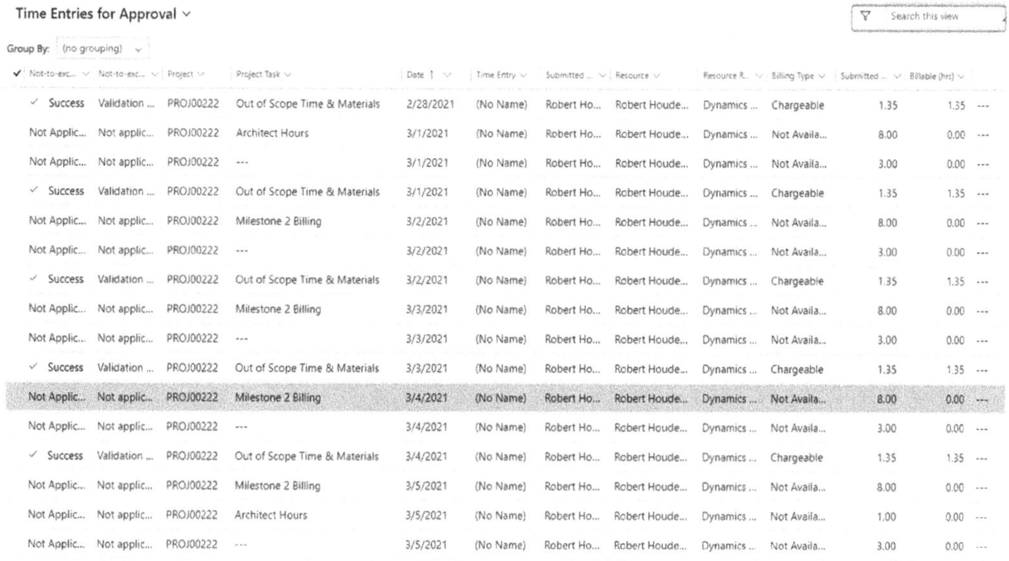
Time Entries for Approval ⌄

Search this view

Group By: (no grouping)

Not-to-exc...	Not-to-exc...	Project	Project Task	Date ↑	Time Entry	Submitted ...	Resource	Resource R...	Billing Type	Submitted ...	Billable (hrs)	
✓ Success	Validation ...	PROJ00222	Out of Scope Time & Materials	2/28/2021	(No Name)	Robert Ho...	Robert Houde...	Dynamics ...	Chargeable	1.35	1.35	---
Not Applic...	Not applic...	PROJ00222	Architect Hours	3/1/2021	(No Name)	Robert Ho...	Robert Houde...	Dynamics ...	Not Availa...	8.00	0.00	---
Not Applic...	Not applic...	PROJ00222	---	3/1/2021	(No Name)	Robert Ho...	Robert Houde...	Dynamics ...	Not Availa...	3.00	0.00	---
✓ Success	Validation ...	PROJ00222	Out of Scope Time & Materials	3/1/2021	(No Name)	Robert Ho...	Robert Houde...	Dynamics ...	Chargeable	1.35	1.35	---
Not Applic...	Not applic...	PROJ00222	Milestone 2 Billing	3/2/2021	(No Name)	Robert Ho...	Robert Houde...	Dynamics ...	Not Availa...	8.00	0.00	---
Not Applic...	Not applic...	PROJ00222	---	3/2/2021	(No Name)	Robert Ho...	Robert Houde...	Dynamics ...	Not Availa...	3.00	0.00	---
✓ Success	Validation ...	PROJ00222	Out of Scope Time & Materials	3/2/2021	(No Name)	Robert Ho...	Robert Houde...	Dynamics ...	Chargeable	1.35	1.35	---
Not Applic...	Not applic...	PROJ00222	Milestone 2 Billing	3/3/2021	(No Name)	Robert Ho...	Robert Houde...	Dynamics ...	Not Availa...	8.00	0.00	---
Not Applic...	Not applic...	PROJ00222	---	3/3/2021	(No Name)	Robert Ho...	Robert Houde...	Dynamics ...	Not Availa...	3.00	0.00	---
✓ Success	Validation ...	PROJ00222	Out of Scope Time & Materials	3/3/2021	(No Name)	Robert Ho...	Robert Houde...	Dynamics ...	Chargeable	1.35	1.35	---
Not Applic...	Not applic...	PROJ00222	Milestone 2 Billing	3/4/2021	(No Name)	Robert Ho...	Robert Houde...	Dynamics ...	Not Availa...	8.00	0.00	---
Not Applic...	Not applic...	PROJ00222	---	3/4/2021	(No Name)	Robert Ho...	Robert Houde...	Dynamics ...	Not Availa...	3.00	0.00	---
✓ Success	Validation ...	PROJ00222	Out of Scope Time & Materials	3/4/2021	(No Name)	Robert Ho...	Robert Houde...	Dynamics ...	Chargeable	1.35	1.35	---
Not Applic...	Not applic...	PROJ00222	Milestone 2 Billing	3/5/2021	(No Name)	Robert Ho...	Robert Houde...	Dynamics ...	Not Availa...	8.00	0.00	---
Not Applic...	Not applic...	PROJ00222	Architect Hours	3/5/2021	(No Name)	Robert Ho...	Robert Houde...	Dynamics ...	Not Availa...	1.00	0.00	---
Not Applic...	Not applic...	PROJ00222	---	3/5/2021	(No Name)	Robert Ho...	Robert Houde...	Dynamics ...	Not Availa...	3.00	0.00	---

Figure 10.1 – Time Entries for Approval screen

This can be overwhelming when first looking at it. However, using the **Search this view** function, you can limit the records you see to something more manageable. With each entry, you can open the entry and view whether or not a team member has put in proper notes in the **External Comments** field.

Some project managers will add this field to the approval screen to validate and ensure that the billing notes are included. To approve a transaction or a group of transactions, a project manager will typically group together projects and then tasks—maybe even down to the team-member level—and validate that the time entries are correct.

The following screenshot shows time entries filtered to only show transactions I want to select and approve:

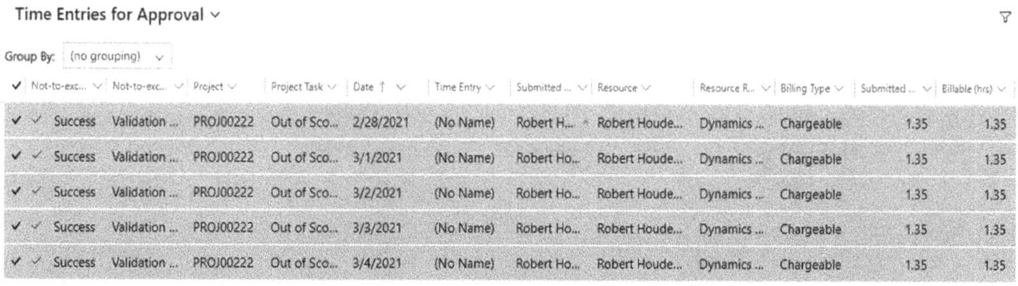
Time Entries for Approval ⌄

Group By: (no grouping)

✓	Not-to-exc...	Not-to-exc...	Project	Project Task	Date ↑	Time Entry	Submitted ...	Resource	Resource R...	Billing Type	Submitted ...	Billable (hrs)
✓	✓ Success	Validation ...	PROJ00222	Out of Sco...	2/28/2021	(No Name)	Robert H...	Robert Houde...	Dynamics ...	Chargeable	1.35	1.35
✓	✓ Success	Validation ...	PROJ00222	Out of Sco...	3/1/2021	(No Name)	Robert Ho...	Robert Houde...	Dynamics ...	Chargeable	1.35	1.35
✓	✓ Success	Validation ...	PROJ00222	Out of Sco...	3/2/2021	(No Name)	Robert Ho...	Robert Houde...	Dynamics ...	Chargeable	1.35	1.35
✓	✓ Success	Validation ...	PROJ00222	Out of Sco...	3/3/2021	(No Name)	Robert Ho...	Robert Houde...	Dynamics ...	Chargeable	1.35	1.35
✓	✓ Success	Validation ...	PROJ00222	Out of Sco...	3/4/2021	(No Name)	Robert Ho...	Robert Houde...	Dynamics ...	Chargeable	1.35	1.35

Figure 10.2 – Time entries grouped for ease of validation and selected for approval

Clicking **Approve**, as highlighted in *Figure 10.3*, generates the approval of these transactions and results in *actuals* in the system. However, some transactions may not meet the criteria for approval. For example, the following highlighted transactions are missing a task and will need to be rejected:

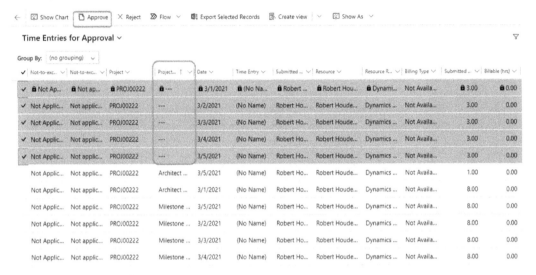

Figure 10.3 – Time entries grouped showing missing project task

Upon clicking **Reject**, you will want to send a reasonable explanation for the rejection back to the team member, as shown here:

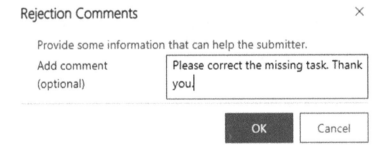

Figure 10.4 – Rejection feedback loop

The team member will then see that they have two lines in their timecard where one has been marked **Returned** and the other **Approved**, as shown here:

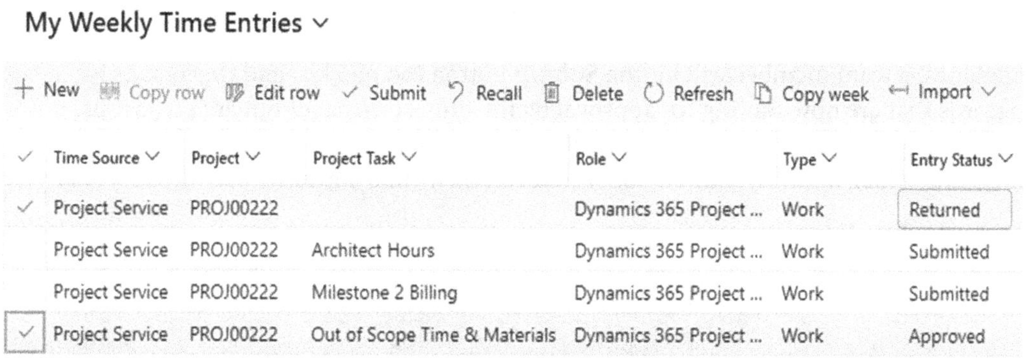

My Weekly Time Entries ⌄

+ New   ▦ Copy row   ▧ Edit row   ✓ Submit   ⤺ Recall   🗑 Delete   ◯ Refresh   🗋 Copy week   ⤺ Import ⌄

	Time Source ⌄	Project ⌄	Project Task ⌄	Role ⌄	Type ⌄	Entry Status ⌄
✓	Project Service	PROJ00222		Dynamics 365 Project ...	Work	Returned
	Project Service	PROJ00222	Architect Hours	Dynamics 365 Project ...	Work	Submitted
	Project Service	PROJ00222	Milestone 2 Billing	Dynamics 365 Project ...	Work	Submitted
✓	Project Service	PROJ00222	Out of Scope Time & Materials	Dynamics 365 Project ...	Work	Approved

Figure 10.5 – The team member's view of their timecard

At this point in the process, we anticipate the team member will correct the necessary time information and will submit as appropriate, and then work through the process with their project manager.

Some companies automate the notification of timecard rejection by sending an email notifying the team member of the rejection. I advise caution in doing this or performing this within the context of regular work hours.

For example, there is nothing more demotivating for a team member than to receive a timecard rejection message on a Friday night when getting ready to go out with family or to some other function. The importance of timecard approvals and processing for a project business is that the time entered turns into money in the billing system. When one timecard is missing or time is rejected and not reprocessed, this results in missed money coming into the billing cycle.

Some team members have stated something such as *"But we will bill that time out sometime later—why the rush?"* The answer is that it is all about the cash flow for the business. If you are not able to bill out USD $50,000 this week due to late timecards, that is $50,000 that will not come into the business for yet another week or more. That cash flow can be used for paying payroll, funding capital expenditures for items such as laptops, or securing other opportunities.

Furthermore, when you miss entering time, you are also likely to forget to bill every hour you worked. This is called **revenue leakage**, which is a clever way to say you are missing hours, resulting in missing dollars.

However, there are times when team members themselves need to recall their time entries.

Recalling time and expense

Sometimes, a team member will hit the **Submit** button too quickly, and this results in timecards that are now waiting for approval by the project manager but are erroneous. For this, Project Operations provides the **Recall** function, as shown in the following screenshot, which allows a team member to recall their time entries:

My Weekly Time Entries ∨

+ New   ⊞ Copy row   ⊞ Edit row   ✓ Submit   ↺ Recall   🗑 Delete   ⟳ Refresh   ⧉ Copy week   ⟵ Import ∨

	Time Source ∨	Project ∨	Project Task ∨	Role ∨	Type ∨	Entry Status ∨
	Project Service	PROJ00222		Dynamics 365 Project ...	Work	Returned
	Project Service	PROJ00222	Architect Hours	Dynamics 365 Project ...	Work	Submitted
✓	Project Service	PROJ00222	Milestone 2 Billing	Dynamics 365 Project ...	Work	Submitted
	Project Service	PROJ00222	Out of Scope Time & Materials	Dynamics 365 Project ...	Work	Approved

Figure 10.6 – A team member recalling their timecard

Upon doing so, the time entry goes into draft mode and can therefore be modified. The result is a clean record that can be resubmitted for approval.

The system will also allow you to recall an already approved time entry, but it will enforce some business rules and compliance around it. The first thing it does is present you with a dialog box to input a **Reason for Recall**, as illustrated in the following screenshot:

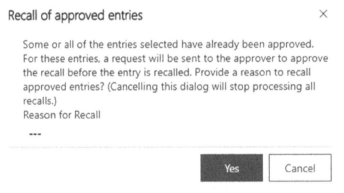

Recall of approved entries   ✕

Some or all of the entries selected have already been approved. For these entries, a request will be sent to the approver to approve the recall before the entry is recalled. Provide a reason to recall approved entries? (Cancelling this dialog will stop processing all recalls.)
Reason for Recall

Yes   Cancel

Figure 10.7 – The reason for recalling an approved entry

This could be any valid reason. One may be that between the time you realized you made a mistake and the time you went back to correct it, your project manager may have already approved the time. This happens. So, then, the project manager has an approval view called **Recall Requests for Approval** that will process these requests.

However, time or expense entries sometimes need to be corrected after they have been approved and processed through. For this, there are time correction capabilities.

Using time corrections and exception handling

Things happen and changes sometimes need to be made to timecards even after they have been approved. This is common and Project Operations has facilities to help you with this.

To correct a time, a project manager or other qualified individual will navigate to the **Project Operations | Sales** area and select **Approved Time**. We will dig deeper into the time-correcting process in the next section.

Time corrections

The process of making time corrections is generally conducted by a project manager or billing administrator who is qualified to handle the transactions that result from this process. The following screenshot shows a couple of transactions we know need to be corrected:

Figure 10.8 – Time correction

When we do this, we are going to be presented with a journal that will produce the time corrections for us. The journal has a **General** tab, as with many other functionalities.

The **Time Entry Corrections** tab is where the complexity of this process resides, as illustrated in the following screenshot:

Figure 10.9 – Time Entry Corrections details

Moving hours from one project to another or one task to another is a very common need in a project business. In our scenario, we are moving hours from the **Milestone 2 Billing** project task to the **Architect Hours** project task. Clicking **Save** and then the **Preview** button will generate the proper accounting entries for the reversal, as illustrated in the following screenshot:

General   Time Entry Corrections   Journal Lines   Related

○ Refresh   Run Report ∨   Excel Templates ∨   ⋮

✓ Description ∨	Transac... ∨	T... ∨	Doc... ↑ ∨	Start Date/Time ∨	End Date/T... ∨	Project Co... ∨	Project ↑ ∨	Task ∨	Transaction... ∨	Role ∨	Bookable R... ∨	Quantity ∨	Unit ∨
...	Cost	Time	2/8/2021	2/8/2021 12:0...	2/8/2021 ...	123 Architects.	PROJ00222	Milestone 2 Billing	...	Dynamics 365	Robert Houdes	-8.0000	Hour
...	Cost	Time	2/8/2021	2/8/2021 12:0...	2/8/2021 ...	123 Architects.	PROJ00222	Architect Hours	...	Dynamics 365	Robert Houdes	8.0000	Hour
...	Cost	Time	2/9/2021	2/9/2021 12:0...	2/9/2021 ...	123 Architects.	PROJ00222	Milestone 2 Billing	...	Dynamics 365	Robert Houdes	-8.0000	Hour
...	Cost	Time	2/9/2021	2/9/2021 12:0...	2/9/2021 ...	123 Architects.	PROJ00222	Architect Hours	...	Dynamics 365	Robert Houdes	8.0000	Hour

Figure 10.10 – Time correction reversing entries

Notice in the preceding screenshot that there are two cost entries coming out of the **Milestone 2 Billing** task and two cost entries entering the **Architect Hours** task.

This completes the transfer of costs from one task to another. However, what about sales transactions? Since this is a fixed-price contract line and task, this is only a cost-impacting transaction. Therefore, no selling transactions needed to be generated.

However, should this have been a time and material contract line type, the transactions in *Figure 10.10* would have been multiplied to include the sales side of the journal. Clicking **Confirm** from the menu will process the journal to completion. There are other exceptions that the system can handle as well.

Exception handling

In Project Operations, you can have a regular journal entry that you can add and remove transactions from. You can also have a time correction journal and an expense journal, as shown in the following screenshot:

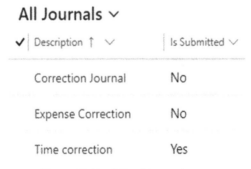

All Journals ∨	
✓ Description ↑ ∨	Is Submitted ∨
Correction Journal	No
Expense Correction	No
Time correction	Yes

Figure 10.11 – Mixed journal types

Notice that the **Time correction** journal is submitted and processed, while the other journals are not. They can be filled in to completion as well, following the same process as for the time entry correction.

The regular journal entry, however, is unique in that you can use this to produce transaction-specific charges to a project, shown as follows:

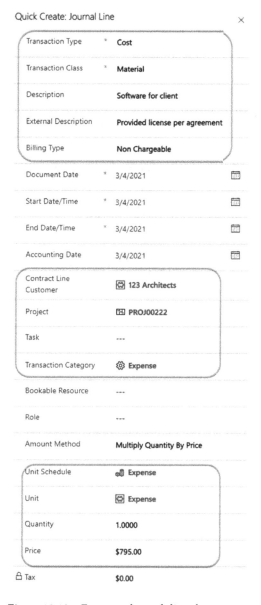

Figure 10.12 – Expense charged directly to project

The preceding screenshot shows a software expense charged directly to this project through the use of a journal entry. A note for the accountants out there right now who are curious about this entry: this is not an *accounting journal entry*. However, the results of this will directly integrate with the project's profitability, thus affecting its net profit. Some systems call this a project charge.

The different transaction types include the following:

- **Cost**: Creating a cost against a project
- **Unbilled Sales**: Entry of unbilled sales to a project, to be billed later in the billing process
- **Billed Sales**: Entry of billed sales to a project, to show as revenue against a project
- **Resourcing Unit Cost**: Used for entering cost transactions against a specific resourcing unit
- **Inter-Organizational Sales**: Used for entering sales transactions against a specific resourcing unit

You can assign transaction classes, including the following:

- **Time**: Charging direct time to the project
- **Expenses**: This could be integrated expenses from Concur, Gorilla, or Expensify
- **Material**
- **Milestone charges**
- **Fee**: Any fee not otherwise part of a project
- **Retainer**
- **Tax**

These are typical billing types:

- **Non-chargeable**
- **Chargeable**
- **Complimentary**

The combination of all these factors gives you a robust set of capabilities in the project journal entry transactions. For project cost accountants, the preceding screens should look and feel similar—if not in exact terms, context, and impact—to a project's ledger.

Many project businesses track project profitability within the Project Operations app itself. Some others who are integrated into Finance and Operations may feel more confident having this data and system of records in Finance and Operations.

This work performed—such as corrections to time, expenses, fees, costs, and sales— should always be entered by a qualified individual that understands the accounting impact of their actions.

Summary

In this chapter, we learned how to approve time and expenses through the system. We processed approvals into actuals that affect the project cost and billing.

We outlined how team members can recall their timecard lines to enhance the processing of their time handling. This ensures the highest quality of transactions. We also outlined how timecards and expenses can be corrected and have their respective journal entries processed through the system. Finally, we outlined how the journal entry function provides a depth of project charges against a project's net profit.

As a result, at this point, you should be fully prepared to manage any exceptions that are encountered. Furthermore, you should now be ready for the next chapter.

As we enter into *Chapter 11, Project Accounting and Operations*, we will bring this overall business process flow to a conclusion by discussing and outlining project accounting and operational factors.

Questions

1. Where do project managers access approvals?
2. How do you reduce a view to a manageable number of records?
3. What happens when a time entry is approved?
4. What happens when a time entry is rejected?
5. Can a team member recall an approved time entry?
6. Can a project manager or administrator correct a time entry?

7. What is the result of a time entry correction?

8. How do you correct an expense entry?

9. How can you enter costs against a project without an expense report or other transactions?

10. Which transaction types are supported in a journal entry?

11

Project Accounting and Operations

In this final chapter of our book, we are going to turn time into money! The preceding chapters have built everything up to the ability to perform billing and accounting for our work products. In this chapter, you will understand the implications of the billing methods we have chosen and you will see how they drive invoicing.

Furthermore, once billed, the conversation will turn to how we can make use of the data that has been generated. So, let's get this chapter started!

In this chapter, you will learn about the following topics:

- Recap of our learning
- Getting an overview of the billing process
- Invoicing
- Finance and Operations integration
- Costing and profit
- Learning about reporting and analysis

By the end of this chapter, you will know how the project operations system generates project accounting transactions.

Technical requirements

To perform the tasks in this chapter, you will need the following:

- An Microsoft 365 account and an Azure AD login

- A Microsoft Dynamics 365 Project Operations (C) license

- Potentially a Dynamics 365 Finance and Operations license

- A Microsoft Project Plan license

- The Project Billing Administrator security role

- A Finance and Operations accounting role and integration role suitable for running the integration

Please visit the following link to check the CiA videos:

```
https://bit.ly/3abRHw7
```

Recap of our learning

We have journeyed together through 10 chapters and are now entering this final chapter together. In the past 10 chapters, we looked at the foundation of what a project-based business is and what the needs of that business model are. We then learned that project-based businesses are focused on delivering the project commitments that have been made to their clients.

When we looked at the Microsoft Project Operations solution, we outlined how we can build upon the Microsoft 365 and Dynamics 365 frameworks to provide users with an experience that is integrated with everything Microsoft. The benefit of this is that while leveraging the Microsoft framework, we can also gain some significant improvements for our people, processes, technology, and data.

When we looked at the Microsoft 365 framework closely, we outlined some of its key benefits by identifying how it gives you an overall platform for success, including Outlook, Teams, SharePoint, and OneDrive. With this framework, we can remove the context switching that happens when a user has to specifically *log into* an app, versus having their work integrated into their daily life.

In the next chapter, we walked through the deployment options for your project operations system, which ranged from Dynamics 365 CE-centric deployments to heavy Finance and Operations deployments. We outlined a number of key questions you should ask yourself and your firm before advancing too far into the deployment.

We also took the liberty to set up a few customizations that make sense for a project-based business. Using the Power Platform, PowerApps, and Power BI solutions, we built on top of the project operations foundation to make the solution work best for you and your firm's needs.

Then, we got into selling contracts and winning business. Project-based businesses are not transactional but relational. Therefore, the need to build out contract lines that reflect special client- or project-specific rates is key to meeting client demands. We also learned that we have many contract types that will directly feed into the project's billing and invoicing, as well as have a tremendous effect on revenue recognition.

During this time frame, we learned the importance of roles in terms of the pricing and costing models. We built out roles per Org Unit and also specified generic roles that drive our ability to staff and plan for resources.

For the practice manager, we outlined how they would manage backlog and how that backlog works to drive utilization throughout the business. When focusing on demand, we also needed to support the talent that makes the business a success. Due to this, we worked through skills and certification management routines and incorporated these into the staffing model.

For businesses that take a more centralized approach to their staffing and resourcing requirements, we walked through how to generate resource requirements and how they become resource requests, which fulfill the demand in the system. Skills, certifications, location, and other factors come together to provide sophisticated decision-making capabilities for scheduling.

When we continued down the road to project success, we worked squarely with the project manager to provide expert management for all the facets of the project. The project manager is presented with a sophisticated interface for developing plans, which includes task, board, and timeline views of the same data so as to support more traditional waterfall planning, as well as agile methodologies. The project manager is empowered to make course corrections to the project to keep it on track while incorporating change orders and other elements of correction.

The team member activities we covered included the most popular activity we all do every week: time entry! This also included expense entry, submitting our time and expenses, and learning how to handle exceptions and things that cause us to have to correct entries.

This led us to the point where we are able to handle and make entries that drive project cost, sales, time, and expense corrections that affect the project's financial health.

Now, we are ready to look at project accounting and operations. In this chapter, we are going to learn how to turn time into dollars and provide benefits for the business with the revenue we generate! So, let's get into it!

Getting an overview of the billing process

The billing processes in project operations will be different, depending on the type of deployment you have. Reflecting back, we have three different deployment types that we can use in project operations:

- Lite deployment – deal with proforma invoicing: This is a Dynamics CE-only deployment of project operations and is integrating with external ERP systems.

- Project operations for resource/non-stocked-based scenarios: This is the integrated version of Dynamics CE Project Operations to Finance and Operations.

- Project operations for stocked/production-based scenarios: This is the Finance and Operations-only deployment.

In this chapter, we are going to focus on the Lite deployment – dealing with proforma invoicing processes – because this particular deployment, with the out-of-the-box integration Microsoft provides into Finance and Operations for the billing functions, *is* the project operations for resource/non-stocked-based scenarios. Let's put this a different way:

Lite deployment + Microsoft Dual Write Integration + Finance and Operations = Project Operations for resource/non-stocked-based scenarios.

Therefore, by covering the project operations Lite deployment, we will cover the majority of the work before any project operations data is integrated into any accounting system, whether it's a Finance and Operations one or any other system.

The project operations for stocked/production-based scenarios is primarily conducted within the Finance & Operations – Project Management and Accounting functionality, so the majority of that conversation is beyond the scope of this book.

As you may recall, in *Figure 3.1 – Project Operations Unified Environment*, we covered each of the functional areas. To build upon this, the following diagram outlines the billing processes we will cover:

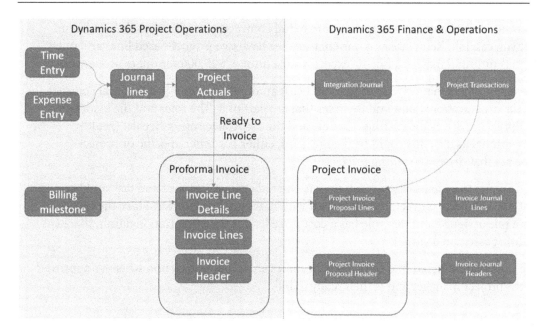

Figure 11.1 – Billing Processes in Dynamics 365 CE Project Operations integrated with accounting

The left-hand side of the diagram contains everything in Dynamics 365 CE – Project Operations in terms of producing the invoicing details in project operations and then integrating them into Finance and Operations. The right-hand side of the diagram contains the accounting system, which shows Finance and Operations as a primary scenario here.

With this information as a backdrop, let's view the impact of the billing methods, contract types, and invoicing options we have performed previously.

Billing methods, contract types, and invoicing

Within project operations, the **Project Contract** and its related **Contract Lines** drive the overall billing methods, which results in invoices. In project operations, there are two main types of billing methods: time and material and fixed price. Let's take a look at time and material contracts first as this is the most direct translation of time into money!

Time and material

With the time and material billing method, you are billing a specific selling rate for every increment of an hour that's been billed for each resource. Your costing is proportional to the hours that are charged by the team member performing that specific role.

A not-to-exceed contract is a time and material contract with a limit on the maximum that you can bill. Remember, in our contract, we have two project-based lines and one of them is time and material, not-to-exceed with a limit of $25,000 for out of scope work.

The components that drive your sales and cost amounts in a time and material contract are the organizational unit and the roles that are part of it. The roles and the associated cost price list drives the costing. The role and the associated sales price list (multi-dimensional as it is, this could be the rate card, either customer-specific or project-specific) that drives the selling price.

These come to a conjunction when time is entered against a project and task and because that has a project contract line associated with it, we get a sales price. Since the resource has a role assigned and that role has a cost price list for the organizational unit, there is a cost that associated with it.

The time that's entered into the system becomes an **actual** transaction when it's approved by the project manager and is then ready to bill.

Fixed price

Then, you have your fixed-price contracts, which have variations, including invoice schedules, milestones, retainers, and fees, as well as the ability to bill out an amount as needed throughout the contract.

Invoices in project operations are billed out on a defined schedule or as part of monthly or other billing cycles.

Time that's entered against a fixed-price contract is only going to cost the contract and not generate any sales transactions, since they are conducted at the milestone invoice level.

Invoicing

Invoicing is the mechanism that transforms our time into money. Invoices are physical representations of the price lists we set up previously and should accurately reflect the agreed upon rates.

The first thing we are going to do is bill out our first fixed-price milestone as per the project contract and line items. To do so, we must begin in the **Project Operations | Sales** area. We must then go to the **Billing** section and select **Fixed Price Milestones**.

This first milestone is to be billed up-front before the work begins, so let's get to it!

Milestone invoice

Let's get our milestone billing ready and generate an invoice. Our first invoice is due **03/07/2021**, as shown in the following screenshot:

Figure 11.2 – Project Contract Milestones

To begin milestone billing, navigate to the project invoice in the sales area and perform the following steps:

1. With the first milestone selected, click **Ready to invoice**.

2. Next, in the **Project Contract**, we are going to select **Create Invoice** in the top-right of the contract This will create an invoice automatically for us, as shown here:

Figure 11.3 – Project Contract Invoice

3. It is important to note that in many integrated environments, either the **Ready to Invoice** step or clicking **Confirm** is the key integration point (project invoice status) that triggers the integration into the accounting system's invoicing system. It is important to ensure that all the elements of our project-based lines are correct. Once we have ascertained this correctness, we can proceed. The result is that we have a contract line of $50,000 that is ready to invoice. We can see this in the preceding screenshot.

4. From the vertical ellipsis to the right of **Flow**, we can now choose to create a proforma invoice by selecting **Word Templates** and choosing **Invoice**. This Word Template can be modified to reflect the type of invoice format you wish to use. Furthermore, it is common to have a different fixed-price format and a distinctly different time and material invoice format. The following screenshot shows the invoice templates (Word Templates) that have been uploaded to project operations:

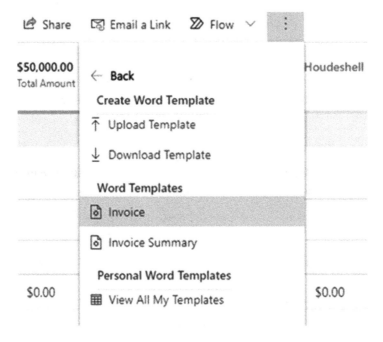

Figure 11.4 – Project Proforma Invoice

Like all Word Templates, this project invoice is customizable and you can make it look as professional as you want using the Microsoft Word template in project operations.

Next, we need to bill out our subscription for project operations.

Product-based billing

As an overall solution, Dynamics 365 CE produces product-based and project-based billings. The **product-based billings** could be for physical products or they can be for subscription services, as we have in our example. It is important to note that we have a unified billing environment that is driving this functionality.

The product to bill out is visible in the **Project Operations | Sales | Billing** section and on the **Product Billing Backlog** screen. Here, select the product and then select **Ready for Invoicing**.

Since we are using a unified billing environment, we will begin our product billings from the project contract, just like all our other project billing functions. From the project contract, click on **Create Invoice**; the system will create a product-based invoice as well.

In the section highlighted in the following screenshot, we are billing out one line item of 20 units at $125 per unit for the extended amount of $2,500:

Figure 11.5 – Product Proforma Invoice

The same integration and invoice printing processes apply. Clicking **Confirm** sets the billing status to **Confirmed**. Next, we need to bill out some *Out of Scope* time that was entered and approved.

Time and material billing

To bill out the time that's been entered and approved, we will begin with the **Project Operations | Sales | Billing** section and on the **Time and Material Billing Backlog** screen. Here, select the lines/time we want to bill and then select **Ready for Invoicing**.

From the project contract, click on **Create Invoice**; the system will create a time and material-based invoice as well. Similar to the steps previous to this, we are now creating invoices for the highlighted *Out of Scope* item shown in the following screenshot:

Figure 11.6 – Project Out of Scope Time and Material Proforma Invoice

The same integration and invoice printing processes that were covered in the previous sections apply. Clicking **Confirm** sets the billing status to **Confirmed**.

Combined billing

Combined billing is really how a biller or administrator will function within project operations. Combined billing simply means that when all the backlog transactions are set to **Ready to Invoice**, we are putting all the transactions together into one invoice. This is a billing process that would require a specially formatted invoice to show the details behind each of the billing scenarios. This process also works at the contract level to provide a more convenient grouping.

For this chapter, we have printed out (and/or integrated) each of these three scenarios individually.

In reality, the process you will follow will include confirming billing backlogs for everything (milestones, products and time, and materials) at one time and then putting them all onto one draft invoice for preview, presentation, and confirmation.

Let's take a look at what happens when you integrate into Finance and Operations.

Finance and Operations integration

Historically, Finance and Operations has been its own Project Accounting solution with time and expense entry, invoicing, revenue recognition, and significantly more.

Microsoft has combined the best of project operations in the Dynamics 365 CE world with the Project Accounting capabilities in Finance and Operations. They have done this by creating an integrated environment where the project operations CE components are augmented with an integration technology solution called **Dual Write Core and Dual Write Orchestration**.

Once enabled on the CE side and the Finance and Operations side of the system, the user experience is to process transactions in CE where they originate while integrating them into Finance and Operations, which is where accounting takes place.

To look into this further, let's look at how we can create and integrate an accounting transaction.

The project operations system produces *actuals*, as shown here:

Active Actuals ∨

✓	Transaction Type ∨	Transaction... ∨	Adjustment Stat... ∨	Docum... ↓ ∨	Project Contract ID ∨	Project Contract Line ∨	Project Contract... ∨	Project ID ∨	Task ID ∨
	Cost	Time	---	3/4/2021	New Project Need	Out of Scope	123 Architects	PROJ00222	Out of Scope Time & Materials
	Unbilled Sales	Time	---	3/4/2021	New Project Need	Out of Scope	123 Architects	PROJ00222	Out of Scope Time & Materials
	Billed Sales	Milestone	---	3/4/2021	New Project Need	New Project Software	123 Architects	PROJ00222	Milestone 1 Billing - Define and Design
	Billed Sales	Time	---	3/4/2021	New Project Need	Out of Scope	123 Architects	PROJ00222	Out of Scope Time & Materials
	Unbilled Sales	Time	---	3/4/2021	New Project Need	Out of Scope	123 Architects	PROJ00222	Out of Scope Time & Materials
	Cost	Time	---	3/3/2021	New Project Need	Out of Scope	123 Architects	PROJ00222	Out of Scope Time & Materials
	Unbilled Sales	Time	---	3/3/2021	New Project Need	Out of Scope	123 Architects	PROJ00222	Out of Scope Time & Materials
	Billed Sales	Time	---	3/3/2021	New Project Need	Out of Scope	123 Architects	PROJ00222	Out of Scope Time & Materials
	Unbilled Sales	Time	---	3/3/2021	New Project Need	Out of Scope	123 Architects	PROJ00222	Out of Scope Time & Materials
	Cost	Time	---	3/2/2021	New Project Need	Out of Scope	123 Architects	PROJ00222	Out of Scope Time & Materials

Figure 11.7 – Project actuals

These actuals represent the operational view of the work that's been completed against projects in project operations. When integrating with Finance and Operations, we are integrating with the Project Management and Accounting system. This means that we are populating journals in Finance and Operations, which are populating the project ledger and then subsequently the general ledger.

Therefore, to get into the general ledger, Microsoft has employed the concept of an integration journal to manage these accounting transactions.

Integration journal

Integration is performed via **Project Management and Accounting (PMA) | Journals | Project Operations Integration journal**. Bringing these records into the system involves running *the periodic process >> Import from staging table*. The integration can bring in actuals based on a comparison to find actuals that have not been integrated since the last execution, and then integrates them into one of the following user-specified groups:

- **Days**: Actuals are grouped and journaled by days.

- **Months**: Actuals are grouped and journaled by months.

- **Years**: Actuals are grouped and journaled by years.

- **All**: All actuals are grouped and journaled, regardless of any date-driven factors.

The results of this are that each project actual transaction has a corresponding line in the **Project Operations Integration Journal**. This means that there will be a similar breakout to the actuals shown in the preceding screenshot.

The system is accounting date-driven and will post to the accounting date that's brought across in the integration. If the period is closed and locked out, then the result will be a posting to the first date in the next open ledger period.

Resource specifications in the integration are meaningful to the Project Operations – CE side of things, but are only informational for Finance and Operations Project Management and Accounting. This is to provide the detailed information needed for customer invoicing.

Financial dimensions

Financial dimensions are notably a Finance and Operations feature that is worth explaining in the context of Project Management and Accounting. You can set a default financial dimension for customers to create a customer dimensional view.

Dimensions can also be set for project contracts through the PMA module in Finance. For fixed-price/milestone contract lines, financial dimensions can be set up to help report on contract types and performance.

Project funding sources can be set in **PMA Project Contracts** via the **Related Information | Funding Sources** tab. This can be helpful for grant management.

For the project itself, the dimensions are pulled through from the customer, contract line, or project, depending on which dimension is more complete. For example, if the customer has a financial dimension but is not on the contract line or project, the customer dimension will be used. If the contract line has a dimension, then this dimension will be used. If the project has a dimension, it will be used to dimension the transactions.

Revenue recognition

The processing of revenue recognition in project operations is primarily conducted through the Finance and Operations – Project Management and Accounting functionality. The setup and complexity of revenue recognition in PMA is beyond the scope or context of this book. However, it is important to factor in that there will be a revenue recognition process regardless.

Whether you're using Finance and Operations PMA revenue recognition or some other accounting system, **Generally Accepted Accounting Principles** (**GAAP**) will require some formulaic calculation of revenue recognition. So, let's talk about what plays into this for a project accountant.

The project itself, along with its tasks, budgeted hours, and dollars, is a large factor in the revenue recognition process. Combined with the contract type and the percentage of the project that's complete, we can calculate the revenue to be recognized. This is typical for a fixed-price contract.

In our project's example, we have a total project contract value of $125,000 being billed out three times. We are currently at 15.61% Cost Consumption for the project, which represents about $19,512.50 in revenue. We can recognize this based on a cost model. The result of this calculation is that deferred revenue will be reversed by $19,512.50 and that the revenue will be recognized or credited for $19,512.50 for this period.

In Finance and Operations PMA revenue recognition, this is a similar approach to the Total cost-actual cost to complete method. There are many others that are beyond the scope of the context of this book.

> **Note**
> With all accounting statements made in this book, the statements are for example purposes only and may not represent your needs or intended results. Please seek professional accounting assistance where necessary.

Taxes and proforma invoices

For all the invoicing we performed in the *Invoicing* section, the invoices that were produced are good for presenting to the client but are potentially missing some critical data.

Taxes are one element of data that may be missing from the invoice. Typically, tax calculations are provided in Finance and Operations through an Avatax web service integration or some other tax integration. The same can be done on the proforma invoice, but it would be highly duplicative.

Furthermore, a proforma invoice is an invoice that the accounting department will generally need to duplicate in their accounting system. This is due to the nature of the invoice needing to be paid by the client and that payment being tracked and recorded. Again, this would be duplicative if we did this in project operations and in Finance and Operations or any other accounting system.

Costing and profit

The project operations system will track costing and profit within the system, as well as make this available through other tools such as Power BI. Within project operations, some key areas where we see actual cost impacts appear as the project's progress is on the front page of the project itself.

In the following screenshot, we can see that we have already charged a number of costs for the project through our time entries and approvals and that these expenses have been entered and approved. To see this, open the **Project** screen from the **Project Operations** menu:

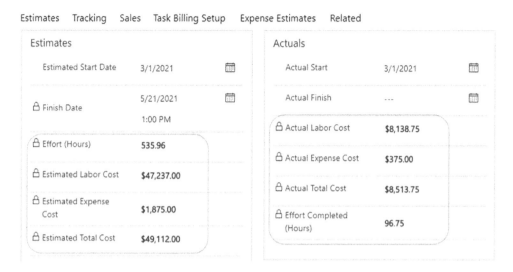

Figure 11.8 – Estimates versus Actuals

Here, we can see that we have an estimated labor cost of **$47,237** and an actual labor cost of **$8,138.75**. The estimated expenses of **$1,875** versus **$375** have been entered and approved.

The goal of the project operations system is to provide accurate accounting for the actuals transactions on the same screen so that we can compare them with the estimates.

Now, let's get into some of the reporting and analysis the system provides.

Learning about reporting and analysis

The purpose of reporting and analysis is to provide performance metrics to the users of the system who are responsible for project performance. To provide this, we have a few options that will provide value to the system.

With project Operations, dashboards are provided out of the box. As you may recall, Dashboards are available from **Home | My Work | Dashboards**. This section will provide you with dashboarding information that can be leveraged by your users.

Project Operations Dashboards

Project operations **Dashboards** are specifically designed visual graphics that are built upon views of the data in project operations. Specifically designed for the personas in use in a project business, these dashboards can have security assigned to them, expanded to include more data, and are generally made into what the users want and need to manage for the project business.

When viewing dashboards, you get to choose your dashboard and set it as a default:

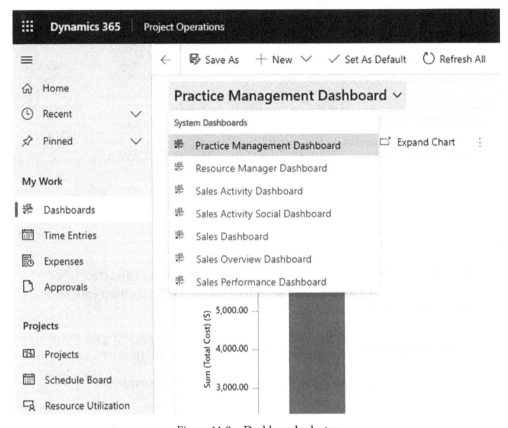

Figure 11.9 – Dashboard selector

As shown in the preceding screenshot, many dashboards are visible to the users of a Dynamics 365 CE system that go beyond project dashboards. For example, there are dashboards for sales, service, activities, and much more.

The most common dashboard for the leadership team is called **Practice Management Dashboard**. This dashboard provides the following critical dashparts:

- Current month versus prior month – Cost

- Current month versus prior month – Gross margin

- Current month versus prior month – Sales

- Current month versus prior month – Total hours

- Active Role Utilization

- Current Month Cost

The goal of these particular dashparts is to give you a starting point for what real information the practice manager may need.

Similarly, the Resource Manager Dashboard provides unique views around active resource requests, active role utilization, and resource demand distribution.

These dashboards can be modified in terms of both visual appearance and information. They are security enabled, which means you can only present the relevant information to your audiences while leveraging the security within Dynamics 365.

The power of the Microsoft Power Platform includes the ability to utilize Power BI Reporting to build even more sophisticated dashboards. To build on these further, these Power BI dashboards can be directly integrated into a project operations dashboard to enhance the system.

Power BI Reporting

Throughout this book, we have seen a few examples of how Power BI is used in forecasting or in other facets of the project operations world. While there are numerous examples we can build from, my experience has been to fully identify and vet the requirements of each individual client before prescribing the right reporting solution.

For example, a quick web search turns up a number of very beautifully formatted, graphics-intensive reports that, when looked at in their own context, represent some really great work! Furthermore, some are of a quality that you would want to mimic in terms of their structure, data elegance, and presentation layering.

However, things change when we look at the reality of each client's user base, report consumption habits, and the decisions that are based on each of these. Therefore, you must consider how best to structure the overall project operations data and your most valuable information first; then, the rest of your reporting will fall in line.

For example, in the *Finance and Operations integration* section, we discussed the use of dimensions in a Project Operations world connected to a Finance and Operations world. Dimensions allow for some sophisticated reporting functionality for the users of project operations.

When using Power BI, you can pull from both Project Operations Dataverse information as well as Finance and Operations information. This information combines into one view to provide a sophisticated join of information, from the front end of the solution to the accounting end.

Since we're talking about Microsoft Technology, it is important to know that some clients will have a hybrid solution approach, which provides Microsoft Technology with a data warehouse and potentially Power BI on the frontend to generate and render the reporting needed for the user base. With this approach, there is unlimited potential for results.

Summary

In this chapter, we concluded our project operations conversation by reviewing some of the key elements of the project operations system, including contract types, finance and operations, and reporting and analysis. This hopefully has helped pull together the key concepts and learnings throughout the book.

In terms of contract types, we reviewed time and materials contracts and compared them to fixed-price contracts. We learned how the project that we built out with its various contract lines all came together in the invoicing processes. We then billed out our milestone invoice and printed a proforma copy. After that, we billed out our product and time and materials billings. In all of these, we learned about the integration points of our invoices and the other *actuals* transactions in the system.

Next, we reviewed some of the key elements in the Finance and Operations integration, including the Integration Journal, Financial Dimensions, and Revenue Recognition. When working in an integrated environment, these are important concepts as they will drive some enhanced functionality further down the line in the implementation.

Finally, we covered Power BI's capabilities and why you will want to use Power BI as a tool to pull together data across systems, and then combine it into a unified reporting structure for your users.

It is at this point that I thank you, the reader, for following along this journey with me. As we close out this chapter, remember that the journey begins by taking some first steps in the right direction. Not every facet of the material that's been covered in this book will apply to your implementation, but every implementation will contain some facets that were covered in this book. It is with this that I look forward to our next book journey and hope that our paths cross again soon!

Questions

1. Which deployment models were used to exemplify project accounting in this chapter?

2. In a time and materials project, each hour of time is transformed into what?

3. In a fixed-price contract, does the sales price per hour get calculated?

4. In a fixed-price contract, does the cost per hour get applied to the contract?

5. When invoicing a milestone, what initiates the fact that the milestone is to be placed on an invoice?

6. What is a common integration point for an invoice to be integrated into accounting?

7. True or false: Project Operations has robust tax engine capabilities and will therefore render a complete invoice in the CE system.

8. Can a single project invoice include time and material, product, milestone, and retainer billings?

9. The Finance and Operations Integration Journal is date-sensitive to what degree?

10. What is the benefit of financial dimensions?

Assessments

Chapter 1

1. A project business provides skilled and certified services delivered by people to achieve a project's purpose.

2. **CRM** stands for **customer relationship management,** and more specifically for Microsoft, the solution is called Microsoft Dynamics 365 **CE (Customer Engagement)**. Dynamics 365 CE provides the project seller account management, contact management, and the ability to enter and process opportunities and quotes, which become the project contracts that you deliver against. This can also be called the *bid-to-win* cycle.

3. The sales methodology is the firm's ability to receive leads in the system from the marketing team and qualify them against the firm's ability to deliver.

4. The **WBS** is the **work breakdown structure** that will be summarized and presented to the potential client. The level of detail presented and the level of detail tracked in the estimates are usually different. The client presentation is more summary-level and can easily be translated to hours, rates, and project pricing.

5. The **statement of work (SOW)** is the key document that we see across many project businesses. It guides and drives the work to be performed and outlines the remuneration expected from the client for this work. SOWs can be of different types: short forms, long forms, fixed fee, time and materials, and many more variations.

6. The red pill!

Chapter 2

1. At a personal and business level, OneDrive is totally tightly integrated into your Office 365 environment to protect your firm's most valuable data.

2. Microsoft SharePoint is used to protect contracts, statements of work, service agreements, and other documents. SharePoint is frequently integrated into Project Operations.

3. Microsoft Project for the web is used within Project Operations – there are project tasks to provide Gantt charts, timelines, and boards to manage projects effectively.

4. The PowerApps editor (`make.powerapps.com`) is the tool to modify your Dynamics 365 CE/Project Operations environment while also allowing you to build new, model-driven applications.

5. Trick question! It is the Project Operations app!

6. Project Operations Team Member – so a team member can have just a limited palette of features.

7. False. Project Operations is available on a per-user, per-month licensing arrangement depending upon your licensing source or cloud service provider.

8. False. Although built on top of the Microsoft model-driven PowerApps, Project Operations can and does integrate with other CRM systems. However, it does work better together with Microsoft's own technology, of course.

9. Microsoft Dynamics 365 for Finance and Operations – utilizing the project management and accounting functionality and integrating through dual-write integration.

10. To match the revenue and cost of a project throughout the accounting periods.

11. Project profitability is the margin derived after subtracting out the project costs from the project revenue on a project and sometimes task basis.

Chapter 3

1. Yes, Azure AD drives all the authentication needed to use Dynamics 365 CE, Project Operations, Project for the web, and other components related to Project Operations.

2. Dynamics 365 CE – Sales is not required to use Project Operations since it can be integrated with Salesforce.com and other CRM systems. However, you get a benefit from using Dynamics 365 CE if it is integrated.

3. Dynamics 365 for Finance and Operations is not required to use Project Operations since many firms will integrate with an existing accounting or ERP system. However, Finance and Operations will give the firm a benefit relative to expense policies, revenue recognition, billing, and project costing.

4. Lite deployment – deal to proforma invoicing.

5. Project Operations for resource/non-stocked scenarios.

6. Procuring licensing and applying the correct licenses to the users.

7. `https://admin.powerplatform.microsoft.com/` provides you with the ability to set up a new Dynamics 365 CE environment and allows you to add Project Operations as an app.

8. The **Advanced Settings** area will drive a number of system-wide configuration choices that will impact all users in the system.

9. From the settings menu, select **Options | Set Personal Options**.

10. In the Project Operations **Settings** area in the lower-left portion of the app.

Chapter 4

1. True. The result of a lead generates the monetary opportunity.

2. **Client (Account)**, **Contact**, and **Opportunity**.

3. The **Timeline** tracks the activities in a lead and carries it forward into the **Opportunity** records as well.

4. Qualified.

5. The business process flow.

6. **Opportunity Lines**.

7. False. You need to have a Dynamics 365 CE license.

8. False. You can use a custom field to integrate into a logical library format, which can then be used either with a CE license or without to access the documents.

9. Use a **Text** field with a URL format and expand the field size to 4,000. Add it to the form of your choice.

10. Click on the **Close as Won** button.

Chapter 5

1. Project contract. The project contract is a project-based variation of the order entity.

2. False. Most all projects will have multiple invoices generated.

3. Milestones. Milestones are created to reflect the contractual agreements in a statement of work.

4. True.

5. False. In our example, we are mixing fixed-price and time and material contracts.

6. Provides a schedule of milestone invoice-generation dates.

7. Time and materials, since time and materials contracts require a selling rate to bill out the hours.

8. The multidimensional pricing model allows for pricing at a rate card-, client-, and project-specific level.

9. False. If set up properly, labor cost rates can be used to track all costs against a project.

10. False. Project costing is a sensitive topic. I suggest working cross-functionally through a firm to gain agreement on what a project cost is.

Chapter 6

1. Direct staffing model

2. True

3. assignments and bookings

4. True, but you can customize a solution to perform this function

5. Billing prices, costing, and filtering in the schedule board

6. **Bookable Resource Characteristics**

7. **Quality of Work**

8. Forward-looking—mostly driven by hours, not dollars

9. Revenue forecasting, which can be built upon the Project Operations system using Power BI

10. Utilization

Chapter 7

1. A role is a type of resource that carries with it costing, pricing, and scheduling characteristics.

2. Work breakdown structure.

3. **Specify Pattern.**

4. False. Generating requirements will show on the schedule board.

5. Resource requests are used to specify more details behind a resource need.

6. False. Additional requirements for the generated project requirement flow directly through to the schedule assistant.

7. True. From the **Book** button, you can book a resource directly.

8. Hard and soft booking terms may vary from one company to another as they are ways of communicating commitment to a project.

9. **Full**, **Percentage**, and **Even Distribution** allocations can potentially overbook resources.

10. From the Schedule Board, without any filters and with the right timelines highlighted.

Chapter 8

1. The business process flow provides a system-configurable set of stages and checklists that can guide a project professional through a project.

2. In an external accounting scenario, the project name field may be the primary key for the integration of a project. Although you can change this field out of the box with Project Operations, in an integrated environment this would be undesirable. Therefore, consider that if you are using this as a key field, you may need to add some logic behind the handling of this field and set it to read-only.

3. True. The customer record must be set up in the accounting system as a customer with credit terms, valid contracts on file, and all the company's processes and policies followed.

4. **Grid**, **Board**, and **Timeline**.

5. The **Board** view.

6. The **Team** tab allows you to add resources to your team and then assign them to the appropriate tasks.

7. The **Estimates** tab has both the cost and the selling price of resources.

8. False. Change orders can be tracked as a task in the project but there is currently no out-of-the-box functionality.

9. True. Teams can be set up to present a significant amount of information across Teams channels.

10. The highly configurable **Dynamics 365 App for Outlook** allows team members to input their time without needing to launch the Project Operations website.

Chapter 9

1. True. Time entry is a weekly process, but time can also be entered daily and submitted weekly.

2. Team members must be set up as a resource and have an associated role that drives costing and selling. They must also be set up for a project and a task.

3. External comments are the client-facing notes that flow through to billing.

4. The copy week function is used and can be used to choose from previous weeks.

5. **Import Exchange Appointments**.

6. True. This helps manage the quality of data.

7. Dynamics 365 App for Outlook with the proper configuration for time entry.

8. False. Microsoft Teams with the Dynamics 365 app is a powerful combination of capabilities beyond just time and expenses entry!

9. False. Many companies will utilize Project Operations but many others will utilize Concur, Gorilla Expense, or Expensify and integrate that data.

10. Click the record selector for the line(s) you wish to submit and select **Submit** from the menu!

Chapter 10

1. From the **Project Operations | Projects** area, choose the **Approvals** menu. When you do, you will be presented with the **Time Entries for Approval** screen.

2. Using the **Search this view** function, you can limit the records you see to something more manageable.

3. Approved time entries become **actuals** in the system.

4. It returns to the team member as **Returned**.

5. Yes, but there is a **Reason** box that needs to be supplied.

6. Yes—from the **Approved Time** screen, entries can be corrected.

7. A series of transactions to reverse the time related to both cost and sales.

8. The **Journals** screen has an expense entry correction type.

9. Through the journal entry with its various transaction types.

10. **Time**, **Expenses**, **Materials**, **Milestone charges**, **Fees**, **Retainers**, and **Taxes**.

Chapter 11

1. Lite deployment – deal to proforma invoicing, but with reference to the Finance and Operations integration.

2. Each hour of time is transformed into a monetary equivalent based on the billable hours sales rates.

3. No; in a fixed-price contract, the sales price is determined by the invoicing schedule.

4. Yes, because a cost is calculated to determine the project's profitability when it's completed.

5. On the **Project Contract Milestones** screen, the milestone is selected and set to **Ready to invoice**.

6. When the invoice is **Confirmed**.

7. False. The Project Operations system will produce a proforma invoice, with tax being added in the accounting system.

8. Yes, the system has this capability out of the box.

9. The Finance and Operations integration journal groups journals by one of the following: days, months, years, or all.

10. When properly set up and utilized, financial dimensions can provide a great detail of reporting clarity when they're used in conjunction with Power BI.

`Packt.com`

Subscribe to our online digital library for full access to over 7,000 books and videos, as well as industry leading tools to help you plan your personal development and advance your career. For more information, please visit our website.

Why subscribe?

- Spend less time learning and more time coding with practical eBooks and Videos from over 4,000 industry professionals

- Improve your learning with Skill Plans built especially for you

- Get a free eBook or video every month

- Fully searchable for easy access to vital information

- Copy and paste, print, and bookmark content

Did you know that Packt offers eBook versions of every book published, with PDF and ePub files available? You can upgrade to the eBook version at `packt.com` and as a print book customer, you are entitled to a discount on the eBook copy. Get in touch with us at `customercare@packtpub.com` for more details.

At `www.packt.com`, you can also read a collection of free technical articles, sign up for a range of free newsletters, and receive exclusive discounts and offers on Packt books and eBooks.

Other Books You May Enjoy

If you enjoyed this book, you may be interested in these other books by Packt:

Microsoft Power Platform Enterprise Architecture

Robert Rybaric

ISBN: 978-1-80020-457-7

- Understand various Dynamics 365 CRM, ERP, and AI modules for creating Power Platform solutions

- Enhance Power Platform with Microsoft 365 and Azure

- Find out which regions, staging environments, and user licensing groups need to be employed when creating enterprise solutions

- Implement sophisticated security by using various authentication and authorization techniques

- Extend Power Apps, Power BI, and Power Automate to create custom applications

- Integrate your solution with various in-house Microsoft components or third-party systems using integration patterns

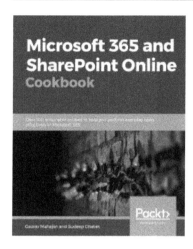

Microsoft 365 and SharePoint Online Cookbook

Gaurav Mahajan , Sudeep Ghatak

ISBN: 978-1-83864-667-7

- Get to grips with a wide range of apps and cloud services in Microsoft 365
- Discover ways to use SharePoint Online to create and manage content
- Store and share documents using SharePoint Online
- Improve your search experience with Microsoft Search
- Leverage the Power Platform to build business solutions with Power Automate, Power Apps, Power BI, and Power Virtual Agents
- Enhance native capabilities in SharePoint and Teams using the SPFx framework
- Use Microsoft Teams to meet, chat, and collaborate with colleagues or external users

Implementing Microsoft Dynamics 365 Customer Engagement

Mahender Pal

ISBN: 978-1-83855-687-7

- Explore the new features of Microsoft Dynamics 365 CE

- Understand various project management methodologies, such as Agile, Waterfall, and DevOps

- Customize Dynamics 365 CE to meet your business requirements

- Integrate Dynamics 365 with other applications, such as PowerApps, Power Automate, and Power BI

- Convert client requirements into functional designs

- Extend Dynamics 365 functionality using web resources, custom logic, and client-side and server-side code

- Discover different techniques for writing and executing test cases

- Understand various data migration options to import data from legacy systems

Microsoft Power Apps Cookbook

Eickhel Mendoza

ISBN: 978-1-80056-955-3

- Build pixel-perfect solutions with canvas apps
- Design model-driven solutions using various features of Microsoft Dataverse
- Automate business processes such as triggered events, status change notifications, and approval systems with Power Automate
- Implement AI Builder's intelligent capabilities in your solutions
- Improve the UX of business apps to make them more appealing
- Find out how to extend Microsoft Teams using Power Apps
- Extend your business applications' capabilities using Power Apps Component Framework

Packt is searching for authors like you

If you're interested in becoming an author for Packt, please visit `authors.packtpub.com` and apply today. We have worked with thousands of developers and tech professionals, just like you, to help them share their insight with the global tech community. You can make a general application, apply for a specific hot topic that we are recruiting an author for, or submit your own idea.

Leave a review - let other readers know what you think

Please share your thoughts on this book with others by leaving a review on the site that you bought it from. If you purchased the book from Amazon, please leave us an honest review on this book's Amazon page. This is vital so that other potential readers can see and use your unbiased opinion to make purchasing decisions, we can understand what our customers think about our products, and our authors can see your feedback on the title that they have worked with Packt to create. It will only take a few minutes of your time, but is valuable to other potential customers, our authors, and Packt. Thank you!

Index

D

E

www.ingramcontent.com/pod-product-compliance
Lightning Source LLC
Chambersburg PA
CBHW060518060326
40690CB00017B/3314